Empire of Hope

EMPIRE OF HOPE

The Sentimental Politics of Japanese Decline

DAVID LEHENY

CORNELL UNIVERSITY PRESS
ITHACA AND LONDON

First published 2018 by Cornell University Press

Printed in the United States of America

Library of Congress Cataloging-in-Publication Data

Names: Leheny, David Richard, 1967– author.
Title: Empire of hope : the sentimental politics of Japanese decline / David Leheny.
Description: Ithaca : Cornell University Press, 2018. | Includes bibliographical references and index.
Identifiers: LCCN 2018013765 (print) | LCCN 2018017540 (ebook) | ISBN 9781501729089 (pdf) | ISBN 9781501729096 (epub/mobi) | ISBN 9781501729072 | ISBN 9781501729072 (cloth : alk. paper)
Subjects: LCSH: Political culture—Japan—History—20th century. | Political culture—Japan—History—21st century. | Emotions—Political aspects—Japan—History—20th century. | Emotions—Political aspects—Japan—History—21st century. | National characteristics, Japanese. | Japan—Politics and government—1989–
Classification: LCC JQ1681 (ebook) | LCC JQ1681 .L45 2018 (print) | DDC 306.20952—dc23
LC record available at https://lccn.loc.gov/2018013765

For Satsuki Takahashi

CONTENTS

ACKNOWLEDGMENTS

In the process of writing this book, I incurred debts I can never repay, although I hope the many people who provided advice, assistance, and support are aware of the depth of my gratitude. Five institutional settings were especially important. At the time of the 2011 tsunami, I was completing a period as a visiting professor at Hitotsubashi University's Institute for the Study of Global Issues, where I benefited immensely from the generous support of Yoshiko Ashiwa, Jonathan Lewis, and Kazuhito Onozuka, as well as advice from Ikuya Sato of Hitotsubashi's School of Commerce. Yasuhiko Sugiyama was a sterling research assistant. I then spent six months at the University of Tokyo's Institute of Social Science, where friends and mentors such as Yuji Genda, Hiroshi Ishida, Naofumi Nakamura, Gregory Noble, and Shigeki Uno provided essential introductions and insights that profoundly affected this work, even late in the drafting phase. Several years later, a summer affiliation with the University of Tokyo's Institute for Advanced Studies on Asia allowed me to do much of the research on Viet and Duc Nguyen, and my brilliant colleague

Jin Sato has been unfailingly supportive, even when appropriately and constructively skeptical of some of my more speculative flights of fancy. Across these periods, Kiichi Fujiwara and Takashi Inoue of Todai's Faculty of Law have been exceptionally knowledgeable and enthusiastic sounding boards.

I finished much of the manuscript during a year as the Toyota Visiting Professor at the University of Michigan's Center for Japanese Studies. I could not have asked for a better environment in which to complete the work, and I am especially thankful for support, advice, and critique from Leea Allerding, Yuen Yuen Ang, Erin Brightwell, Yuri Fukazawa, Brad Hammond, Chris Hill, Reggie Jackson, Jennifer Robertson, Peggy Rudberg, Ann Takata, and Jonathan Zwicker. Kiyo Tsutsui deserves a special shout-out for everything from brilliant insights into the theories and case studies of my project to the tickets to an unforgettable Michigan–Michigan State football game. Along with my wife and son, I owe many thanks to the Tsutsui family and the Pok-Wagner family for making our stay in Ann Arbor so much fun.

My decade at Princeton provided me with resources, support, camaraderie, and engagement that will remain incalculable in their benefits, and I remain especially grateful to my peerless colleagues in the East Asian Studies community for including me as one of theirs for ten years. I simply could not have thought through the book's concerns without my many long conversations with He Bian, Amy Borovoy, Janet Chen, Ksenia Chizhova, C. P. Chou, Tom Christensen, Steve Chung, Martin Collcutt, Tom Conlan, Christina Davis, Tineke D'Haeseleer, Ben Elman, Shel Garon, Tom Hare, David Howell, Erin Huang, John Ikenberry, Martin Kern, Mike Laffan, Federico Marcon, Seiichi Makino, Sue Naquin, Keiko Ono, Willard Peterson, Franz Prichard, Anna Shields, Brian Steininger, Jackie Stone, Joowon Suh, Buzzy Teiser, Atsuko Ueda, Haruko Wakabayashi, Andy Watsky, Kerim Yasar, and Everett Zhang. Friends from across the university—particularly Gary Bass, Mark Beissinger, Peter Brooks, Anne Cheng, Leslie Gerwin, Mike Laffan, Serguei Oushakine, and Kim Scheppele—profoundly affected the shape and questions of this project. Without the professionalism and kindness of Lisa Ball, Richard Chafey, Brandon Ermita, Jeff Heller, Patty Lieb, Chao-hui Jenny Liu, and the late June Balint, my career at Princeton would have foundered embarrassingly. I need to thank especially Donna Musial-Manners and Amber

Lee, whom I would describe as two of the finest people in the world even if I were not so indebted to both of them in so many ways, large and small.

For all sorts of advice, access, and guidance, I also want to thank Baba Osamu, Rich Calichman, Rebecca Copeland, Alexis Dudden, Hanai Kazuyo, Rob Hellyer, Yuichi Hosoya, Kiguma Seigo, Eiich and Yumi Kuwana, Mashiba Azuki, Stuart Ridgway, Richard Samuels, Christina Schwenkel, Katherine Tegtmeyer-Pak, Sawada Yukako, Dan White, Joshua Winchell, and Evan Young. And I am very grateful as well to my new colleagues at the Graduate School of Asia-Pacific Studies at Waseda University, particularly Gracia Liu-Farrer, Seio Nakajima, Glenda Roberts, Chikako Ueki, and Shujiro Urata for their shrewd insights and their support in the closing stages of the project. Audiences at Princeton, Wake Forest, Waseda University, the University of Tokyo, the International Research Center for Japanese Studies, the University of Michigan, Tsukuba University, City College of New York, Dickinson College, Harvard, and Washington University graciously listened and always challenged me to improve my arguments and my research. Financial support from the University of Michigan, Waseda University, and Princeton University was essential to the research and publication of this book, and I am grateful to all three institutions. This book is published with support from Waseda University's English Academic Book Publication Support Subsidy.

Although I did not realize it at the time, Peter Katzenstein and Takashi Shiraishi got me started on this project when they asked me to write a chapter about popular culture and soft power for their book *Beyond Japan*. I agreed to write it not out of any prior grasp of the topic but rather because I had already committed to coauthoring (with three others) another chapter of the book, and I felt guilty about being in the book workshop when I had done little more than draft a handful of pages under the watchful eyes of my coauthors. I couldn't have known at that time how that chapter would end up shaping the trajectory of this book, and I thank them for their generous advice and, as always, peerless intellectual leadership on that project. Portions of chapter 4 appeared in previous form in "A Narrow Place to Cross Swords: 'Soft Power' and the Politics of Japanese Popular Culture in East Asia," in *Beyond Japan: The Dynamics of East Asian Regionalism*, edited by Peter J. Katzenstein and Takashi Shiraishi, © 2006 Cornell University and published by Cornell University Press.

If I had one piece of advice for first-time authors, it would be to work with Roger Haydon at Cornell University Press. He has worked assiduously, with firm recommendations but unfailing good humor, to encourage me to make each of my monographs far better than it otherwise would have been. For this reason, any reader of my books should be at least as grateful to Roger as I myself am; whatever disappointments he has ultimately experienced with my final drafts, he has spared readers almost as much pain as the embarrassment he's spared me. Other members of the team at Cornell—especially Carmen Torrado Gonzalez, Karen Hwa, Ellen Murphy, and Donald Pharr—have each contributed in ways that have not only improved the book but also served as a continual reminder of the press's unmatched professionalism. Thanks too to Sandy Sadow, who kindly and adroitly prepared the book's index.

Anyone who reads a full manuscript for a friend or a colleague is a special kind of saint, particularly at a time that so many of us have too many obligations to too many colleagues and students to meet them all. And so I will simply say that I do not have the words to thank appropriately Allison Alexy, Todd Hall, David Johnson, and Ayako Kano. Each was kind enough to read a messy version of the manuscript and to make his or her points in ways that preserved the last strands of my self-confidence through the drafting process; each offered trenchant, critical observations that taught me a great deal both about my own work and about how to be a better colleague myself. Henry Laurence and an anonymous referee read and evaluated the manuscript for Cornell University Press, and I am deeply grateful to both for their insightful comments, suggestions, questions, and recommendations. My esteemed friends and colleagues Paize Keulemans and Shawn Bender both offered superb, timely advice on individual chapters, each of them improving the project at crucial moments. Shigeki Uno, Naofumi Nakamura, and Yuji Genda were particularly kind to read a late version of chapter 6 to check its logic, accuracy, and clarity. Whatever the book's remaining problems, it is stronger for the advice that all of these readers provided. The blame for remaining errors or failures in judgment rests solely with me.

The research and writing process was part of an emotional roller coaster for me for reasons that extend beyond the manuscript. I'm glad to have a child, sad to have lost my father, grateful to be married, excited about a trans-Pacific relocation—all of which happened as I struggled to complete the book. And so a special shout-out to my family and everyone who has kept us, and one another, going since my father's death: Cara, Vivienne, Mark, Mom, Nari, Richard, Michael, Eileen, Paul, Lena, Kobe, Yurie, Hidemoto, Tom, Koko, John, Sharon, and Jean. I hope that my godfather, Ben, and my dad are catching up on old times somewhere. This book, however, is dedicated to Satsuki, who has been my most consistent and most active interlocutor since I began this research. She introduced me to the story of Beto-chan/Doku-chan and also encouraged me to examine the *Ehime Maru* accident, both of them becoming key chapters of the manuscript. She spoke, informed, chatted, and argued with me about the book's argument over a number of years. And she then sustained and challenged me in ways that are too numerous to list but too important to leave unaddressed. She has my boundless love and my everlasting, humble gratitude.

CONVENTIONS

Japanese names are given in Japanese order (family-given) except in those cases when authors or scholars routinely publish or write in English, giving their own names in Western order.

Diacritics have been used in Japanese but generally not in Vietnamese, mostly because the limited number of Vietnamese terms and their context will make their meaning clear without them. I have omitted them in Japanese words or names that are typically rendered in English without them (e.g., Tokyo).

Empire of Hope

1

Maybe They Will Smile Back

In September 2011, about six months after the cataclysmic earthquake, tsunami, and nuclear disaster in the country's Northeast, Japanese theaters screened a new film by director Fukasaku Kenta. Known mostly as the screenwriter of the unhinged thriller *Battle Royale* and the son of its legendary director, Fukasaku Kinji, he made in this case an adaptation of Hada Kōta's book *Bokutachi wa sekai o kaerukoto ga dekinai* (We can't change the world). The addition of an English-language subtitle, *But We Wanna Build a School in Cambodia*, makes the film's story a bit less of a surprise than it otherwise might have been. Say what one might about the film—charitably, a middling cinematic achievement—it delivers what it promises. Its university-student protagonist, feeling aimless and uninspired by Japan's options, enlists his friends in a possibly quixotic and poorly defined effort to build an elementary school in rural Cambodia. Although the film is, predictably, about the personal transformations of the young Japanese volunteers, particularly the one played by heartthrob Mukai Osamu, it features Cambodia as a place of almost unending

Figure 1.1. Tokyo Skytree, the world's second-tallest structure, July 2012

poverty, illness, and misery, populated by good-hearted and decent people who deserve the same chances that the befuddled and largely talentless heroes have had. Indeed, the crux of the film's ethics comes when Mukai's character, facing challenges from cynical classmates, says "I just think if we go there with smiles, maybe the children of Cambodia will smile back."

There are, of course, *many* smiles in the film but also a plethora of tears, encouraging speeches, and even a belittling harangue, not to mention a despairing howl that features prominently even in the movie's trailer. The kids, after all, do what they do not just because they want to help their new friends in benighted Cambodia but also because they want to find purpose for themselves in a country that had gone off the rails. That, of course, is a political topic, but nothing about the film feels particularly political, even when the kids are confronted by the AIDS pandemic, the legacies of the Khmer Rouge genocide, and the deep inequities that the film shows. Japan is by far Cambodia's largest national donor of international aid,[1] and although aid activists and actors alike may emphasize humanitarian goals, no political scientist would view development assistance as divorced from politics. The movie, like the book on which it is based, is sentimental about its Japanese and Cambodian characters alike, and in its warm humanism it reminds readers both that the Japanese, by virtue of their wealth and education, have something to offer to the Cambodians, just as the Cambodians, through their decency and kindness, can remind their Japanese counterparts of what is important in life. And, as any competent melodramatic film will, it renders much of this through a complex range of showy emotions, at least among the Japanese protagonists. But the movie makes sense only because of its political subtext, one that positions Japan internationally and relies on an implicit story of what Japan had been and what it had become. This book explores the relationships among this story, these concerns about Japan's international position, and the ways in which people describe Japan's national emotions.

In international politics, people (or the nations they constitute) seem to have stunted emotional lives. As Todd Hall has noted, they are frequently angry, sometimes sad, and infrequently but significantly remorseful (as has Germany been with regard to the Holocaust).[2] In a remarkable amount of the public discourse, Chinese people are continually angry, with stories of Chinese rage that reappears each time a diplomatic dispute between China and another country, usually Japan, leads to protests and demonstrations.[3] Of course, the attention to Chinese anger is not uninvited; James Fallows of the *Atlantic* famously wrote a short essay decrying the frequent use of the Chinese government's statements that one thing or another had "hurt the feelings of the Chinese people," and Jessica Weiss, a leading specialist on Chinese foreign relations, has written extensively about the Chinese government's emphasis on the uncontrollable emotionality of Chinese protests as part of its bargaining strategies.[4] In contrast, people in the United States seem anxious or fearful—odd, given their country's vast wealth and global power. But anxiety is so prevalent as an expression of the US psyche that two political scientists have written an award-winning book analyzing how and under what conditions anxiety can be politically exploited by Republicans and/or Democrats.[5] Usually, governments give voice to these feelings, which are tightly circumscribed. We regret the war (or our actions in it). Our nation grieves for the victims of an air disaster (even one that happened primarily to the luckless citizens of another country). We celebrate or are happy for the agreement reached between two rival powers. Confusion, melancholy, bemusement, and consternation, to name but a few feelings that adults have, seem out of the question. Queen Elizabeth herself may not be amused and may use the royal "we" to express it, but "we British are not amused" or "we French are mildly irritated" would seem to be odd statements to utter on the floor of the United Nations. Most of us have messier emotional lives than these collective depictions suggest; indeed, we might describe ourselves as "happy" or "sad" but wonder whether adjectives like that precisely capture how we feel about something or wonder why we do not feel exactly the way we think we should.

The feelings in *We Can't Change the World* run the gamut, at least by the conventions of commercial cinema, but they are shaped profoundly by the story the film tells as well as the larger story against which it is set. After all, Hada's autobiographical book would have sat quietly on the shelves without a cinematic adaptation had it ended with the Japanese kids' giving up and not building the school or with the Cambodians' angry rejection of the gesture. Which studio would have funded a movie promising only failure and despair for its good-hearted but ineffectual heroes? The inspiring we-can-do-it tale not only demands a certain structure but also imposes on it certain emotional demands; there has to be a pattern of enthusiasm and self-doubt along the way before the smiles truly set in.

And this story itself, even if it fits within a well-worn genre of films about determined youngsters who succeed against the odds, makes sense to the Japanese audience primarily because of the larger, implicit one against which it is set. After all, the key characters are recognizable only because they themselves are part of a larger story about Japan that has been told and reproduced for many years. Unlike earlier postwar Japanese (especially men) who faced many opportunities upon graduating from elite colleges, the film's young protagonists are members of a generation that cannot count on a stable pathway into a collective effort to improve Japan's economic success. They are largely unmoored, the beneficiaries of national wealth but the inheritors of a malfunctioning employment system and a national cultural environment that provides fewer obvious chances for meaningful pride in one's achievements or for a sense of purpose. These are Japan's Lost Two Decades, the ones that followed the long period of high-speed growth that almost allowed Japan to escape from America's shadow and to become a regionally and internationally beloved leader; these are the two decades that ostensibly saw Japan's regional and global status recede. Without this background, the characters' decision to go to Cambodia in the first place, not to mention their plan to bring smiles to the people there, would make precisely no sense whatsoever.

This book examines the representation of emotion in Japanese political life and transnational engagement. It differs from many recent treatments of emotion and international politics in two ways. First, rather than taking emotion as a cause—as an independent variable—that drives people's behavior or their rational calculations of interests, it instead places the focus on how and when people speak of national or collective emotions. As do Roland Bleiker and Emma Hutchison in an important article, this book argues that our analytical lens should be placed on a logic of representation rather than on feelings themselves.[6] Partly for this reason, this chapter draws inspiration from recent works on sentimentality and affect in the humanities, which have mined the emotional worlds of literature, cinema, and art, taking the opportunity, for example, to examine how disdained sentimentalism in often-neglected works of literature or negative and seemingly minor emotional expressions in major works provide clues about silenced or marginalized political claims.[7] Second, instead of addressing only those topics considered to be of obvious political or diplomatic importance, it suggests that the relevant representations of national emotion often come in incidents and forms likely to be viewed as everyday life. This is essential in part because when people invoke national emotions—we Japanese are angry, or we Americans mourn, or we Germans are thankful—they likely have political goals in mind, but if the language succeeds, it does so largely by creating the image of an affective community that is not fragmented by the messy, divisive stuff of politics. It is persuasive because it seems to deny politics itself. The recurrence of public emotionality, however removed it may be from actual people's feelings, suggests the enduring appeal of highly sentimentalized stories of nations that create boundaries both for communities as well as for the things that their members can say about themselves.[8] Amending Descartes, we might say that "we feel, therefore we are," which makes the ability to speak authoritatively and convincingly about these feelings important indeed.

Interpreting Emotion in the Political World

Debates about emotion and politics have been productively traced to the classics of political thought, with recent scholarship suggesting that rigid distinctions between the passionate and the rational are intellectually and empirically misleading; they are also plagued by inattentiveness to the gendered nature of knowledge and its construction.[9] After all, despite classical and modern entreaties to keep emotions out of politics—instead using our rational, calculating, and dispassionate minds to come up with sound policy and wise governmental choices—they are of course deeply embedded in the political world: from the enthusiasm of a political rally to the despair one might feel when grudgingly making one's way to the polling station to place a vote between unappealing options only because it feels like part of one's civic duty as a democratic citizen.

Several important developments have strengthened and called attention to this movement. First, increasingly rigorously produced findings from neuroscientific research have shown that people's emotional worlds are deeply intertwined with their calculations and decisions, potentially making emotion central to political choice.[10] Additionally, political science has started to embrace experimental methods like those ideally employed in psychology.[11] Perhaps topping all of this has been the entry of US politics into a particularly anxious/angry era, from the 9/11 attacks through the subsequent disasters of the Iraq war and the larger war on terrorism, and into the 2016 presidential campaign and the Trump presidency, which has focused attention on how fear, anxiety, and anger shape decisions. If rage and fear drive political choices in ways that justify a disastrous military intervention, the routinized use of torture, and the election of a seemingly unhinged television celebrity as the president of the United States, emotion would appear to be an essential focus for political science research: hence the wide interest. But by disciplinary necessity, these approaches strip emotion to a few basic possibilities—anxiety, anger, and the like—creating the brutal simplicity that maps more effectively onto causal models than into the stuff of actual human feelings.[12]

At the same time that political scientists convinced of the importance of emotion have tightened it into testable models, researchers in cultural history and the humanities have begun to rely on affect and emotion to enrich our current reading of the past and to rethink the restrictions of contemporary disciplinary debate. This has sometimes meant the jettisoning of theoretical language that aims to turn the messy stuff of immediate feelings (or affects) into the cognitively processed language of emotion, sometimes a rethinking of the modern condition through consideration of emotional demands reproduced in cultural products, and occasionally an avowedly theoretical emphasis on the cultural dimensions of affect itself.[13] Some pathbreaking recent work on modern East Asian history has read emotional representation into important source material, seeking to understand the development of "public sympathy" in China and the relationships between Japanese settlers and local residents of Korea under the Japanese Empire.[14] Daniel White's excellent 2011 doctoral dissertation explores dimensions of Japan's cultural diplomacy and soft power strategies (a topic that I approach from a different perspective in chapter 4) to highlight the theorized gaps between nonconscious and experienced affects and socially produced emotions. As do Jie Yang in her justly acclaimed study of mental health workers in China and Anne Allison in her influential account of recessionary Japan, White uses affect theory to uncover otherwise hidden features in his close ethnographic research.[15] Although the "affective turn" in the humanities has invited criticism, particularly when it draws—often highly imprecisely and without appropriate context—from neuroscientific findings,[16] it has produced creative and significant rethinking of how to interpret sources and materials. This matters in particular for those politically fraught circumstances when people are prone to make some radical claims about how entire communities or nations feel and how those feelings matter.

The chapters in this book explore how emotional rhetoric and representation have characterized notable moments in Japan's late-twentieth-century and early-twenty-first-century politics and diplomacy. They draw from the existing literature the view that emotion matters in politics, often in ways that cannot be boiled down to simple causal frames and analyses, and that paying attention to it would enrich and uncover material all too frequently obscured in the mainstream political science literature. In doing so the book focuses not on what Japanese people actually feel but rather on how emotions are represented in Japanese politics—and especially on how these representations make sense only against the background of an implicit national story. In her influential study *Upheavals of Thought*, political philosopher Martha Nussbaum argues that rational thought and decisions are unintelligible without reference to emotion and that considering emotion in politics requires attention to narrative. After all, people's attachments and needs are affected in part by the ways in which they order that which is meaningful in their own lives and journeys; it is in part for this reason that Nussbaum finds French novelist Marcel Proust to be especially useful as a guide to the ways in which love and desire develop and play durable roles in shaping people's behavior.[17]

Unlike Nussbaum's book, this one draws more inspiration from quotidian sources, using sentimental representations in public debate, popular culture, and media sensations. *We Can't Change the World* is hardly a match for the artistic sweep and intellectual breadth of Proust, but it provides valuable clues—ones that will be echoed in later chapters—that can help to tease out what emotional references work in Japanese politics, why they do, and how they draw their power from a broad national story. After all, Abe Shinzō's 2012 campaign phrase "Take Japan Back" provided the same kind of implied story line for Japan that Donald Trump's "Make America Great Again" later would for the United States: that the country had lost its glory days and that its aspiring leader would somehow rebuild that greatness in the future.[18] History, of course, does not work in consciously planned stutter steps, but that is beside the point. The slogans aimed to build on and to reaffirm national feelings of pride, of anxiety, of dread, and of hope, all wrapped not just in the momentary urgency of an emotional flush but rather in a longer story of what had happened, what is happening, and what (hopefully) will happen. The emotional rhetoric that each leader deployed made sense specifically against these background stories of an earlier time when the nation worked together as one, unlike the disorderly, menacing present. A good future would be one in which the nation—taken back, made great again—would be able to act collectively and smoothly as it had in the idealized past.

Peter Brooks's now-classic notion of the "melodramatic imagination" provides several relevant clues for interpreting Japan's representations of emotions by detailing the elements of melodramatic narrative.[19] His principal concern was with the nineteenth-century novel's articulation of class differences and anxieties through an identification of virtue as innocence, an excess of emotional expression, and a story driven largely by dark external forces over which the main character has little control. But his argument's wide and continual use, even in some recent work on US politics,[20] reflects its effectiveness in highlighting relationships between emotion and narrative, as well as the malleability of the form's elements to illuminate different political and cultural contexts. The sources and episodes depicted in this and succeeding chapters trace how a promise of Japan's collective agency emerges from a sentimental construction of innocence, of innate and rediscoverable goodness, as national virtue in the face of a threatening or unpredictable world. When commentators, officials, and scholars describe Japan's global status—its visible role in a world that, virtually all agree, it did not create and does not control—they frequently draw from precisely this story: what we accomplished together, what struggles we face today, and what we must rediscover in order to accomplish together and to earn the world's respect and affection again. *Empire of Hope* argues that Japanese political actors have divergent goals when they invoke national emotion, but their claims resonate particularly when they connect the feelings of the Japanese people to a story of Japan that all of them are expected to share.

This shared story, with its emotional consequences, is a more promising route to explore than is the presumption of nationally shared or nationally distinctive emotions. After all, this specter of emotional difference has been a source of anxiety to scholars working on emotion, many of whom write primarily about their own countries. What if people in different places actually have different feelings? Writing from a neuroscientific perspective, Rose McDermott acknowledges the issue but rejects its relevance, arguing that differences lie more in emotional expression than in emotions themselves:

> The more advanced part of the brain, located mostly in the prefrontal cortex, develops from birth in interaction with the environment and grows largely in reaction to learning from the outside world. That is why people differ from culture to culture, but they share certain basic human processes. For example, all people use language to communicate, but they do not all use the same language.[21]

Others, however, have argued that cultural context has innate consequences for connecting emotion to politics. Even if one might identify general and ostensibly universal emotions (joy, anger, sadness), different triggers would likely produce them in different cultural contexts.[22] Surely, the logic goes, the predominantly Western scholars working in this burgeoning field ought to engage in some reflection about their ability to know the feelings of others, particularly in postcolonial or non-Western societies, before arrogating to themselves the right to make authoritative claims based on a putatively cosmopolitan or universal science of the mind.[23] Even if basic feelings are universal, their political consequences might be highly specific. After all, the social dimensions of emotion—how we communicate our feelings to others, how we experience them together—clearly have political consequences, whether in the ways in which actors creatively deploy them in the fraught circumstances of post-conflict situations or truth-and-reconciliation commissions, or in the ways in which shared experiences of trauma are used to establish collective identities.[24]

These identities might be reinforced or recognized by common performances of emotion—the rending of garments, ululation at weddings and funerals, enraged burning of a foreign-owned store during a demonstration or riot—but even these expressions would likely conceal the great range of feelings and experience of the participants themselves. They also offer, as Jonathan Mercer has noted, the opportunity to depict a community engaging in these practices as irrational, as emotional in ways that cloud rational thought.[25] In his study of Japanese melodramatic literature, Ken Ito notes how often his students point to overriding sentimentalism in much of Japanese popular culture, and indeed one could, for example, produce a lengthy YouTube montage of Japanese film scenes of characters running, crying, and waving to their friends or loved ones seated in departing trains.[26] Even recent action films, such as those in the Sea Monkey (*Umizaru*) series about Coast Guard rescue personnel, usually find time—so much time that it almost seems to be borrowed from another dimension in which nothing pressing is taking place—for emotional overreach: long, tearful confessions and conversations at moments when one might expect that the lead characters might instead be trying to figure out how to safely exit a sinking ship. Sentimentality seems so—well, so Japanese—that perhaps an examination of its political role tells us something about Japan but nothing about much else.

But that melodramatic display of emotion in political life—usually earnest, powerful, and operating according to locally available themes—shows up just as clearly, if inflected differently, in other contexts: from the British National Front's concerns over a national "soft touch" to Russian lamentations over the fallen soldiers of the Afghan War, and from the intense public reaction to Clint Eastwood's *American Sniper* in the United States to Vietnamese debates over the socialist ethics symbolized by East German architecture.[27] My point in drawing from research on melodrama is not that emotions themselves differ;

indeed, this book's next chapter will argue that claims of national emotional difference are themselves political rather than analytically useful statements of empirical fact. Instead, I argue that that we can do better than simple dismissals of difference or rendering them analytically incomparable because Japanese have Japanese feelings, Italians have Italian feelings, and so forth. By drawing attention to the ways in which national narratives shape opportunities for convincing emotional expression, we can highlight context in rigorous, identifiable ways while avoiding unsustainable generalizations that are closer to crude stereotypes than analytical categories. Feelings exist everywhere, as do scripted ways for governments to express them. But their political role—the ways they draw connection between an immediate sensation and larger questions of justice, fairness, order, rights, and the like— reflects the ways in which they appear in the stories that we routinely tell one another to remind ourselves of who we are.

The Story of the Long Postwar

By late 2010 and early 2011, Japanese writers, officials, and academics had been writing with numbing regularity and consistency about two "lost" decades, the nearly twenty years since the 1989/1990 pop of Japan's financial bubble and a terribly long stretch of minimal national economic growth.[28] But what was lost? Many people's wealth, to be sure, although the uneven growth in Japan after the financial crisis has meant radically divergent outcomes, with some having gained immensely through financial deregulation and others having fallen into abject and nearly inescapable poverty from transformations in Japanese employment. Beyond money, was it national pride that had been lost? National spirit? Indeed, at one workshop I attended in Japan in 2015, we spent a substantial amount of time trying to determine what "lost" precisely meant, even if there was little doubt that the word was both appropriate and applicable. I would argue that the broad acceptance of the term, as well as its recognizability across Japan's contemporary landscape, reflects the power of a widely understood story of Japan's postwar era. What mattered in large part was the pervasive sense that Japan's long period of national economic growth had been the result of collective national effort, manifesting itself in Japan's perceived international status by the late 1980s as the next superpower. When the bubble collapsed, that expected future was lost.

Myriad factors likely account for far worse economic outcomes in Japan in the 1990s and 2000s than from the 1960s through the 1980s, but there is no doubt that Japan's economy lost significant ground when compared to other advanced industrial nations and a number of developing economies alike.[29] Throughout these two decades, business and bank failures, media reports of crime and disorder, concerns about longer-term demographic challenges, and representations of the experiences of a new generation of young people with shaky job prospects and precarious economic circumstances together shaped wide dissatisfaction with the country's direction. It was not simply that conditions were bad, although they clearly were for some, but rather the sense that the Japan that had emerged in the 1990s and 2000s was not the future Japan imagined back in the 1960s, 1970s, and 1980s, when people were encouraged to believe that Japan's future would be better, richer, and more successful than its past. That it demonstrably was not, at least not for many, led people to question whether Japanese still had the ability to work as a national community to recreate that earlier story, the one in which collective endeavor would lead to national success.[30]

That earlier story smoothed out a number of the rough edges in the country's emergence as an economic superpower. Japan's immediate postwar years were ones of shortage, poverty, and fear as national defeat had left it occupied by a US government that, whatever its loftier goals, also wished to make Japan a strong ally in the looming cold war with the Soviet Union. This meant substantial reconstruction funds as well as crucial and continuing access to the US market for Japanese goods. When Prime Minister Yoshida described the Korean War—the human catastrophe for Korea and the other Cold War–era antagonists—as a "gift from the gods," he was referring not to the carnage overwhelming the peninsula but rather to the market for Japanese goods. Manufacturing firms rebuilding their factories after the devastating bombing campaigns that had ended the Pacific War found that the US armed forces were generous and reliable customers, and the capital amassed at this time assisted in rapid leaps to full reindustrialization.

Of course, the rapid leaps were not painless ones. Divisions among firm owners, workers, teachers, and farming and fishing families were energized by the redevelopment of Japan's prewar party system. Although communists were purged by the US occupation, Japanese Socialists (JSP) represented a powerful force that was defeated in the 1955 election only by the defensive coalition of two conservative parties to form the Liberal Democratic Party (LDP), which would remain in power for most of the next fifty years. Whether motivated by outrage that members of the wartime regime remained in power (either as bureaucrats or as members of the LDP) even through Japan's democratic transition, motivated by desperation to avoid incorporation into an anticommunist US empire, or motivated by efforts to make amends for Japan's brutal wartime behavior, Japanese leftists challenged the conservative government, particularly in the defense of workers' rights and in militant fidelity to the "pacifist" constitution. Between violent strikes such as the one at the Miike mine or incidences of environmental catastrophe such as mercury poisoning in Minamata, early postwar Japan was fraught with diverse tensions, the most famous symbolized by the 1960 riots of the US-Japan Security Treaty. Prime Minister Kishi Nobusuke—himself anathema to Japanese leftists because of his key role in the wartime government, particularly in the economic management of Manchuria—had planned to have the treaty's passage well in hand for the scheduled visit to Tokyo by President Dwight Eisenhower. When the minority JSP members blockaded the Diet to prevent the LDP from passing it, Kishi chose to have the police arrest the querulous opposition rather than to negotiate; his legacy was cemented when hundreds of thousands demonstrated in the streets around the Diet building, with one student dying in the melee. Kishi resigned, and the Eisenhower visit was delayed permanently.

Kishi's successor, Ikeda Hayato, was himself a former member of the Ministry of Finance, and his spectacular success at crisis management culminated in his announcement of the Income Doubling Plan. Not much of a policy innovation itself, the plan was really Ikeda's announcement of what he had been told by key economic officials: that the Japanese economy was expected to double in size within ten years. In essence, Ikeda personalized this expectation by emphasizing that the average per capita income would double by the end of the decade. Countless books have been written to explain the Japanese "miracle," with opinion divided over the importance of strategic state guidance, entrepreneurial activity by Japanese firms, or the way in which the Japanese electoral system rewarded national growth combined with regional redistribution.[31] Scholars and practitioners aimed to uncover the secrets of Japanese economic success, but it was increasingly narrated as an accepted fact of life to late-twentieth-century Japanese.

This, of course, took an extraordinary amount of work, though not always as conscious political propaganda; similarly, the popularity of "greatest generation" references in the United States is not the result of a formal agreement about how to portray those who fought in World War II and then participated in the postwar growth of the US economy and its military might. Particularly in the 1980s, Japanese bookstores were teeming with works about the miracles of Japanese-style organization, various knockoffs of Ezra Vogel's classic *Japan as Number One,* and even laudatory references to English-language accounts that were increasingly positing Japan as a threat to the United States. These were accompanied by public relations efforts to promote rural areas as the "real" Japan, deserving both generous development schemes as well as personal expenditures by tourists from the wealthier cities. Advertising campaigns widely promoted ideas of a unified middle class that needed the same commodities, with personal electronics and fashion accessories joining their predecessors such as air conditioners and television sets. Overlaying much of this were routine references to a unified Japanese cultural identity—including some notion of a shared history of samurai and poetry, of warm humanism and community. Equally central was intense attention to Japan's international position, both its long-term and subordinate spot in a US-led security order and its increasingly visible position as an economic and technological pioneer, particularly among other Asian states. No one coordinated these messages, but they fed on one another in ways that reaffirmed the commonality of a culturally unique nation finally coming into its own as a global leader, having long worked at doing so.

So it is no exaggeration to emphasize the conservativeness of Japan's prevailing postwar political ideology, at least in the widely reproduced images of traditional family structures and gender relations, of paternalistic employee-management connections, and of a state that, whatever the occasional foibles of its more comically corrupt legislators, had the best interest of citizens at heart. For many, these images would have not even seemed particularly political, let alone conservative. Government social policies, though far from a social democratic ideal, played important redistributive functions, and many were established largely because of direct cooperation between bureaucrats and progressive forces.[32] In the construction of Japan's "long postwar" as a democratic, peaceful era marked by a rupture with the prewar past (rather than by any of the substantial continuities), there has also been a substantial depoliticization of the nation's story after the war.[33] Indeed, much of the voluminous work on Japan's social and political debates over the past twenty years emphasizes how a shared set of anxieties and a shared mission for national restoration often elide the bitter divisions between Left and Right in modern and contemporary Japan.[34] It is not that people have been tricked into believing that there were no Anpo riots, no fights over pollution, no labor strikes, no student violence; it is rather that these events sit at the ragged, contested outskirts of public memory, not at postwar Japan's heart.

In the midst of the post-bubble era, director Yamazaki Takashi located that heart at one of Tokyo's most recognizable landmarks. His 2005 film *Always: Sunsets on Third Street* was a major box-office success about families in a ramshackle neighborhood in central Tokyo in the mid-1950s.[35] Bolstered by strong, showy performances and occasionally impressive digital images of postwar Tokyo in the shadow of the under-construction Tokyo Tower, the film swept Japan's Academy Awards. The film's artifice is both obvious and deliberate, as befits a film based on a manga; characters are lovable and self-evident caricatures, occasionally pulling off vaguely superhuman feats as they work to improve the lots of their families with the pride and optimism of a country that had emerged from defeat and was on the threshold of an economic miracle. Its sequels continue the story in 1960 and conclude in 1964, when Tokyo welcomes the world to the Olympics.

In one sense, the *Always* film series might resemble *Forrest Gump*: a great deal is effaced in their representation of the Country That Used to Be. Like *Forrest Gump* (in which terribly sad things, such as racism and the Vietnam War, keep happening to our developmentally disabled US hero through absolutely no fault of his own or really of anyone at all), *Always* and its sequels might be seen as presenting a national past in which success emerged largely from a nose-to-the-grindstone perseverance and personal integrity, certainly not from systemically predatory behavior or from an imperial past for which anyone bears responsibility. But the corny humor and exaggerated sentiment—typical for manga—make for a certain guiltless charm. The one constant in the first film, the thing that overshadows all of the characters even as it seems to result from their diverse acts of diligence and kindness, is the Tokyo Tower itself. As the film progresses, we see the tower continually growing and then finally achieving its height of 333 meters, taller than the Eiffel Tower, on which it was modeled.

To examine in more depth how the Tokyo Tower's construction in *Always* (or its post-construction popularity in *Always 2* or that of the 1964 Tokyo Olympics in *Always 3*) symbolically mirrors the growth of postwar Japan would be to belabor the exceptionally obvious. It might suffice to say that it represents postwar Japan as a country of national striving to rebound, to grow, and to be modern. In this vision, growth implicitly results from collective national enterprise rather than from the somewhat less appealing combination of preexisting economic institutions, access to a Cold War US market, labor bargains that limited wage growth in favor of security for an important subset of workers, or family patterns that made children and women particularly dependent on male breadwinners, whatever their individual moral qualities or cruelties. The vision is almost militantly apolitical; there are no battles between police and labor unions, no fights over Japan's relationship with the United States or its former colonial territories, and little that is more contentious than an otherwise good-hearted garage owner's comically short fuse. The movie's only villainous character, a wealthy and cruel industrialist, might have offered the opportunity for a critique of class difference. In the end, however, he earns only a few moments of screen time, far less than do the many symbols of collective effort, such as the teenage girl who becomes a beloved member of her employer's home after she arrives as a job-seeking bumpkin from the countryside. Japan grows together, with the politics—over who gets what, when, and how—relegated to background noise if even acknowledged in the first place. It together becomes a powerful, functioning, modern economy, supporting but also buoyed by its multigenerational families. And Japanese ostensibly *feel* it together, as the final shots suggest, with leading characters, now spread across the capital city, individually gazing up proudly and admiringly at the newly completed Tokyo Tower.

The nostalgia of the *Always* films is not a simple desire for the better days of the past. After all, even when viewed through the movies' rose-colored lenses, the past occasionally seems like a mess: no air-conditioning, few television sets, grief over the deaths of friends during the war, the threat of absolutely crushing poverty. But two central themes seem to make the 1950s—in reality, marked as much by environmental despoliation, struggles over political radicalism, and intense labor upheavals as by national economic growth—an appealing alternative to the 2000s, when the films themselves were made and earned large and enthusiastic audiences. First, people back then seemed able to work together and cooperate, despite their foibles and differences; back then, Japan seems to have had a spirit of community. Second, and largely because of that spirit of togetherness, people could look forward to a bright future, a Japan that would be better ten years down the road than at that moment. The real backdrop to the films is therefore not the 1950s and the early 1960s but rather recessionary Japan and its absence of hope.

Stories of Hope

Although the most rapid expansion of the economy occurred before the early-1970s energy crises, even after 1973 the Japan's GDP grew at a robust annual rate of roughly 5 percent through the end of the 1980s. Until the 1986 Plaza Accord, in which the Reagan administration bowed to domestic political pressure to limit Japanese exports to the United States, an undervalued yen kept Japanese products artificially cheap and foreign products comparatively dear. The rapid expansion of paper wealth when the yen virtually doubled overnight resulted in a massive Tokyo property and stock bubble involving not just major firms but also hundreds of thousands of smaller investors who engaged in risky borrowing for their real estate and capital investment plans. Despite the deafening pop of Japan's stock and property bubbles in 1990–1991, a broad emphasis on national decline became far more noticeable only when the late-1994 collapse of a set of financial institutions was followed immediately by the January 1995 Hanshin-Awaji earthquake, in which six thousand perished, mostly in Kobe, and then the lethal March attack by the Aum Shinrikyo cult on Tokyo's subways with sarin gas. Both were noted as calamitous government failures: the former for a Katrina-like national response that left Kobe's organized-crime families and a developing nongovernmental organization (NGO) network as among the first responders on the scene, and the latter for crime and intelligence units focused nearly exclusively on aging leftists rather than on other potentially obvious threats, such as a millenarian cult led largely by chemists and engineers. To many observers, the events seemed not to be separate phenomena but like snowballing elements of the unraveling of modern Japan; by mid-1995, the phrase *aimai na fuan* (vague anxiety) was becoming a mainstay in titles of books and articles in leading opinion monthlies.[36]

Like *Always*, the disconnected, partly fictionalized episodes of the popular 1990s NHK series *Project X* take a nostalgic look backward, usually to some group of hardworking Japanese businessmen and technicians who overcome setbacks before completing one of the many industrial or infrastructural milestones of the long postwar.[37] The differences with the 1990s and 2000s could hardly be starker. With banks and financial firms failing, major Japanese companies such as Nissan being sold off to foreign investors, a new generation of young students facing dire job prospects, and a rapidly aging population facing a looming pension crisis, Japan was anything but the unified, optimistic powerhouse that the television programs and films suggested it once had been. Worse yet, there seemed to be few reasonable prospects to staunch the bleeding, with each reform—Prime Minister Hashimoto's financial "big bang" deregulatory measures, Prime Minister Koizumi's privatization of the postal savings system, Prime Minister Abe's multidirectional "Abenomics" package—spurring momentary enthusiasm but little sustained confidence in the country's economic prospects.

Many of Japan's most important economic concerns revolve around the aging population, but this lack of confidence in the future—a stark departure from Japan's previous postwar generations—has inspired myriad studies of the economic and employment insecurity facing the young. As sociologist Mary Brinton has noted, for nonelite younger workers the breakdown of traditional pathways from school to workplace has in some ways created an untethered "lost generation" that is alienated from social institutions that functioned largely because of their tight connection to conventional education and employment. For years, the problem was widely seen as a moral one, with selfish, materialistic youngsters choosing an irresponsible lifestyle of part-time and short-term jobs, delaying marriage and families, and frequently living with their parents into their thirties. Brinton calls particular attention to work by the labor sociologist Genda Yūji in turning the discussion toward the structure of labor markets and its consequences for the young.[38]

Although the United States has now had one president from Hope (Arkansas) and another extolling its audacity, only Japan has a Genda, who has spearheaded major research projects to create national hope. After more than a decade of publishing widely read and highly empirical accounts of labor market dysfunctions and their consequences for the young, Genda took the lead in establishing the *Kibōgaku* project (perhaps translated most clearly as Hope-ology, although it is generally rendered in English as "The Social Sciences of Hope"). This multiyear project officially ran until 2009 at the Institute of Social Science at Japan's most prestigious institution of higher education, the University of Tokyo. Among the many publications to have emerged from the project, the core is the four-volume edited set, enthusiastically blurbed by one of contemporary Japan's most famous novelists, Murakami Ryū.[39] Murakami had himself diagnosed a need for national hope in his 2000 novel *Kibō no kuni no ekusodasu* (Exodus of the country of hope), about a mass defection of 800,000 students from Japan's junior high schools, inspired by one teenager who had set off on an anti-landmine expedition to Pakistan; they ultimately form a network that challenges global capitalism and Japanese political authority. Genda, in his introduction to the "social sciences of hope," quotes Murakami's famous line in the novel: "We have everything in this country. Really, we've got just about anything one could want. The one thing we don't have is hope."

We return to the "social sciences of hope" in chapter 6, emphasizing both the durability of hope in discussions of contemporary Japan as well as its essential and recognizable place in a longer story about the country. Japan's national story—rebirth from the trauma of war, collective effort for national growth, an Icarus-like plunge in the wake of the putative materialism and greed of the 1980s—has become so pervasive that it acts nearly like a genre, shaping the ways in which other stories are mapped onto it and the kinds of emotional payoffs they are supposed to create. For example, a Hollywood romantic comedy will likely follow a mismatched couple who start by annoying each other, discover their feelings for each other, face humorous obstacles (a snobbish girlfriend, a lecherous boss), and finally—crucially—confess their feelings to each other, with the closing credits fortunately arriving before the myriad conflicts and challenges of marriage, disease, or economic vulnerability. A dark mystery novel can throw all manner of red herrings and minor scares at a detective before a final, violent confrontation that she or he solves, but with continuing doubts and anxieties about the human condition. The surprises may lie in the details of the path but not in its structure; a grim ending would doom a romantic comedy's viability, just as a thoroughly upbeat resolution would turn away the fans of an ostensibly gritty thriller. And so it is with the narration of national political events, which, regardless of their details, will usually be folded into a larger story of a country: America's continuing revelation of greater levels of human liberty, Japan's collective effort to build national prosperity and autonomy. The "social sciences of hope" project reflects an intellectually audacious effort to understand how hope is generated and built in challenging environments. But its existence itself, like its durable goals, reflects a larger national story about Japan's past, present, and anticipated future.

The Ending People May Have Wanted

Anticipation matters. It matters in politics, it matters for the study of politics, and it matters in the ways in which we express ourselves in politics. A day before the massive 2011 tsunami that devastated Japan's northeastern coast, Japan's most renowned and widely read monthly magazine, *Bungei Shunjū,* released its April 2011 issue. The cover story was a staple sort of feature for the magazine, a collection of short essays by dozens of famous politicians, intellectuals, writers, and artists around a central theme. This time, the question was "Is *This* the Japan We Wanted?"[40] Needless to say, most answers were varying shades and intensities of "no"; why even frame the question this way if the answer would likely be "yes"?

In his famous study of narrative, Peter Brooks calls attention to the act of reading and particularly to the desires of readers themselves.[41] After all, a writer or speaker telling a story does so in part with the understanding that the listener or reader wants to reach a certain point, a climax. Brooks's psychoanalytic examination of narrative theorizes in part about the sexual element of this desire, but the book's focus remains resolutely on the complicity between reader and author in propelling a story forward, ideally toward an ending that—with or without surprises—ought to be satisfying. Indeed, this is what the large story of Japan's postwar economic miracle was supposed to have created, a satisfying outcome in which the collective endeavor of the Japanese would ultimately allow the country to occupy a respected leadership role in the world. Different political actors have viewed this differently. Some nationalists have aspired to taking the mantle of leadership away from the Western powers that had mismanaged and colonized the world, leaving Japan with a masochistic reading of its own history rather than a celebration of its long-term culture. Many leftists have envisioned a Japan that would lead by moral example as a peaceful economic superpower with top-tier technology and limited inequality, able to bring along other countries under Japanese tutelage. And even those political advocates of a middle-ground approach, viewing Japan as a complementary player in international politics, argue that Japan's economic miracle and collaborative example would make it a widely respected contributor to global solutions.

The expected endings have differed, but the vast majority of public claims about Japanese aspirations have been built on the shared story about Japan's past and the challenges it had recently confronted. And this is partly why, for all the differences in their political views and approaches, nearly all of the respondents in the *Bungei Shunjū* feature could register disappointment in what Japan had become by spring 2010. Japan might still meet each writer's desires, but it had not yet done so, and there would need to be some kind of national recommitment to make this happen.

The broad familiarity of this narrative makes it not just politically useful—after all, political figures make strategic decisions all the time about what stories to tell and how to tell them—but also compelling and even central to what a community is. Stepping outside of this story of what postwar Japan achieved and how it achieved it risks running afoul of core expectations of listeners, readers, viewers, or voters. This is much same way that US Republicans and Democrats, despite their very different views of the nation's history, will still likely emphasize a continuing, if frequently threatened, national drive toward liberty. It was crystallized in the Revolutionary War, remained central to the Civil War (whether to the northern abolitionist movement or to Confederate "states' rights"), and has been the cornerstone of a twentieth century that may, depending on the speaker, be marked primarily by World War II's victory over fascism, by the civil rights movement's challenge to US apartheid, or by the Cold War triumph over Soviet communism. Stories like this work in large part because of the ways in which people are encouraged to invest themselves emotionally in stories of their community.[42]

Indeed, some of the most striking work on politics in recent years has viewed the ability to tell compelling stories as an essential factor in the success of social movements and social organizations in promoting collective action, convincing members that they are part of a larger narrative that unites personal and social change.[43] Focusing specifically on Japan, Richard Samuels has considered the ways in which "captivity narratives"—that is, a preexisting narrative structure, with general roles and defined courses of events—can be deployed by political actors to shape, in this example, the meaning of abductions of Japanese and South Koreans by North Korea.[44] Samuels here notes the central tension in narrative analysis in politics. On the one hand, we tend to privilege political agency—the ability of self-interested political actors to make choices that further their own goals. The popular use of narrative in political punditry (as when someone "shapes the narrative") implies that the storyteller who sits on top of events really knows the truth but makes strategic decisions regarding how to tell the story to convince (or perhaps to fool) credulous citizens into supporting the storyteller's position. But Samuels also calls attention to existing narrative structures over which the storyteller has limited control and even those in which the storyteller himself or herself is unwittingly playing a role. And this matters in large part because a narrative implicates speaker/author and listener/reader alike in the drive toward an ending, not just a programmatic goal, to which they expect their own actions to lead.[45]

Sentimental Episodes and Emotional Stories

This book's chapters examine issues and episodes in ways that highlight the connections between an overarching Japanese postwar narrative and the kinds of emotions expressed within them; they also call attention to the gaps between these public expressions of emotion and the complex, messy reality of people's emotional lives. To that end I have chosen cases that might be remembered in Japan more for the pathos, enthusiasm, grief, or pride that each ostensibly engendered than for the potentially divisive politics at work. For example, chapter 2 examines the momentarily volatile but now mostly forgotten *Ehime Maru* accident of 2001, when a fisheries training boat filled with high school students was struck and sunk by an American nuclear submarine. Soon overshadowed by the 9/11 attacks and Japan's subsequent efforts to support the US

"War on Terror," this accident briefly approximated a diplomatic crisis, resolved when the United States famously raised the boat and located eight of the nine dead aboard, including three of the four high school students who had been killed. This chapter challenges arguments about the cultural specificity of emotion, arguments that were themselves central to the dispute and its resolution. In doing so, it traces the representation of Japanese emotionality by actors in both Japan and the United States, showing how expressions of national emotion built from a common story about the US-Japan relationship. These agreements allowed a diplomatic solution that elided—even suppressed—the messier story of personal grief associated with the victims and their families. The more positive reactions from the Japanese side emphasized a limited form of Japanese agency in the alliance: the ability to achieve "mutual understanding" through US acknowledgment of Japan's distinctive emotions, however unsustainable these claims of distinctiveness were.

In chapter 3 we turn to the 1980s Japanese saga surrounding Nguyen Viet and Nguyen Duc. The conjoined twins "Beto-chan" and "Doku-chan," understood to be victims of the US use of Agent Orange during the Vietnam War, became celebrities in Japan when they visited for medical care at age five. Two years later, they were surgically separated, with Japanese financial and medical assistance, in Vietnam. Vietnam sits uneasily in Japan's postwar narrative, a mostly forgotten victim of Japanese military control that became far more relevant in the 1960s as Japanese argued over their government's complicity in US violence against the country. This chapter engages debates about Japan's postwar cultural, economic, technological, and political role in Asia, particularly as a country that was the victim of US violence, then lost its war but temporarily won the postwar, able to provide qualified but meaningful help to those most traumatized by US hegemony. In doing so, it follows recent work on the affective representation of politics, showing that the sentimentality of the story highlights a longer story about Japan's regional and global positions.

That anxiety about international status would become an overwhelming feature of debates in post-bubble Japan, and chapter 4 introduces the "soft power" craze that served as a kind of response. Chastened by the country's economic decline and the new difficulty of celebrating a distinctive Japanese Way in which the country could provide regional or global leadership, Japanese officials and writers expressed great enthusiasm about the country's "soft power" resources—the popular culture products that were making post-bubble Japan the cool center of a hip, transnational global culture. First identified by the American political scientist Joseph Nye but long disdained by political science for its conceptual fuzziness, soft power has perhaps been particularly meaningful as a way of countering the expected consequences of political or economic decline. The chapter draws from literary theorist Lauren Berlant's recent work on "cruel optimism," arguing that her investigation of emotional modes in US cultural life offers tools for considering how and why an empirically unsustainable concept such as soft power could have so rapidly become an appealing policy guide in recessionary Japan. Largely devoid of specific content despite their putative connection to Japan's "digital content industries," soft power proclamations became an opportunity for an expression of national pride so capacious that they could incorporate almost any image of what kind of Japan would be admired around the world, and what good that admiration would do.

The background story of Japan's postwar era and the future it had ostensibly promised is central to the emotional representations in these episodes and to the effacement of potentially divisive political issues over Japan's relationship with the United States, over its moral responsibilities in Asia, over the kind of society Japan ought to become. To consider how the reproduction of narrative reflects emotional expectations, chapter 5 analyzes the work of Caramel Box, a popular contemporary theater group in Tokyo. Tracing the development of the play *The Empire of Light,* this chapter looks at the reproduction of certain narrative structures and their emotional beats as a necessity in a complex, competitive market. It does so by showing how a story by a well-known science fiction writer could become part of Caramel Box's highly stylized repertoire when reimagined within the melodramatic framework that the company had developed over a quarter century. In drawing more explicitly from narrative theory, the chapter also suggests how these works display a certain structure of conservative politics, one in which characters' previous and deviant choices are emotionally rationalized through their reintegration with the social world around them. By focusing closely on Caramel Box's relationship with its overwhelmingly female audience, the chapter also calls attention to its negotiation of a broader set of social and moral claims in bubble-era and post-bubble Japan. The company's repertoire is avowedly

apolitical, yet its systematic resolution of personal crises, through characters' reckoning with prior choices and their reintegration into loving,
accepting social environments, provides a hint of what a Japanese politics
of hope might resemble.

Chapter 6 returns to the "social sciences of hope" project established
by the University of Tokyo in 2004. Focusing on Kamaishi, a declining
steel town in Japan's periphery, the empirical contributions in the project aim to trace the institutional foundations through which the town's
citizens were striving, with some measure of success, to keep hope alive
in the city despite its economic burdens. This chapter articulates the
ways in which a certain generation of Japanese scholars—those who
had had reason to expect a brighter future than the present with which
they were contending—tried to account for and to encourage patterns
of entrepreneurship and development that might bring hope anew to
those in their twenties. It also examines how emotional representations
of Kamaishi's fate during and after the 2011 tsunami, which killed a
thousand of the city's residents, could reshape and rechannel the meaning of national hope itself.

In keeping my focus largely on sentimentality, I have deliberately
steered away from Japan's fraught regional relationships, particularly
with China and Korea: the neighbors both most willing to criticize Japan
for its seeming impenitence regarding colonial and wartime practice as
well as most able to challenge Japan for regional leadership. Bluntly, I
have been reluctant to engage these relationships to avoid doubling down
on recent debates that, while continually important, have been explored
extensively in both English and Japanese in recent years, including in
accounts that frame the relationships through emotional lenses.[46] Instead,
I focus on Japan's relationships with the United States and with Southeast Asia because both have been particularly salient to concerns about
Japan's status in postwar Asia as the subordinate partner in an alliance
that primarily reflects US hegemony and as a frequently praised aid donor
and economic model for Southeast Asian governments that have been at
times eager to extol Japan's leadership and celebrate its friendship. China's ominous rise and Korea's continual reminders about Japanese war
responsibility provoke, among other things, anxiety, guilt, and anger in
Japan; these feelings are ineluctably political. The episodes in this book
call attention to the possibilities that a long national narrative affords for

the sentimental representation of Japanese emotion, often in ways that conceal the politics itself.

To that end, my interpretive approach has asked a similar basic question—how were people expected to feel when the story reached its expected or desired conclusion?—but looked to different sources in each case: the voluminous newspaper accounts of the Nguyen brothers, the public government reports in the *Ehime Maru* accident and the Tōhoku earthquake, and the narrative variation between the Caramel Box play *The Empire of Light* and the science fiction story on which it is based. And these cases reflect a wide array of publicly articulated feelings: grief, gratitude, pride, despair, and hope. Focusing on the usual suspects in political science research on emotion, such as anger or anxiety, is as limiting as considering politics to be only the stuff of regular elections or civil wars. Most of our political judgments, feelings, and feelings about politics emerge in the spaces between these convulsive tremors, and they transcend simple judgments of nationalism, collective fear, or public rage. Our collective sentiments feel ordinary, common, and justified when they fit well with what we already know to be our past and what we expect to be our future.

For this reason, the concluding chapter, "Everything Sinks," looks explicitly at Japan's future, or rather at the future that Japan was supposed to have. It examines in particular how Japanese intellectuals, artists, and officials express, often emotionally, how they are coming to grips with a global environment in which Japan's malaise is the norm rather than the exception. Although I refer to some rethinking of the postwar narrative that necessitated a study of national hope in the first place, I pay further attention to the ways in which Japan's global status is buttressed by its position as the vanguard, the "problem pioneer," whose solutions and efforts might bring hope and intellectual and cultural guidance to the imperiled, sinking world around it. And the chapter considers what it might mean for Japan to force a smile in the hope that the world will smile back.

2

SOULS OF THE *EHIME MARU*

Oranges can float on the surface of the ocean for a spell before rotting or disintegrating against the force of heavy waves. Particularly when they spill out together—from a damaged crate or a bag that falls over the side of a boat—they are likely to spread slowly apart, even as they move, nudged by current and wind, in the same general direction. In summer 2001, Glen Watabayashi of the US National Oceanic and Atmospheric Administration (NOAA) explained the drift patterns of oranges to Naval Pacific Meteorology and Oceanography Center researchers who had been tasked with plotting the best way to raise the *Ehime Maru*, a Japanese fisheries training boat sunk in a collision with the nuclear submarine *USS Greeneville*, and to bring it to a shallow-water recovery site (SWRS) near the coast of Hawaii. There it would be searched by US and then Japanese divers to locate the remains of the nine Japanese missing and presumed dead. Raising and moving the ship, however, risked releasing some of its fuel oil into the open sea, where it might drift toward the coast. The operation's supervisor, US Navy Rear Admiral William Klemm, had dictated that "Not

Figure 2.1. Divers searching the *Ehime Maru*, November 5, 2001
Source: US Navy photo by Chief Petty Officer Andrew McKaskle

a single teaspoon of oil will get onto any Hawaiian beach," hardly an easy guarantee, given the size of the *Ehime Maru* and the unprecedented complexity of the salvage operation.[1] The oranges represented an opportunity to predict how oil from a ruptured tank might disperse once the boat was relocated to the SWRS, where US Navy divers would begin the famous search of the sunken boat for the bodies of nine victims, including four high school students and two teachers from their school.

The story of the *Ehime Maru*—its deadly collision, the resignation of embattled Prime Minister Mori Yoshirō, the US Navy's salvage mission, and the boat's final scuttling—was covered extensively in the news, and it might subsequently have offered endless lessons for observers. It could have become a component of a story of Japan's weakness and capitulation within the American empire, with the US government offering a few scraps of remorse only because of the extent of potential damage to the relationship. It could have been viewed in retrospect as an episode of human loss and the struggle to achieve justice. It might have become a story of doing the right thing even when such a choice is personally costly. It was momentarily described as an inspiring story of an alliance that overcame an obstacle—namely, public outrage and grief over the grim fates of a group of sailors, teachers, and students—by overcoming cultural difference.

But this story of a maritime disaster—one potentially redolent with meaning for Japan's global status and security—was swiftly overcome by events. After all, just a few weeks before the boat's salvage in October 2001, which might have been a major news story in the United States as well as Japan, nineteen airline passengers armed with box cutters managed to crash their hijacked jets into the World Trade Center and the Pentagon. Analysts routinely referred to it as the most devastating attack on the United States since 1941, when Japan's Imperial Navy laid waste to much of the US Navy base at Pearl Harbor. Seventy years later, at the time of the 9/11 attack, Pearl Harbor welcomed the *Chihaya,* a Japanese submarine rescue ship tasked with assisting in the recovery of the bodies from the *Ehime Maru.* And the September 11 attacks provided the opportunity for hawkish governments in Tokyo and Washington alike to reinvigorate the US-Japan alliance in a manner that would render the *Ehime Maru* diplomatic tension—the deaths of nine people, the tortured apologies, the hand-wringing over the future of the US-Japan relationship—more or less meaningless. Japanese leaders had long viewed the alliance with the United States as the indispensable core of Japanese national security, and US strategists had similarly understood Japan to be an irreplaceable asset in a very dangerous neighborhood. For all the talk of the success of cultural sensitivity, it is difficult in retrospect to imagine how, particularly in the wake of an alliance-testing attack, things might have turned out much differently. In part because of the heightened rhetoric in Japan and to some degree the United States, the most powerful leaders in both countries were focused on crisis management primarily as damage control; not a single teaspoon of oil from the broken ship would be allowed to stain the alliance itself.

This chapter retells the story of the *Ehime Maru*'s collision with the *Greeneville,* focusing particularly on the way in which both governments emphasized US respect for a distinctive Japanese emotionality as the driving motive behind the US raising of the ship. In doing so, it argues that this representation of national emotion was simultaneously sincere and deeply misleading. After all, there is no doubt that a wave of grief for the boys swept through Japan in the wake of the disaster, accompanied by combinations of outrage, frustration, and anger at the United States. Surely no figures lied when emphasizing the importance of recovering and returning the victims' bodies so that their families might perform proper funerals. But these statements demonstrably overstated the differences between US and Japanese emotions about death in general and the accident in particular, and they camouflaged deep differences within Japan itself, seemingly especially with regard to the victims' families. Emotion matters, of course, but states do not feel, and their leaders are at best imperfect representatives of their people, whose emotional lives are fraught, elastic, and complex.

The *Ehime Maru* case shows the ways in which emotional claims by governments can obscure the messy complexity of people's feelings, but it does more than that as well. Journalists and scholars routinely display their savvy by looking at how officials seek to manipulate emotions—fear, anger, anxiety—to achieve their policy goals. But the *Ehime Maru* case shows two governments working assiduously to cooperate and to compromise, to preserve their alliance in the aftermath of a terrible accident. By stipulating that Japanese and Americans had different emotional responses to death—despite the absence of evidence to support this—commentators and officials in both countries laid the groundwork for an effort that would overcome these largely fictive differences, offering "mutual understanding" as a way of resolving the crisis. These efforts therefore helped to depoliticize what might otherwise have been understood to be a deeply political (and, for some, deeply felt) division between the two countries, one that ostensibly robbed Japan of anything more than token agency: the ability to have its feelings noticed by its alliance partner. A critical reading of the *Ehime Maru* case thus draws attention to the politics of emotional expression—particularly in the construction of national bodies of feeling through official claims about collective feelings.

Reports of the Accident

The *Ehime Maru,* a training vessel owned by the Uwajima Fisheries High School in Ehime Prefecture, was used principally for training and research expeditions for the high school's students.[2] Even with a population of over

90,000, at least after the 2005 legal consolidation of several smaller villages into the city, Uwajima would still be considered by most in Japan to be rural. Fisheries continue to represent a major industry in Japan, especially important to smaller coastal cities like Uwajima. With a secondary school system stratified by test scores and often segmented by areas of interest, Japan has a number of high schools that focus on training students for the marine sector, whether as fishers, marine scientists, maritime engineers, or employees of one of the nation's many seafood processing companies. Albeit distinctive, Uwajima High School, with its nearly 200 students (about 70 percent of them boys), is far from unique, and it might be considered characteristic of smaller, more "traditional" coastal towns far from major population centers.[3] It would later become an occasional source of irritation in the Japanese press that American media outlets routinely referred to the *Ehime Maru* as a fishing boat rather than as a training vessel, which in theory could somehow reduce the horror of its sinking or the demise of nine of its crew, although most American sources were clear in repeating that the victims included a number of high school students on a training expedition. The purpose of the trip—to train a group of rural high school students in the myriad difficult tasks associated with deep-sea fishing—was relatively straightforward in the Japanese press, requiring little elaboration or explanation.

The *Ehime Maru*'s training run had been scheduled for seventy-four days, and at noon on February 9 it had departed Honolulu, where a brief stopover had allowed for the repair of a broken air-conditioning system. Less than two hours later, the high school students, their teachers, and the boat's formal crew heard two loud noises and felt the boat shake; within five seconds the boat lost all power, and diesel fuel began to spray onto the fishing deck. The *Greeneville*'s rudder had opened a nearly three-foot-wide gash across the boat's bottom, with immediate damage rising vertically as far as eleven feet. With the lower decks plunged into darkness and diesel fuel and seawater filling the boat, the students—who had just finished lunch—were forced to move quickly either from the crew mess or their bunks to the mustering area behind the pilothouse. With or without lifejackets, those who could jump off the boat or into life rafts escaped, although others were apparently swept away by the waves or were trapped inside the boat, which sank in less than five minutes. The oil slick that covered the water made it especially difficult for those not already in lifeboats to reach safety. Most of the crew members were rescued by Coast Guard divers, but nine remained missing.[4]

The *Greeneville's* flamboyant and popular commander, Scott Waddle, had made the nuclear submarine one of the most respected in the Pacific fleet, and it was for this reason that it was chosen to host a group of sixteen civilians, designated as the navy's "distinguished visitors," who were part of an organization dedicated to erecting a memorial to the ship on which Japan surrendered to the United States, the *USS Missouri*.[5] Two of them were allowed to sit at the helm and control stations when Waddle demonstrated one of the most entertaining parts of running a nuclear submarine. Having already executed a set of high-speed turns and gone to periscope depth to check the surface for other vessels, Waddle ordered his apparently surprised crew to execute an emergency deep dive. This maneuver is usually followed by an emergency blow: forcing high-pressure air into the ballast tanks and thus driving out water as rapidly as possible in order to make a sudden and jarring trip to the surface. The distinguished visitors who were not fortunate enough to be at the controls of the ship were so shaken by the ballast-blow maneuver that they were reportedly grabbing whatever they could to stay upright. Seconds before the bridge would have reached the surface, the guests and crew heard a loud sound and felt the submarine shake, with Waddle asking one of his final questions as an active submarine commander: "What the hell was that?"[6]

The same question might have been asked by the seemingly bewildered Japanese prime minister, Mori Yoshirō. Having become prime minister through a widely reviled backroom deal occasioned by former Prime Minister Obuchi Keizō's sudden illness and coma, Mori's nearly comical gaffes and malapropisms—from a campaign photo unwisely showing him in rugby shorts to his puzzling, 1939ish reference to Japan as a "divine nation with the emperor at its head"—had already rendered him a lame duck within the ruling Liberal Democratic Party. But on hearing the report that the *Ehime Maru* had been sunk by a US nuclear submarine, and with nine missing and feared dead (including four boys from a rural high school), Mori made the ghastly decision to finish his round of golf, reaching the nadir of his failed term in office; he would be forced to resign by the end of April. Within weeks of the sinking, one of Japan's most astute diplomatic and political observers, the international relations scholar Tanaka Akihiko, argued that it was Mori's behavior that actually spurred the problems that ensued. By appearing to be unconcerned about the missing and their families, Mori lost the opportunity to be a credible representative of Japanese anger and grief toward the United States. Doing so would also have allowed him more space to emphasize the unshakable importance of the alliance. It would be natural to protest and to express anger, but the thing that ought not be forgotten, in Tanaka's eyes, was that the United States was Japan's most valuable ally.[7]

Other English-language accounts have already examined the crisis-management efforts that the United States undertook in the wake of the accident. Curtis H. Martin traces the tensions between the United States and Japan in the *Ehime Maru* case, arguing that although security concerns and domestic politics mattered in both nations, many of the frictions were cultural in nature, particularly in regard to demands for an apology as well as for the recovery and treatment of the bodies of the missing. Martin evinces some wariness about cultural stereotypes of the United States and Japan, but he locates several of the friction points as emanating from the differences between Japan's "collectivist" culture and America's "individualistic" one.[8] Indeed, expressions about the cultural differences between the United States and Japan were central to the diplomatic efforts between the two countries, and numerous accounts have taken them to be of foremost importance in their ultimate success. From this perspective, the especially deep salience of apology in Japanese culture—presumably because of the special importance of the community and the individual's responsibility to behave in a manner that protects its harmony—made it all the more crucial for US efforts at "image repair" to involve "mortification" (deep, abject apology).[9]

At least in terms of sheer numbers, there was no shortage of apologies. President George W. Bush, Secretary of State Colin Powell, Secretary of State Donald Rumsfeld, Ambassador Thomas Foley, and US Navy Admirals Thomas Fargo and William Fallon were among the many officials to express their regret to Japan and the victims' families within days of the accident. In some ways the tardiness of a statement from Waddle himself became a convenient focal point for the discussion, although even he made a public apology a few weeks after the crash. Ambassador Foley ascribed the delay to the importance of protecting the subject of a legal inquiry, but Waddle himself later wrote that he had been eager to apologize and was disappointed that the navy had sent top officials rather than him to do so.[10] Apologies like these may have done little to assuage the anger and grief in particular of the families who had lost their loved ones, especially as it became more clear that safety decisions inside the submarine had likely been compromised by efforts to showboat for the civilians. That these civilians were reportedly wealthy executives courted by the US Navy as boosters in its public relations efforts made the situation even less defensible. One might conclude, therefore, that the apologies were meaningless or insufficient. But they were extensive enough that *Washington Post* columnist Richard Cohen famously (and controversially) wrote that enough was enough: Japan should move on, as the United States had apologized sincerely for a mistake, particularly to an ally that was notoriously unwilling to accept responsibility for its own behavior in World War II.[11]

Several limited US steps that might have demonstrated remorse or reflection followed, including disciplinary actions against Waddle and several officers on the *Ehime Maru,* a mild redrafting of the guidelines for the handling of distinguished visitors, and extensive payment as compensation for damages to family members, other victims, and the Ehime prefectural government. One might judge these to be either obvious and responsible initiatives by a government at fault or simply as empty maneuvers in a dysfunctional and unbalanced alliance, one that continued to threaten public safety. Scholars like Gavan McCormack and the late Chalmers Johnson have argued extensively that the US-Japan relationship has been marked by deep pathologies related to the long-term presence of bases on the territory of a wealthy but supposedly pacifist military ally (though with one of the world's largest budgets for national security).[12] Although different regions in Japan have experienced mishaps and accidents involving the US military—the Japanese fishing crew irradiated by a US nuclear test in 1954, a plane crash into an elementary school five years later—Okinawa has been at the center of many of the most appalling incidents. The 1995 rape of a twelve-year-old girl by three US Marines in Okinawa became a flashpoint in local and national politics[13] as did, to a lesser extent, the molestation of a fourteen-year-old by another Marine five years later.[14] Okinawa, therefore, represents a war-torn victim of the US-Japan alliance, made dependent on funding related to the presence of bases and seen as something of a colonial outpost by the Japanese and American governments alike.[15] With so many bases in Japan, critics could (and did) argue that the *Ehime Maru* accident represented not only a risk for those who might be sailing in the open seas near Hawaii but also "potentially a problem for all Japanese" (*nihon kokumin zentai no mondai de aru hazu da*).[16]

Viewed from this perspective, the most telling aspect of the case would likely be the desperation of the Japanese government, despite its rhetorical support for the families, to repair the relationship as quickly as possible, as well as the US unwillingness to prosecute Waddle through a court-martial. Though forced to resign, he was honorably discharged with a military pension, enraging many Japanese writers, politicians, and journalists, not to mention family members themselves. As Martin notes, the US Navy "vigorously defended" the distinguished visitors' program, arguing that the visitors' being onboard did not contribute to the accident, though the National Transportation Safety Board would later conclude that "their presence on the submarine and the manner in which they were accommodated by the crew, especially the [captain], had an adverse impact on the safety of operations."[17] Waddle's own account—which walks a delicate line between taking responsibility for the accident, which he does repeatedly, and subtly sharing it with others—leaves little doubt that had he been court-martialed, the distinguished visitors would have been part of the discussion, at least as a mitigating factor in the case. In describing the accident in his 2002 memoir, Waddle writes the following:

> Our sole mission was to entertain a group of distinguished visitors. We had no other reason for going to sea that day. . . .
>
> As for the fourteen Texans, I knew little about them. I'd heard that several of them were visiting Hawaii to participate in a golf tournament benefiting a project restoring the retired battleship *Missouri,* but I wasn't even certain of that. Nor did it matter to me. All I knew was that the Navy wanted to impress them. My goal for the day was to provide them with a short voyage they would never forget. . . .
>
> The *Greeneville* crew performed with precision that day, putting the submarine through its paces, negotiating the maneuvers as though they were driving a car through the cones on a test track. The submarine pitched from side to side and up and down as we went through our "angles and dangles," and the distinguished visitors were loving it! Everyone was enjoying the ride and having fun, and one of the guests was taking pictures as his fellow guests hung on as though they were on a ride at Universal Studio's Islands

of Adventure theme park. I could barely suppress a smile as I watched the expressions of joy and amazement on the faces of our distinguished visitors. Even Captain Brandhuber seemed to be impressed. . . .

The emergency dive is an evasive maneuver that thrusts a submarine far below the surface in a hurry, which was exactly what I wanted to do, since we were running short on time. I couldn't linger any longer. . . . Sure, I was probably pushing them too fast, but I always pushed our crew. I was confident in their abilities and I was confident in myself. Besides, I was eager to further impress our guests. . . .

I ordered an emergency main ballast blow, the procedure that would shoot the seven-thousand-ton *Greeneville* from a depth of about four-hundred-feet to the surface in a matter of seconds. It was the ultimate roller coaster ride, a life-or-death desperation order that every commander hoped he'd never have to implement in reality, yet a procedure we practiced occasionally to make sure we were prepared. Each of the twenty submarines operating in the waters near Hawaii practiced an emergency blow at least once a year, either for training to verify that the ship's emergency systems worked correctly or for demonstration. Today, our blow would be for all three purposes, but mostly for show.[18]

It is entirely possible, of course, that political considerations were irrelevant to the court of inquiry's recommendation "against court-martial due to the absence of any criminal intent or deliberate misconduct on his part."[19] But Waddle's account, if aired by the defense in a criminal inquiry (as any competent defense attorney surely would have done), would have put the distinguished visitors program itself on trial, even in an inquiry conducted within the relatively safe confines of the US Navy. And this may suggest the limits of the response that the United States was willing to offer. Martin argues that with growing numbers of Japanese voicing grave doubts about the relationship, Americans' willingness to send "costly signals" to Japan provided credibility to the US intentions and goals. But it is also clear that those costs fell within boundaries acceptable to the US Navy; jeopardizing a public relations program that connected the navy to wealthy, powerful, and visible civilians with political clout would not have.[20] And it is worth asking whether, because of the amount of technical skill and physical courage on public display (precisely the point of the distinguished visitors program itself), the navy's subsequent steps represented significant costs at all.

Raising the Dead

In a sense, one of the most pressing and perhaps unexpected demands from the Japanese side provided both governments with a nearly perfect if unlikely solution. The repeated calls for apologies were to be expected, particularly given the growing role of apologies in international relations, and these were readily offered.[21] Similarly, Japan's domestic audience might have reasonably expected criminal prosecution, given the thirty-month sentence given to a Maritime Self-Defense Force commander whose submarine, the *Nadashio,* had struck a passenger party boat off of Tokyo in 1988, killing thirty civilians.[22] Whether because a criminal case could not have been made legitimately or could have been made only at the expense of valuable government programs, this was a step that the navy was unwilling to take in Waddle's case.

But pressure grew in Japan for the United States to raise the boat from a depth of nearly 700 meters in order to locate and return the bodies of the missing. As University of Hawaii Professor George Tanabe, who served as an advisor to the US Navy on Japanese burial rites, explained at the time, the bodies would have to be retrieved to be ritually cremated, which would allow their souls to be unified with their ashes and to be fed during funeral and memorial events to ensure that they would not become "hungry ghosts": "If the bodies of the missing *Ehime Maru* crew members are not retrieved, they cannot be purified by fire, preserved as ashes, placed in safekeeping and prepared for postmortem care. They will remain in anguish, never resting in peace."[23]

The demand for the bodies became a central element of the debate within days of the accident, when the Foreign Ministry made a request to the United States to do so. US Ambassador Thomas Foley, in his last days in Tokyo because of the imminent arrival of his successor for the new Bush administration, sought to allay some of these concerns in a final speech and Q&A session at the Japanese Press Club. Like President Bush and others before him, Foley expressed his deep regret and sorrow, explaining that there would be a thorough investigation and saying, somewhat oddly, "We will strive to obtain the truth of this accident without any effort to disguise or dissemble it or to deny the Japanese government and the Japanese people, as well as our own, in the United States." He did not touch on the developing Japanese request to raise the ship, engaging the issue only obliquely in the Q&A session with Japanese reporters in which he much more directly explained why Captain Waddle's apology would likely be delayed pending the investigation. One journalist, provocatively referring to the dead sailors interred in the *USS Arizona* in Pearl Harbor, raised the issue of cultural difference between Japan and the United States, both in terms of the legal expectations surrounding apologies and the religious traditions involved in locating bodies. Specifically with regard to the bodies, Foley responded:

> Well, I think it is sometimes very difficult for people in each culture to fully appreciate and understand the attitudes in other cultures. When John F. Kennedy, Jr., and his wife were lost in an aircraft accident, they had a ceremony at sea, commending their bodies to the deep in effect. As in the case that you mention, the *USS Arizona*, we often regard the bodies of those lost at sea as a special matter for respect and that there is more attention and demand often; and it is an understandable but different part of the culture in Japan to recover the bodies at virtually every opportunity where it's possible.[24]

Four days after Foley's appearance, Upper House legislator Koizumi Chikashi, a member of the Japan Communist Party, referred to Foley's statement in an agitated Diet exchange with Foreign Minister Kōno Yōhei. Emphasizing his conversations with the family members, Koizumi argued that the issue was not just the boat but rather the Japanese government's willingness to act in demanding the expression of institutional responsibility:

> [Having now had the opportunity to read the letter from the Foreign Minister to the US government,] it's written that the US government is strongly requested, because of the most important request from the families, to raise the boat itself. But in terms of the problem of raising the boat, for the families themselves, the most important issue is, after all, that the navy that's responsible, the government that's responsible, make a clear promise to raise the boat. And that's what they've emphasized.
>
> Even in listening to Foreign Minister Kōno's report, the American side has said that the decision to raise the boat depends on what is technically possible, that that's what they're saying. In other words, the American navy and the American government haven't made a promise (*kakuyaku*) to raise the boat. And that's what is angering the families, according to what I'm gathering from them.

For example, in his speech on February 23rd, Ambassador Foley indicated that in America there is a special dignity involved in being lost at sea, while in Japan it's important to collect the bodies. And in Japan a sincere apology is important, but in the United States, apologies are difficult while a legal process is underway, and so there are some cultural problems and differences, so to speak. This is how he explained it. For me, the most important thing now is that the Japanese government, in accordance with the feelings of the family members, is to be straightforward in ensuring that the American government and navy promise to raise the boat.[25]

Later in the same meeting, Japan Socialist Party stalwart Den Hideo followed Foley's assertion that cultural differences lay at the root of the understanding but then turned it into a discussion of the importance of standing up to the United States. The important thing was not the sanctity of the bodies per se but rather the Japanese government's willingness to assert that American culture could not dictate the terms of Japanese grief:

People my age were raised partly in an education system that emphasized that Americans and British were savages (*kichiku beiei*). But now, I have very friendly feelings toward America as well as Americans themselves, and I have actual American friends. Despite that, it's important to recognize that this thing is really terrible.

At the same time, it's been said that there are cultural differences in the ways in which the American side and the Japanese side are approaching this, and I feel the same way. Actually, for Japanese people, family-centeredness (*kazoku-shugi*) is, so to speak, extremely important. You could probably say the same about all of Asia. America is all about individualism, so even when family members die, it's sad and regrettable, but it's still seen from the perspective of individualism. And that's different from Japan.

You'll remember when ten young Japanese who had gone skiing in Austria died in a cablecar [fire in Kaprun, 1990]. At the time, the country with the largest number of victims was Austria itself, and then Germany was next, with Japan losing ten. But the telling part is that thirty Japanese relatives, the most of any country, then visited the spot. And this really shocked the people in Austria, but it really showed the feeling of Japanese about the importance of their families.

It's the same with America this time, I think. And I actually think that in a sense, it's the perfect opportunity to give a piece of our mind to the Americans, to explain without restraining ourselves how Japanese feel and think.

Americans are under the impression that they themselves are the world's "Number One" [*nambā wan*] in all matters. And isn't it about time for us to say, no, that American democracy, the culture of America, and of Americans, simply isn't the best in the world?[26]

Having already gotten into a testy exchange with the more truculent Koizumi, Foreign Minister Kōno defended American behavior by emphasizing that US leaders were working to overcome the clear cultural gap by trying to "understand" the Japanese side:

Truly, in this incident—whether we call it an "incident" or an "accident"— the sense of how to deal with it afterwards is different in the United States and Japan. But, as I said to Mr. Koizumi as well, there are differences, in this case with the United States. I think it's definitely correct to make sure that the United States is thinking about how to deal with this problem while obviously taking care to consider the feelings of the Japanese people, or perhaps Japan's spiritual culture. In particular, Ambassador Foley has demonstrated a great deal of heart-felt consideration (*kokoro zukai*). He's been ambassador here for an awfully long time and was supposed to return home, having finished his term at the end of this month, but he said that he would stay on a little longer because of this problem that occurred right before his departure. Of course, in America, there are people like this who really understand Japan, though I know that there's a part of America that can't understand. But I believe it's necessary to take efforts to make them understand.[27]

To the LDP-led government, public anger at the United States represented more than just a challenge from Japanese left-wingers, long critical of the alliance. Mori's cabinet struggled to show both backbone in making demands toward the United States while also aiming to limit potential damage to the countries' strategic relationship. This was fraught political territory. Many Japanese conservatives—the core of Mori's support— bristled at American high-handedness and complained bitterly about the US role in crafting Japan's antimilitarist constitution and in writing a version of history that made Japan into a uniquely villainous enemy in World War II in the Pacific. But among them, many tied their hopes for a remilitarized Japan to the political cover and alliance demands from the United States. Pressing the United States in the aftermath of the accident seemed only natural in emphasizing national sovereignty and rights, but jeopardizing the substance of the alliance was risky at best. And some conservatives found Japan's persistence on the accident to be unbecoming of a strong, proud nation.

This led, most famously, to criticism among many readers that the right-wing *Sankei Shimbun* had been insufficiently supportive of the demand to raise the ship, but it also generated some remarkable anger in the pages of conservative monthlies. In one piece in the nationalist *Shokun*, Teikyo University's Takayama Masayuki (also on the editorial committee of the *Sankei Shimbun*) depicted Japan as saying "ee . . . iya da, iya da" (a childish, foot-stamping "No! No!") to US claims that raising the ship might be impossible, before going on to excoriate the United States as a nation of liars constantly demanding that Japan apologize for its alleged war crimes while offering, at best, cheap talk to anyone injured by US violence.[28] On the one hand, Japan's position vis-à-vis the United States was embarrassing, demanding that the United States do the nearly impossible for Japan just because Japan wanted it; on the other, failing to press the United States was tantamount to accepting that the relationship was so unequal that people had no right to complain about even the deaths of high school students at the hands of joyriding American civilians operating a nuclear submarine.[29]

The Japanese request to raise the ship thus reflected something more complex than a rulebook regarding the treatment of dead bodies, and American responses were remarkably unreflective about the larger meaning that the bodies represented politically. In a later letter directed primarily at Japanese readers (and translated into Japanese), the former commander of Naval Forces Japan, retired Rear Admiral Robert Chaplin, emphasized different cultural approaches to the dead bodies as encoded in actual practice:

> This incident caused the USN [United States Navy] to work through the cultural differences of our two countries. In the US, survival charts would be consulted and a timed search would be conducted, after that period of time the search would be concluded and those people not recovered would be declared lost at sea. In Japan one searches until the families of those lost feel it is time to stop. The Japanese culture also desires that the remains of loved ones return to their home country for appropriate services.[30]

This statement is only partly true. Roughly three hundred Japanese are lost at sea most years, usually from fishing boats; despite Admiral Chaplin's claim that the search continues until a family decides it is time to stop, the procedures of Japan's Coast Guard are identical in practical terms to those in the United States. A search continues if it is plausible, based on various factors including weather and temperature, that lives will be saved; efforts to recover bodies may go on a bit longer than that, but searches are ultimately called off when the likelihood of success drops. There are often demands for ships to be raised so that family members can find their lost loved ones, but there is no system in place for determining when it should be done and who is primarily responsible for doing so.[31] It does not challenge the religiosity or sincerity of bereaved families to note that they frequently, even today, must somehow cope without finding their relatives' bodies. As I discuss below, by all accounts the families of victims whose bodies were ultimately returned and cremated expressed solace regarding this outcome. I note simply that this is hardly an automatic demand, one that grows straightforwardly out of the illogical murk of Japanese religious culture. And it does not fly in the face of a more reasonable US approach that both depends on technical institutions designed to predict feasibility and pushes out emotional considerations, as it can be honorable to be lost at sea.

Ambassador Foley's comparison of the *Ehime Maru* accident to the handling of the Kennedy plane crash is even more astonishingly imprecise. Kennedy, flying a small plane, evidently made crucial pilot errors that cost him his own life, as well as those of his wife and her sister. There was an extensive search by the US Navy itself, culminating in the discovery and recovery of the bodies from roughly 100 feet below the surface; they were cremated and their ashes commended to the sea by the navy, in recognition of the Kennedy family's broader contributions to their country. Their lives had not been taken by a foreign military, and the US Navy recovered the bodies despite its having played no role in their deaths and despite the fact that none of the victims had served in the military.[32]

And under other circumstances, the US government has proved itself to be relentless in searching for the bodies of its citizens, particularly its soldiers. Although there are US military cemeteries throughout Western Europe, as well in the Philippines, there are none in any of the other Asian countries—particularly, Japan, Korea, and Vietnam—where thousands of Americans died. Most soldiers who fell there were flown or shipped home, as they have been from Afghanistan and Iraq. US-Vietnam relations have been profoundly shaped, more than forty years after the end of the war, by the continuing efforts to find the remains of servicemen there, many of whom were the subject of decades-long conspiracy theories about slave-labor camps, not to mention crucial elements of major American action films in the 1980s, most notably *Rambo II*.[33] None of this implies that burial at sea (or being lost there) is or should be considered dishonorable by family members. Nor does it suggest that US or Japanese observers were consciously disingenuous in their depictions of cultural gaps.

It does, however, suggest that cultural difference is politically contingent yet so convincing that officials could utter demonstrably untrue things without reflection or fear of contradiction; after all, who would dispute the need to be culturally sensitive when dead children are involved? As Katherine Verdery notes in her study of reburial in postsocialist Eastern Europe, dead bodies themselves can represent a wide variety of meanings, and debates over their treatment require attention to political context.[34] In this case the return of the bodies reflected not just simple demands of accountability but also, as MP Koizumi Chikashi himself argued, the very right to make demands of the United States. Den's subsequent comment about cultural difference is offered not as a simple statement that people approach bodies and religious ritual in different ways but as a critique of US power, or rather one consequence of it: an unwillingness, in his eyes, to admit that the United States might be anything other than "number one." Whatever the victims' bodies meant for the bereaved families who had lost their children, they meant something quite different, and far broader, to debates about the US-Japan relationship. The emphasis on simple cultural difference made by both Ambassador Foley and Foreign Minister Kono moved the discussion away from the tricky questions about power imbalance, national resentment, and high-handed neo-imperialism and left it on much safer terrain: a dispute that could be overcome with mutual understanding.

Understanding and More

The US Navy's most dramatic efforts following the disaster might be considered costly in some ways. By pledging, following an initial inquiry into its feasibility, to raise the *Ehime Maru* and search for the bodies of the nine missing crew members, the navy embarked on a technologically complicated, pricey, and at times physically risky mission that involved extensive use of navy divers, private contractors, and US government scientists. And so much of the US response—repeated apologies and a court of inquiry rather than a court-martial—was decidedly cheap by the standards of international relations, even if consequential for the officers themselves. And the damages that the US Navy would ultimately pay the victims' families and the disaster's survivors represented a tiny portion of the navy's annual budget. The costs, the ones trumpeted by the US and Japanese governments alike, lay instead in the decision to raise the *Ehime Maru* from its resting place, a commitment that seemed meaningful specifically because it would respond to Japanese concerns about the treatment of dead bodies and also because it was so technically challenging.

This was not, of course, the first military foray into deep-sea salvage and not the first time in which the retrieval of foreign dead would be politically salient. In 1974, working under the cover of a Howard Hughes mining project, the CIA's Project Azorian successfully removed parts of a sunken Soviet nuclear submarine, although much of the material was lost.[35] The bodies of two Soviet sailors recovered in the debris that made it to the surface were given an official burial at sea, complete with a ceremony in English, videotaped in front of a US flag and a Soviet naval flag. The presiding officer referred to the transnational brotherhood of sailors killed in duty. Mixing Christian and Norse imagery in reference to the duty of the warrior and the transcendental meaning of death, he said:

> The fact that our nations have had disagreements does not lessen in any way our respect for them or the service they have rendered. And so, as we return their mortal remains to the deep, we do so in a way that we hope would have meaning to them. . . . We therefore commit these crew members of this ship to a proper resting place to join the Valhalla of sea heroes who have gone before them. We commit their remains to the deep, looking for the resurrection of the body when the sea shall give up her dead, and the life of the world to come. Amen.[36]

After watching the sermon, the viewer witnesses a red cargo crate holding the dead Soviet sailors as it is lifted by a rope winch and dropped into the sea, where the camera follows it into the water. One next sees the red square in the dark sea for only a moment before it disappears, replaced only by the brief froth on the surface. The tape has been edited, with some of the last moments of speeches and music superimposed over the final video of the cargo crate being dropped into the water.

The story, which became a talking point for Japanese observers during the *Ehime Maru* case, at least offered the possibility that the United States could, in fact, raise the ship from a depth much shallower than the nearly 2,000 meters of the earlier submarine disaster.[37] It was, of course, a different event, and the at-best-partial success of Project Azorian offered little guidance for how the bodies from the *Ehime Maru* might be recovered. Too deep for divers but with human remains too fragile and deeply embedded to be pulled out safely by mini-subs and surface-controlled machinery, the *Ehime Maru* represented a key technical challenge that prevented a US guarantee to recover the bodies for several weeks. After an exploratory determination that the *Ehime Maru*'s hull could likely withstand the strain associated with a straight pull toward the surface, the navy contracted with the oil firm Halliburton, itself controversial because of its deep connections to Vice President Richard Cheney and to the US military, to secure the use of its drilling platform the *Rockwater II* for the maneuver.[38]

The oceanographic team designed a simple experiment to contribute to the computer modeling already under way. Armed with a GPS unit and two bushels of twenty-five oranges apiece, a small boat released one bushel at low tide and one at high tide to chart the direction of the wind and ocean currents, trying to determine whether a SWRS might be located to allow divers from the US Navy and the Japanese Maritime Self-Defense Forces (MSDF) to examine the wreck carefully to locate the men and boys still missing from the February disaster.[39] Even by this stage, with the *Ehime Maru* still nine miles south of Oahu and nearly seven hundred meters below the ocean's surface, the extraordinary technical demands of the mission had been the subject of wide debate in military, industrial, and oceanographic circles. Just to safely anchor the crane barge required unusual construction choices. The mooring relied on an unconventional and costly set of open-ended steel tube piling partly because the usual corrosion risks facing steel underwater were judged to be relatively unimportant given the short-term nature of the *Ehime Maru* project and also because the emergency nature of the project militated against cost cutting. Besides, steel was viewed to be significantly better at punching through the hardened coral reefs dotting the ocean floor around Hawaii.[40]

On October 12, 2011, the *Rockwater II* used two cranes, one on each side, to lift the *Ehime Maru* from its resting spot in a series of short increments to reduce the risk of a frayed cable that would have effectively left all of the wreck's weight on one side of the barge, flipping it over. Moving slowly closer to the coast of Oahu, the *Rockwater II* was ordered to stop late on the night of October 13 because of impending darkness and tidal change, spilling more diesel oil into the sea. It seems to have been the right call, as the *Ehime Maru* leaked oil overnight into the darker, deeper waters. Only when tidal conditions were viewed to be favorable—as determined by the dispersal patterns of the floating oranges—were the *Rockwater II* and its precious cargo permitted to enter the SWRS, where teams of navy and MSDF divers awaited the opportunity to search the hull for the bodies of the accident's victims.[41]

After being laid at a depth of roughly thirty meters, the *Ehime Maru* was allowed to settle for a day before teams of navy divers began to recover the victims, following instructions to place the remains into body bags feet first in deference to Japanese Buddhist traditions.[42] Eight were discovered within a week of the beginning of the search dives, with the ninth victim later declared lost at sea after several more weeks of searches. US divers continued the search and the collection of personal effects and removal of hazardous materials and fuel from the ship before turning over the operation to Japanese MSDF divers, who completed weeks of further dives. On November 25 the *Ehime Maru* was lifted and towed to deeper water and laid in its final resting place.

The level of detail available in official US reports is fascinating in its technical specificity, nearly matching the subsequent reports in industrial and peer-reviewed scientific journals explaining the mooring and drilling operations, the lifting and moving of the *Ehime Maru,* and the identification of the victims.[43] By all accounts, this was a remarkable, unorthodox operation that demonstrated great technical sophistication and physical effort. The Discovery Channel even broadcast a well-regarded and highly flattering documentary, *Deep Salvage,* dramatically tracking the physical perils awaiting US divers as they searched the ruined training boat, all as part of a mission to repair a frayed US-Japan relationship.

As Captain Bert Marsh, director of Ocean Engineering and supervisor of Salvage and Diving at the Naval Sea Systems Command, wrote in the official newsletter to navy divers,

I urge you to read and take pride in what your community has accomplished. As I mentioned to the MDSU ONE Divers, when assigned to determine if raising the *EHIME MARU* and recovering the remains was feasible, I knew I had an ace-in-the-hole with the MDSU located at Alpha docks on Hickam AF Base. My confidence was fully justified. They not only succeeded in recovering the remains and personal items, they became America's best Ambassadors to Japan. Through their meticulous awareness of cultural issues and the establishment of an exceptional working relationship with their Japanese counterparts, they restored trust between our two countries.[44]

Later in the same newsletter issue, another US Navy salvage specialist wrote:

The full impact of the success of the operation will probably never be known. What is already clearly apparent is that eight families of those nine unfortunate crewmembers have been able to bring home their loved one and that the ninth family has been greatly assisted in their grieving process. Everyone who participated in the recovery has assisted in accomplishing an act of kindness that will be remembered for a long time.[45]

In his later letter directed to Japanese working with the US Navy in Japan, Retired Rear Admiral Chaplin emphasized that the *Ehime Maru* recovery project, which continued through the aftermath of the September 11 attacks, had cemented an emotional bond between the two countries. He addressed one particular moment shortly after the 9/11 attacks, when a bereaved family contacted him as they still awaited word of whether their son's body would be found:

I received a letter from a family that had lost a son in the accident. The letter stated that the family watched the television reports of the horrible events happening in the United States. They knew they would have to wait for the recovery of their son because they were certain that the US Navy would focus on this war on terror. But to their surprise the Navy continued the recovery operations of *Ehime Maru,* and because of this, this family truly understood the meaning of freedom.[46]

Admiral Klemm is quoted in the navy's final press release from the recovery operations, referring specifically to the Mizuguchi family, whose seventeen-year-old son Takashi was the one victim whose body had not been found. His words are the most emotionally open of the press release itself, but they also reflect a certain construction of the grieving process that may have been somewhat foreign to Japanese audiences:

> [The divers] have overcome significant technical difficulties in order to provide *closure* to the families of the missing crew members. The gratitude they showed us justified the operation. We are pleased that we were able to recover the remains of eight crew members, but our prayers continue to be with the Mizuguchis (the family of the ninth missing crew member) in their loss.[47]

Klemm's reference to "closure" seems both natural and intuitive, but it is the one word I have struggled to translate when I have lectured about the *Ehime Maru* accident in Japanese. It is not that the concept does not exist; I can explain it, using a fairly long phrase, as the moment when people can turn the page on some kind of painful decision or personal loss, when one can move on. It makes sense in a way. But trying to translate it also forces one to think about its weird artificiality in American English as well. I know no one whose grief for a loved one, particularly a child, is really closed, even if they have somehow gotten on with their lives; surely Klemm, whose handling of the recovery efforts has been widely hailed, did not mean anything ghastly or insensitive in his statement. But referring to closure seems to have signaled the finality of the US Navy's extraordinary efforts as well as to general public acceptance in Japan, not the end of the story for the families themselves. Julian Barnes's justly famed statement on grief in his masterful novel *Flaubert's Parrot* captures something of the lingering fragments of grief, the ones that cannot be summed up by a word such as *closure,* therapeutic or administrative demands notwithstanding: "And you do come out of it, that's true. After a year, after five. But you don't come out of it like a train coming out of a tunnel, bursting through the downs into sunshine and that swift, rattling descent to the Channel; you come out of it as a gull comes out of an oil-slick. You are tarred and feathered for life."[48]

We will return below to the conflicted responses of the victims' families, but for the moment it is worth noting the ways in which the salvage operation was represented. By virtually all accounts, this was a remarkable feat that involved extensive planning, technological sophistication, and difficult and possibly dangerous physical work. But the accounts were plentiful and public, and although they uniformly addressed the "tragic" loss of life and some figures, such as Admiral Klemm, emphasized what the US Navy "owed" the families, they usually represented the operations not as atonement or compensation but rather as diplomatic gestures made necessary specifically because of the cultural particularities of the Japanese and rendered possible because of the skill and dedication of the navy. Whether in the August 29 invitation to the news media to photograph US Navy divers practicing for the search of the ship or in the link to the "Mobile Diving & Salvage Unit One" Web page, the *Ehime Maru* recovery operation became an opportunity to showcase the immense technological capacity and personal bravery of US Navy personnel.[49] Few people have the opportunity to become distinguished visitors like the executives aboard the *Greeneville*. As the navy's description of the program notes, "People considered for this program are selected based on their ability to share their experience with the largest possible audience. Embarkations of journalists, community leaders or celebrities that gain mass media exposure greatly assist our recruiting and educational efforts by allowing thousands to share in the experience."[50] But a larger number can see photos, read reports, and watch television documentaries focusing on the extraordinary skill with which the US Navy tended to the cultural sensitivities of the Japanese, who became, in these public accounts, grateful admirers who were then able to move on with their lives.

Alliance of Emotion

The public relations mission was in many ways a success, particularly in displaying the cooperation of the US and Japanese naval forces. The most sympathetic Japanese portrait of US efforts appeared in the highly conservative monthly magazine *Seiron,* published by the *Sankei Shimbun.* *Seiron* is hardly an unalloyed fan of the United States, with no shortage of articles lambasting the United States for high-handedness, for having drafted Japan's "peace constitution" and many of its most important early postwar laws, and for enforcing on Japan a self-flagellating view of the country's wartime history. The United States represents a convenient bogeyman for the Japanese right wing, particularly when the problem under consideration is the kind of moral turpitude that has crept into a materialistic, individualistic postwar Japan. Under other circumstances, however, the United States can play the role of a normal and even honorable country, one that has the proud and capable military that Japan should. In 2002 *Seiron* published a lengthy piece—which had appeared in a different form in the *Sankei Shimbun* itself—by Japan Maritime Self-Defense Commander Hayashi Hideki, who had served as the JMSDF's liaison to the US Navy's Pacific Fleet in Honolulu. With the *Ehime Maru* incident, he was drafted into the stressful position of interpreter between the Japanese families and the US Navy, as well as guide to Japanese manners and mores for the American officers entrusted with apologies and other direct contact.

Hayashi indicates that he had been apprehensive about even serving as interpreter, given the likelihood that family members—not recognizing him as a JMSDF officer but rather as a representative of the US Navy—might turn their anger and grief on him. Family members of the victims had arrived in Hawaii shortly after the accident, and many would return frequently through the administrative hearings on Commander Waddle and the long process of searching for their loved ones. In explaining his decision to take up the task, he emphasizes the danger that the crisis posed to the alliance, implying that only skillful diplomacy based on genuine understanding could protect the US-Japan relationship:

> I thought: To save the friendly relations between the United States and Japan from this continuing crisis, there is no one but the MSDF officers who have worked so hard for stability in the Pacific for fifty years. Even if we're taking risks, we have to prevent a crack in the very monolith (*todenba*) that the US Navy and Japan Maritime Self-Defense Forces represent in the US-Japan relationship.[51]

Given the immense media attention that the *Ehime Maru* case drew during the initial months and then around the actual lifting in the fall, Hayashi's dramatic account may well be understandable even if it seems, in retrospect, a bit overblown in the implication that the military relationship was in serious trouble. After all, Hayashi acknowledges that his commitment was, if anything, widely shared. When a JMSDF diver was injured during one of the training runs in Hawaii before the actual search of the ship and had to be hospitalized briefly, he begged the *Chihaya*'s captain to allow him to stay. Hayashi writes that he reportedly said (*uttaeta sō desu*):

> It's okay with me even if I have to have another surgery here in Hawaii, so please don't make me return home until we have fulfilled our duty (*saimu o mattō suru made*). . . . I represent the Maritime Self-Defense Forces, and I was dispatched here for the families, as well as to maintain the friendly relations of the United States and Japan, so I cannot return home until we have completed the mission.[52]

Although the point of his article is largely to praise American efforts while detailing his own role (which he remarkably does with unfailing and appealing modesty), parts of the article seem aimed to demonstrate the professionalism and respectability of Japan's naval forces as well. From the end of the Cold War onward, there has been considerable attention in Japan to burnishing the image of the Japanese military, much of which is done through emphasizing both its humanism and its capability. But this does not make it uncontroversial, so Hayashi's reference to the *Chihaya*'s entrance into Pearl Harbor, with the Hinomaru (Rising Sun) flag flying proudly along with the JMSDF flag, as the moment when he remembered his love for a country is a deeply political act, even if one unattached to an explicit policy agenda.

Indeed, the article is wrapped up not in its commentary on security politics, which is scant at best, and not in its coverage of the actual sinking of the *Ehime Maru* or of legal responsibilities toward the families. It is instead connected intimately to an unbridled emotionalism that is virtually absent in any of the English-language accounts. Hayashi reports on a day late in the search, toward the end of October, when the US Navy chartered a private boat to take family members out to the SWRS where the *Ehime Maru* rested. They pulled up near the dive platform and threw flowers over the side while loudly calling out to their lost loved ones. One of them, representing the group, asked Hayashi to send a message over the radio to the divers on the platform, informing them how grateful they were for their hard work. Hayashi did so, and one of the divers answered that they appreciated the family's words and feelings, and that they would continue to do their very best. When Hayashi relayed this to the families over the boat's microphone, they began to wave at the divers on the platform, all of whom waved back, along with their commander. At this point, the family members began to cry, as did Hayashi himself. The US naval officer in charge also cried, followed by all of the other navy personnel.

It is a crucial moment in the article but not its climax, which comes when Hayashi had to explain that the JMSDF divers, having searched for weeks after the end of the US mission, had been unable to locate the last body, that of seventeen-year-old Mizuguchi Takeshi. It had been weeks since the discovery of the eighth victim, and the Mizuguchi family had clearly been apprised of the likelihood that their son would never be found. Two days before the final dive, Mizuguchi's mother, Yoshiko, reportedly made cookies and gave them to the crew of the *Chihaya* as they continued their efforts, which at this point boiled down to the search for only her son's body. The JMSDF called off the search, and Hayashi explained to Mizuguchi's parents that the divers took the opportunity to leave in his boat locker flowers and some cookies that his mother had baked so that when he came back to the locker, he would see the flowers she had left for him and be able to eat the cookies. He then gave the parents photos that had miraculously survived on Mizuguchi's digital camera aboard the boat, including from his birthday celebration two days before the fatal accident. It seems to have been an extremely meaningful moment for the one family unable to be reunited with the remains of their lost son, and it caps what Hayashi describes as the most difficult but memorable year of his career in the JMSDF.[53]

The lesson that Hayashi draws is inseparable from both the grief and the sympathy, and particularly from the determination to work together to do the right thing, to be respectful of cultural difference while seeking out what makes us all human. Right-leaning publications such as *Seiron* typically display at best mixed views of the United States, with many of the critiques circling around the US designation of Japan as the aggressor in World War II, forever doomed to pay in apologies and shame. And indeed, even Hayashi—who no doubt heard plenty about the history of the relationship during his work as a liaison with the US Navy—refers to tension in his final comments about his year as translator for the *Ehime Maru* recovery project:

> As we saw from the reactions to the terrorist attacks in America on September 11th, there are many differences in our value systems and the way

we feel about things. Frequently there are differences in the way we think about history (*rekishi ninshiki*), and sometimes it's thought that it'll be hard to overcome that. But even with these differences, we need to make sure the alliance continues. What's more necessary than anything else, I think, are experiences that we share. If we work together and overcome problems together, we'll understand one another better and will help trust grow. In the end, what drove me was the belief that "People love one other, people grieve when others die, and that won't change." This is a truth of life, and it goes beyond east and west, and new and old.

As I have tried to describe, the US Navy, as people and as an organization, moved on a very steep road to meet whatever challenges and overcome all obstacles, unwilling to accept failure, in order to keep the promise that they made to the families to raise the boat. I will never forget what I learned from them about the wonderful tradition of "honor" (*meiyō*) of the US Navy.[54]

The Limits of Shared Emotions

Only in the final lines of Hayashi's article, written as a postscript by *Seiron* editor Kataoka Yūri, are we reminded that, as of the writing of the article, there were still ongoing legal disputes in the *Ehime Maru* case. The bereaved were united in pressing the United States to retrieve the bodies, but the outcome was far messier and fraught with continuing anguish than a story about US-Japan rapprochement, based on American sympathy for Japanese feelings, might imply. The US Navy was, by all accounts, eager to resolve the case without public dispute and offered extensive financial compensation not only to the families of the victims but also to the survivors and to Ehime Prefecture for the loss of the boat itself. After the completion of the legal negotiations, the final payments amounted to roughly $30 million, with nearly $12 million going to Ehime Prefecture and almost $17 million to the families of the victims and to other survivors.[55] Ikeda Naoki, one of the Japanese lawyers representing the families, later noted that this was more than the victims could have expected in a Japanese court but that what they wanted most—real punishment for the offender—remained out of the question. The payments and other steps, which included a meeting between the victims' families and top navy brass, showed "collaborative American joint action to show consideration for the bereaved families."[56]

Unlike the search for bodies, the compensation was never described as dictated by culture, although it might easily have been. After all, the relatively high compensation paid in an US court might have been described, however inaccurately, as reflecting different judgments about the value of human life or of institutional responsibility for its loss. Similarly, the payments to survivors, often explained with reference to their need for post-traumatic stress disorder (PTSD) treatment, would have been unlikely just a few years earlier. PTSD had itself become a mainstay—say, a cultural fact—in Japanese social and political analysis only after the 1995 Kobe earthquake, rapidly becoming an element in Japanese debates about the nation's own contributions to post-disaster relief.[57] And yet both in Japan and the United States, the compensation itself was relatively uncontroversial and unexamined—understood perhaps as driven by political exigency but not by cultural strangeness regarding life and death.

The financial compensation, however, had not been depicted as central to the demands of the bereaved families and was not expected to bring them solace; they would have to get it, if possible, from the return of their loved ones' remains. And solace would, by most accounts, remain elusive. Terada Ryōsuke and Masumi, who had lost their son Yūsuke, would become known as the most vocally angry parents, with Ryōsuke shouting at Waddle at the Hawaii military inquest in April. The Teradas had addressed their feelings before the raising of the ship at a June 8 Tokyo meeting titled "Investigating the Truth of the *Ehime Maru* Incident." In their presentation they connected their anguish primarily to the sense that the real story of the collision was being withheld, reportedly saying through their tears, "Since the accident, a lot of feelings have just been frozen in place. We don't recover from our sorrow; it only grows. We plan to continue telling anyone we can, without hesitation, about the accident."[58]

For them, at least, the return of their son's body seems to have been immensely meaningful. In a study of the way in which the bereaved families understood the relationship between souls and dead bodies, a young religion scholar, Nawa Kiyotaka, used reports from the *Ehime Shimbun,* the regional newspaper, to emphasize that the bodies were not simply material things (*mono*) but could actually be analyzed as living things (*shōja*). In these reports, the parents were crucial figures. After the memorial service at which Yūsuke was cremated, Ryōsuke apparently spoke to his son's ashes late into the night, as if he were still alive, saying, "You've arrived in a different form, but I'm so relieved that you've come back home, where you are loved."[59] His mother explained how intolerable it had been for his body to lie inside the wreck for many months: "[His] training uniform and the underwear in which they'd found him had been covered with heavy oil that had hardened into clay. . . . The smell was so awful that it hurts the eyes, and I realized how that it must have been a terribly brutal experience for him to be lying in that oil for eight months."[60] Nawa concludes that their behavior and attitudes fit well with the view of noted religion scholar Sakurai Tokutarō's theory of the relationship between the soul and body in Japanese Buddhism: the soul is immediately separated from the body, then briefly returns to it. Then, after a proper funeral, it moves on to the next world, although there must be periodic memorials and prayers for it to move smoothly and comfortably between this world and the next.

In December 2002, retired Commander Waddle made a trip to Japan to apologize directly to the families and to lay flowers at a memorial in Uwajima, near the high school. In a postscript to Waddle's book, the only part written in the third person, Waddle's return is described as bringing "closure" to the families of the victims. In reality, almost all refused to meet with him, a decision sometimes interpreted as reflecting their continuing anger and sometimes as a statement that they had moved on with their lives and that having to deal with his highly publicized visit, in the glare of the media spotlight, would reopen old wounds. Terada Masumi herself reported that she could not decline the opportunity to meet with someone offering a genuine and wholehearted apology (*seishin-seii shazai*) but decided to see him in Tokyo at a closed meeting without reporters. According to a subsequent report by the families' attorney, while showing Waddle photos of Yūsuke, Masumi described her son's life and love for him until Waddle himself broke down in tears. This confirmed Waddle's basic decency and humanity to Masumi but also seems to have been hollow and anticlimactic for her; her son's death was not something to be gotten over, especially with an institutional rather than human culprit at fault: "As for my son whom I loved desperately, who was everything to me—the fact that he was taken away from me by the crew of the *Greeneville* with Captain Waddle in charge, it doesn't erase his life for me. I can't forgive them for the accident itself. But I think it's possible in a sense that Waddle himself is a victim of the Navy as an organization."[61] She reportedly remained tormented with self-reproach (*jiseki*) that although she had reconciled herself to her son's death and Ryōsuke had finally been convinced that the *Greeneville* had not been steered deliberately into the *Ehime Maru*, she had been unable to forgive Waddle completely.

In describing her comments to reporters afterward, attorney Ikeda Naoki portrays Masumi in a manner that resembles Barnes's depiction of the messy impossibility of real closure from mourning, a concern that seems to have extended to the Uwajima community itself. In Ikeda's telling, parents of survivors had, like the Ehime prefectural government, been eager for the support that a more rapid resolution and settlement might bring, including in the form of funding for PTSD therapy for their children. The bereaved families had pushed for further concessions, including the return of the bodies, a formal apology from the navy, and commitments to change procedures to prevent accidents like this from taking place in the future. But they were also expected to grieve and to continue along an emotional process according to a timetable that fit with broader political and media narratives. Quoting Terada Masumi's request that the mass media respect the different ways in which family members responded to the loss of their loved ones, Ikeda points out that she and her husband had been the target of intense local pressure within their tight-knit, rural community, likely mirroring statements from outside that were filtered through the town: that they could not stand up to the US Navy, that the navy had already admitted that it was at fault, that their family members were dead and would not be coming back. It was simply time for a kind of closure: to accept the outcome and to stop making trouble.[62]

Emotional Agency

My point is not that the understandable grief of parents should overwhelm a bilateral political relationship or that the *Ehime Maru* case should have been handled differently. After all, whatever else the decision to raise the boat might have accomplished—to demonstrate America's friendship with Japan, symbolize US respect for Japanese cultural missions, provide an opportunity to showcase US technological and physical prowess—it seems to have provided at least some solace, though probably not "closure," to bereaved families. Although I have emphasized the production of cultural difference as having a number of functions in the *Ehime Maru* salvage operation, I do not wish in any way to doubt the religiosity of the families or the meaningfulness of their loved ones' return. One might point as well to the connections that were built between Japan and, in particular, Oahu, where local civil society organizations (especially those led by Japanese Americans) played key roles in memorializing the accident and tending to the families during their trips to Hawaii.[63] Telling this story as one of US cruelty or indifference toward Japan, or as Japan's simple acceptance of US power, would badly misrepresent the complex relationships among the actors and diminish the hard work that many did to restore the bilateral relationship, care for the victims, and/or pull the shipwreck to shallow water to retrieve the bodies.

But to tell the story as simple alliance management, or as one of mutual respect, would just as surely misrepresent what could be resolved and what could not, as well as the complex interests involved in and affected by the outcome. My goal here has been to emphasize that the construction of family grief as, in effect, national grief allowed for decisions that might have been more deeply meaningful to the families than to Japan as a whole but that offered them no real resolution. They did not become what at least some seem to have hoped: the standard-bearers for a more equal partnership between the United States and Japan or for a revised alliance that would somehow have been able to turn back or correct earlier alliance cruelties, such as the careless irradiation of a fishing boat or the gang-rape of a child. Nor could they become the eager cheerleaders of a US Navy that had taken their loved ones from them, no matter how well-intentioned and diligent some of its subsequent efforts had been. As at least the residents of Uwajima seem to have noticed, the aftermath of the *Ehime Maru* accident was messy and partial.

But, as a national matter, it was rapidly forgotten. In February 2011, a few short weeks before the earthquake that killed thousands in northeastern Japan, memorials were held in Hawaii and Ehime to commemorate the ten-year anniversary of the disaster. But the accident had long since been eclipsed by US-Japan cooperation in the war on terror, by the video of Prime Minister Koizumi air-guitaring while visiting Graceland with President George W. Bush, by nationalist Prime Minister Abe Shinzō's anger at and then capitulation to a US congressional resolution demanding Japanese apologies to the "comfort women," by Prime Minister Hatoyama Yukio's calamitous mishandling of the relocation of US bases in Okinawa. No longer a symbol of two countries forever divided by culture, it had become instead yet one more instance of successful alliance management: the application of diplomatic technique and administrative finesse to solve the problems, or perhaps "heal the wounds," caused by the sinking.

Less than a month after the accident, noted international relations scholar Soeya Yoshihide came close to predicting this in his testimony to the Survey Group on International Issues in the Upper House of the Japanese Diet. The first presentation that afternoon had been from former ambassador Edamura Sumio, who had emphasized something akin to the conventional wisdom: that it was the role of diplomacy to overcome obvious differences in value systems (*kachikan*), such as that symbolized by the Japanese request that the US Navy search for the dead bodies. Soeya, with an American doctorate and moderate views on Japanese security politics, took the conversation in a different direction. The previous week, at the invitation of Admiral Blair, Soeya had joined a group of Japanese in a three-day program that included a tour of a nuclear submarine of the same class as the *Greeneville* as well as briefings at the Naval Headquarters. Emphasizing that he did not wish to be impolite about it, he pointed out that he felt as if he, and Japan as an alliance partner, were being "handled sensitively" (*senshitibu ni atsukatteiru*)—the same way he had felt about US efforts in the aftermath of the 1995 rape case.

Like the other speakers, he ranged widely in his comments; this was, after all, a panel on international issues, not only the *Ehime Maru* case. In tracing the difficulties and dangers of Japan's diplomacy, Soeya referred specifically to the way that young people like his own students at prestigious Keio University were likely to be frustrated by Japan's dependent role in the alliance, as well as its seeming inability to speak up forcefully against criticisms from a rising China. Japan's diplomatic status as little more than the junior partner in a bilateral relationship was therefore one of the elements that might fuel an unhealthy nationalism among the young. His views on the incident and its aftermath must be taken in the context of his broader recommendation that Japan develop itself more clearly as a "middle power," one not aspiring to superpower status but willing to have its own military and diplomatic capacity to act independently, thinking actively about the value of the US-Japan alliance rather than considering the alliance as constitutive of Japan itself. The problems were not simply diplomatic or political. They were psychological and nearly spiritual:

> As a result, currently, if you we think about what postwar Japan has become, and we think about how difficult it would be structurally to free Japan from the US-Japan alliance, we end up not even considering the alliance as a choice that Japan, as an agent, has actually made on its own. . . . [From both the Left and the Right] there is lingering discontent about the US-Japan alliance. That means that from whatever direction the debate develops regarding the absence of Japanese autonomy in the US-Japan alliance, the more you cry out for this agency, you end up choking yourself on it. And I feel that within that structure, the loss of agency has actually operated unconsciously in informing these perspectives.[64]

This was an accident for which the US Navy bore undisputed legal responsibility, and there is little doubt, particularly in the context of alliance politics, that it would have been willing to pay a substantial settlement to the families involved. Conversely, there were clear decisions about the treatment of the ship's personnel as well as the maintenance of the distinguished visitors program that flew in the face of Japanese requests and popular outrage. Japanese agency, such as it was, had yielded an expensive and difficult mission that variously demonstrated American technological capacity and ingenuity, bilateral naval cooperation, and mutual understanding, the last of which might be seen either in a Japanese letter about American freedom or in the tears of US naval officers as they waved to grieving Japanese families. In constructing Japan as a body of distinctive national emotion, US and Japanese observers alike provided the opportunity for accounts about grief and reconciliation that could at least allow the alliance to weather the crisis and move on to the next steps. With most of the bodies recovered, and the families facing pressure to stop calling attention to themselves, there was little reason to consider epilogues and a clear desire to declare that all had reached "closure." After all, only a few months later, Japanese Maritime Self-Defense Force ships would be heading toward the Indian Ocean to support their US Navy allies in their new war, this against a nonstate actor in a land-locked country.

The *Ehime Maru* incident and its aftermath might be seen as a perfect case for emphasizing the importance of emotion in international politics, given the undeniably fraught passions surrounding the deaths of blameless civilians at the hands of a military ally, particularly given the youth of many of them. The eagerness of leaders and of analysts to emphasize different cultures surrounding these passions surely provides more evidence of both the importance of emotions and the need to treat them contextually. This chapter, however, has argued that a close investigation of the case suggests that the issue is less emotion itself than the productive power of emotional representation. By invoking national emotion, leaders in both countries helped to reproduce a view of innate cultural difference that could be overcome through diplomatic gesture. They also demonstrated how the invocation of national emotion sets boundaries for the nation as an affective community while helping to discipline unruly elements—the dissipation of the *Sankei Shimbun*'s initial criticisms of the demand to raise the ship, later replaced by *Seiron*'s homage to the US Navy for its honor in doing so—that cut against that notion. If emotional representation can help to solidify the idea of a national community, but the emotional basis for that unity is at least partly mythical (as it clearly was in this case), then it seems essential to consider the logics behind representation itself, not the actual emotions and their putative role in driving political or diplomatic responses. In the following chapters we will turn to the question of how the invocation of emotions within broad national narratives—such as the one in which Japan's national agency was forever compromised in 1945—helps to define their use and their utility.

3

CHEER UP, VIETNAM

A startling pair of photos opens a section on the use of Agent Orange, the chemical defoliant used by the United States military in Vietnam, in the 1983–1990 edition of *Gendai shakai shiryōhen* (Collected materials on contemporary society), an optional reader generally revised every seven years and used to supplement government-approved textbooks in Japanese social studies classes. On the right are the white-gloved hands of someone we might presume to be a medical professional holding the upright, seemingly seated bodies of two tiny infants, both with abbreviated cranial areas, their heads stopping just above their eyes. The text identifies them as having been born without brains. On the left is an infant body seemingly shaped like an upside-down "T," with heads, torsos, and arms at either end and a pair of legs pointing straight up; a third stump rises from the midsection. The head on the left, identified as Beto-chan, is turned away from the camera; the face on the right, noted as Doku-chan, looks directly at the viewer.

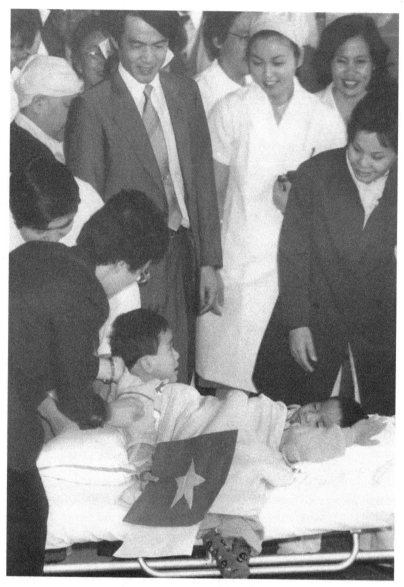

Figure 3.1. Viet and Duc Nguyen, about to leave Japan, 1986

Source: The Mainichi Newspapers

When the photo, credited to the *Mainichi Shimbun,* was taken in 1981, the boys were named Ba and Bon (numbers three and four, respectively, the same way that Ichirō and Jirō—first and second sons—might be names in Japanese). Serving as the tragically laughing subjects of a short selection by the journalist Kutsuwada Takafumi (from his then-recently published book on Agent Orange), Ba and Bon were initially obvious cautionary tales, the innocent victims of a cruel military power and its inhuman use of chemical weapons, leaving behind countless victims. The collection quotes at length a letter to the *Mainichi* about Agent Orange from Murata Kōji, a reader from Kitakyushu City—the city that was scheduled to be bombed on August 9, 1945, before cloudy weather forced a B-29 Superfortress, the *Bockscar,* to move instead to its secondary target, Nagasaki:

> This is clearly the devil's work. And yet it was done by humans. A country that prides itself on being the leader of the world did this ten years ago, but we're still living with the after-effects. It's impossible to think of this any other way than to realize that the ego of a superpower allows for no respect for human life. Sure enough, it's like they just wake up to this, thinking, "well, that's war . . ."
>
> Japan also still bears the scars of war. I don't mean just those from the Pacific War. I mean we can't forget the Korean War, the Vietnam War—the wars that we used as stepping stones, making our economy fat and rich while warping our society. That's the misery war causes, no matter how logically or legitimately militarization supposedly takes place. What we really need is a government that understands that.[1]

With the graphic photos, Kutsuwada's anguished descriptions of his feelings of powerlessness and grief upon meeting the two boys and their caretakers, and Murata's angry missive, we see a number of ways in which Japanese might have interpreted or framed their feelings and judgments about the physical consequences of the US use of Agent Orange during the Vietnam War: medical puzzle and spectacle, a melodramatic rendering of the emotions produced by exposure to the boys, and outrage at a country that would carry out such violence, as well as at their own government for its ghastly complicity in the violence.

Ba and Bon would later be renamed Nguyen Viet and Duc—or Betochan and Doku-chan in Japanese—and by the time the text collection was replaced by a new edition in the early 1990s, they had become almost certainly the most famous living Vietnamese people among postwar Japanese, a distinction likely still held by Duc, the surviving brother. In 1986, with the support of Japan's prime minister, they traveled to Tokyo, receiving medical treatment for Viet's crippling bout with encephalitis; in 1988, Japanese physicians associated with the Red Cross provided medical equipment and training to the Vietnamese doctors who carried out the complicated surgery to separate the two boys. Doing so saved Duc's life, although it left Viet in a vegetative state until his death in 2007. Throughout his adult life, Duc has served as a goodwill ambassador between Vietnam and Japan, appearing on Japanese television and giving interviews to Japanese newspapers, usually to update them on his life, his marriage, fatherhood, and his work on behalf of the Vietnamese disabled, especially the victims of Agent Orange.

This chapter traces the peculiar case of Viet and Duc—virtually unknown in the United States and substantially less famous in Vietnam itself than in Japan—and of the emotional arc of their story in the Japanese media. The *Ehime Maru* accident, discussed in chapter 2, provided an opportunity for Japanese and American leaders to depoliticize a potentially serious disagreement by allowing for a qualified expression of Japanese agency, as well as by demonstrating American recognition of the legitimacy of largely inscrutable Japanese emotionality. The Viet and Duc story is also one that makes sense, particularly in its highly personal and humanistic (and in many ways depoliticized) resolution, only when mapped out against a larger narrative of postwar Japan. In this story the nation's agency is contingent and specific, and relevant particularly to a struggling or developing Asia that Japan can help. This narrative, both partial and elastic, provides fodder both for imagining the complex events in Japan's postwar era as well as for considering the lessons that Japan, which ostensibly reclaimed part of its national agency through peace and through national economic growth, can provide to its less fortunate Asian neighbors.

Sensationally sad episodes can make for gripping media accounts, and who would not hope for a happy ending to a story as heartrending as that of Viet and Duc? This chapter does not argue that only in Japan would they have become the center of media attention or that only in Japan might people want to ascribe happy endings, if only partially, to their own country's interventions. Each story in US papers during the Iraq War and

Afghanistan War about girls going to school, or nongovernmental organizations (NGOs) forming to demand an end to corruption, or groups of American doctors traveling to help the sick and the wounded might speak to a similar desire. Instead, this chapter suggests that considering an emotional representation within the structure of a larger story helps to make sense of how and why it works, and why it begins and ends the way that it does. As chapter 1 noted, a hallmark of the "melodramatic imagination" is the emphasis on innocence as virtue, as well as on the dark threats constantly facing it. That the Vietnamese victims were children provided special opportunities for a sentimental treatment not just of the awful things done to them but also, more broadly, to their country by the United States. It thus offered the chance to imagine Japan's potential and restorative role for them as reflecting Japan's larger contributions to Asia and to the world.

After discussing later configurations of the Vietnam War era in Japan's postwar and especially about how national narratives highlight or extend certain periods while compressing or obscuring others, this chapter focuses on the ways in which lingering debates about Japan's responsibilities fit within the country's emergence as a global success story. The chapter next traces Viet and Duc's appearances in Japanese media and broader political discussions, as well as the complex set of potential motives behind the work of their advocates in Vietnam, in Shiga and Fukui prefectures, and in Tokyo itself. We then turn to the ways in which Viet and Duc's medical care would be remembered and represented in Japan, as well as the moral lessons drawn from it. Finally, we return to larger debates about Japan's global role and about the expectation that the core of Japan's interaction with the outside is premised on a warm humanism that works uneasily alongside the country's economic and technical leadership, particularly of the Asian region.

This gentle humanism that comes to inhabit Japanese treatments of Vietnam's postwar helps in some ways to flesh out the politics of memory of Asian conflict, particularly of the Vietnam War. Although American debates about Vietnam had long focused on the particular sets of interests, missteps, miscalculations, and strategic visions that led to the decade-long US debacle in Vietnam, interest has more recently turned to the memorialization of the war elsewhere. Christina Schwenkel's landmark study of transnational processes in the construction of Vietnamese memories of the American war is perhaps the best-known example, but other scholars working on Vietnam have produced rich accounts of the ways in which the war and its legacies help to shape everyday life there.[2] As Charles Armstrong has noted, South Korean activists for democracy and against militarism have had to contend with the violence carried out in Vietnam by Korean soldiers fighting on the side of the Americans, leading to an intense and complex mixture of emotions and debates about guilt and victimhood.[3] The aftermath of the Vietnam War was, of course, more than an opportunity for the United States to work out its own issues, a solipsism best summed up in the final voice-over in Oliver Stone's Academy Award–winning *Platoon:* "I think now, looking back, we did not fight the enemy; we fought ourselves. And the enemy is in us."[4] It was, in addition to an unspeakable calamity for the people of Vietnam, a defining moment for other countries in East and Southeast Asia—even Japan, which sent no soldiers to the fight. And the melodramatic narrative of Beto-chan and Doku-chan shows how the war's terrible consequences could be pulled convincingly into a story about Japan itself.

In focusing on the ways in which their story was told during their medical treatment and over the years, even as a comatose Beto-chan languished and died, this chapter emphasizes the political roles of sentimentality. Indeed, when I mentioned the story to some Japanese scholars working on the country's international relations, they all acknowledged knowing the story but not having followed it closely; it was a sad human story, not the high politics of regional relations. But recognizing and analyzing the story allow us to consider the breadth with which international relations—or, in this case, Japanese relations with Asia—are legitimated in part because of the deep personal hold that such stories ostensibly have for the public, through accounts like Beto-chan's and Doku-chan's, that can be meaningfully and poignantly drawn into a national narrative.

Postwar Asia in 1980s Japan

Less focused but more sustained than the 1960 protests that ended Prime Minister Kishi's tenure and inspired the ruling party to release the "Income Doubling Plan" to quell unruly demonstrations, Japan's Vietnam War–era demonstrations included challenges to Japanese militarism, authority in Japan's universities, and Japan's postwar capitalism. Altogether more difficult to pin down in terms of causes and goals, these protests were so violent and intractable that they shut down the University of Tokyo (and other universities) for the better part of the year. And in the aftermath of the demonstrations and the government's myriad responses, most participants were drawn safely back into Japan's postwar employment system rather than prison, perhaps voting for socialists or communists, but otherwise doing little to upset the applecart of economic growth.[5] The war, however, remained a central tension. Unlike South Korea's President Park Chung-hee, who provided many thousands of troops to support the US war effort, Prime Minister Satō Eisaku was deeply constrained by public opinion in how far he could go to help the United States. Both because of his ardent anticommunism and his desire to curry favor with the United States to hasten the reversion of Okinawa to Japanese control, Satō's government provided industrial and medical support to American forces in the conflict while maintaining its formal pacifist line (which helped to earn Satō a Nobel Peace Prize during what seems in retrospect to have been a rough stretch for the award, a year after Henry Kissinger won his).[6]

Almost any discussion of Japan's protest movements during the Vietnam War era is likely to provoke debate and backlash. In 2009, when the historical sociologist Oguma Eiji published his massive—even by his prolix standards—two-volume book *1968* (more than 2,000 pages in all), he drew exhaustively (and exhaustingly) from the written record of the era, provoking critiques, among others, that he had created a dishonest "montage" of the late 1960s protest movements without actually talking to any of the participants. The risk, in this view, was that Oguma's book, both because of his position as a leading public intellectual and the work's shelf-bending size, would be taken as the authoritative record of the era.[7] Similarly, when historian Simon Avenell published an article on philosopher Tsurumi Shunsuke, one of the leading figures in the anti–Vietnam War movement, in the well-regarded journal *positions: east asian cultures critique* in 2008, it was followed in the same issue by a trio of responses from the distinguished historians Laura Hein, J. Victor Koschmann, and Wesley Sasaki-Uemura. These commentaries, challenging and contextualizing Avenell's interpretations of Tsurumi's work and the era, together are nearly as long as the article itself. It was an inspired decision by the journal, helping to bring the era's debates to life.[8] It was also highly unusual, showing just how volatile the era remains for scholars.

And for artists as well. After Hollywood-oriented director Harada Masa-to's 2002 film *The Choice of Hercules*[9] dramatized a 1972 crisis in Nagano Prefecture, when United Red Army members took a woman hostage in a mountain inn, from the perspective of harried and frustrated police, the renowned left-wing director Wakamatsu Kōji described it as "full of lies."[10] He responded in 2008 with his powerful but nightmarish three-hour *United Red Army*,[11] portraying the same incident, often viscerally, from the young militants' perspective. It is little wonder that subsequent films about the politics of the protest era, such as Yamashita Nobuhiro's 2011 *My Back Pages,* would aim to sidestep some of the controversy by representing the era sentimentally, with idealistic heroes ultimately confronting and becom-ing demoralized by the violent excesses it contained.

We might view the Viet and Duc story primarily in the still controver-sial, still deeply political memories of the 1960s and 1970s. After all, the activists who identified the boys in Vietnam and many of the commenta-tors would discuss them specifically in the context of the American war that the Japanese government had shamefully if tacitly supported. But they emerged as figures in Japan in the 1980s, an era that is still largely avoided in much of the scholarly record. For example, the third and final volume of *Postwar Japanese Studies,* featuring essays by a distinguished group of progressive Japanese scholars, ostensibly focuses on the 1980s and 1990s, but gives the 1980s short shrift as it moves quickly into an analysis of the post–Cold War era. An introductory conversation between the historian Narita Ryūichi, modern literature scholar Komori Yōichi, and consider-ably younger media studies specialist Kitada Akihiro briefly explores the decade through two of its most important attributes: the apparent success of a putative "Japanese-style capitalism" and the discourses of Japanese uniqueness (*nihonjinron*) that animated public debate. They then turn to the emergent popularity of postmodern thought, particularly with the suc-cess of Asada Akira's famous *Structure and Power: Beyond Semiotics,* to sum up the era's key intellectual contributions.[12] The sense that the 1980s are only barely worth mentioning becomes particularly strong when the volume's first substantive chapter focuses on the period between the end of the Cold War (still in full swing through virtually the entire 1980s) and the 9/11 attacks (not even on the horizon for the Afghan-based Islamist movement of the era).[13] Although conservatives are more likely to express pride in the more overt nationalism of the decade's most prominent prime minister, Nakasone Yasuhiro, they are scarcely more reflective and far from nostalgic, in large part because the decade's climactic financial scandals helped to usher them out of power soon thereafter.[14] Only recently have scholars begin to consider the 1980s as part of modern Japanese history, whether through the semiofficial efforts to codify the "Japanese way" of political economy or the ways in which changing entertainment and leisure systems emphasized self-realization and creativity.[15]

And it was largely in the 1980s that Japan's economic relations with Asia were publicly and proudly depicted as a primary element of the country's statecraft. Shortly after the end of World War II, with the loss of Manchuria and, with communist revolution, any prospect of access to China, Japan's economic policy makers had turned toward Southeast Asia as a potential source of raw materials for Japanese industry.[16] Indeed, the government soon used its reparations treaties in the region as the origins of Japan's development assistance regime.[17] Economic engagement, largely through aid, became a defining feature of Japanese postwar diplomacy.[18] For a time, it was also highly popular, especially after 1989, when the country surpassed the United States as the world's top aggregate donor of development assistance.[19] After all, as the Japanese government continued to defer to the United States on security matters and struggled mightily with the emerging trade frictions that shaped the bilateral relationship for much of that time, there were few arenas in foreign policy that demonstrated clear Japanese agency. Aid was perhaps the leading one, as well as the one most open-ended in its meaning. For some Japanese politicians, officials, and writers espousing Japan's continued pacifist role, aid represented a potential way for Japan to build positive relations with its neighbors without relying on the further development of military force.[20] For others, development assistance was one part of a larger diplomatic strategy that could and should include a more elaborate international security role for Japan, including the peacekeeping missions that might be seen as complementing the developmental goals of aid itself.[21] Official development assistance (ODA) was therefore capacious in its promise, at least as long as Japan's national budget seemed able to sustain it.

Aid, moreover, offered the chance for real diplomatic autonomy, for Japan to engage the world, especially the Southeast Asian nations that were leading recipients, on its own terms rather than in a manner subordinate to Washington's prerogatives. And while Japan also donated aid to South Korea, Taiwan, and, later, China, tensions over Japan's wartime behavior in these countries made relations more fraught than they usually were with Southeast Asian countries, whose leaders normally suppressed anti-Japanese claims while currying favor with Tokyo.[22] In this view, aid was not just money but a means for making Japan a model: bringing the tools and know-how of Japan's high-speed growth to the developing world, especially in Asia. Over time, critics—frequently among the European donors but increasingly among vocal Japanese progressives as well—challenged Tokyo's penchant for "tied" aid that explicitly carved out space for Japanese products or contractors, as well as for the loan-based (rather than grant-based) aid that ostensibly instilled responsibility among recipients. Yen-based loans, critics noted, rendered these countries vulnerable to exchange-rate volatility. Japan's emphasis on infrastructure frequently supported investment plans among Japanese firms, providing ODA funds to support telecommunications or transportation systems necessary to make Japan's joint ventures and overseas factories profitable.[23] For these critics, Japanese development assistance seemed always to enrich Japanese in the process. But for many Japanese officials, Japan's "developmental" emphasis on aid led to good results. For all the talk of sustainability, poverty reduction, democratization, and equality among European and American donors, many in Tokyo preferred to emphasize the bottom line: results. After all, Japan's main aid recipients, clustered in East/Southeast Asia, mostly enjoyed vastly higher growth rates than the Latin American, Sub-Saharan African, and South Asian targets of European and American assistance. The World Bank's 1994 report *The East Asian Miracle* became famous because its split personality—sometimes extolling state-led developmentalist strategies, frequently hewing to the World Bank's typical line on markets and liberalization—resulted from a bitter drafting fight between Japanese economists at the World Bank and the organization's US-trained leaders.[24]

For years, *The East Asian Miracle* was virtually required reading in many Japanese graduate classes about development, frequently accompanying mid-1990s debates about "Asian values." Notable for their connection to authoritarian leaders such as Singapore's Lee Kwan Yew and Malaysia's Mahathir Mohamad, these values connected East Asia's economic fortunes to a kind of cultural background emphasizing some versions of thrift, hard work, family cohesiveness, and loyalty to authority, which supposedly emanated mostly from combinations of Confucianism and local traditions.[25] Mahathir's "Look East" program explicitly made Japan's development the model to which Malaysians should turn. Lee and Mahathir were reacting in part to some of the political triumphalism after the Cold War, perhaps symbolized best by Francis Fukuyama's *The End of History*, with its emphasis on liberal democracy as the last cohesive political-economic order standing after the great wars of the twentieth century. Much of the Asian values discourse resonated with strands of left-wing and right-wing thought in Japan. Politician, novelist, and right-wing provocateur Ishihara Shintarō, for example, whose *The Japan That Can Say No* had deliberately poked Washington in the eye in 1989 with its emphasis on Japanese technological superiority as a match for Washington's arrogance, coauthored a dialogue with Mahathir titled *The Asia That Can Say No*.[26] Although views within Japan about developmentalism and Asian values were far from uniform, it was common to see even relatively liberal accounts of economic change refer to cultural patterns that allowed the countries of East Asia to learn from the Japanese model more effectively, and with more affection, than they could from the West.

Because the Asian values debate has attracted so much attention in English for the anger against Western—generally meaning US—pressure and condescension, it has masked the warmth with which images of Asian community are frequently represented in Japan. Even Japanese proponents of "Asian values" rarely presented Asians as an angry collective mob turning away top-hatted, monocle-wearing Western imperialists; they were instead people with similar, traditional values, following Japanese guidance toward a better tomorrow. Indeed, much of the popular representation of Asia in Japan is deeply nostalgic, with other countries (particularly the ones not burning Japanese factories or forcefully demanding that Japan apologize more profusely for atrocities and sexual enslavement in World War II) serving as imagined sites for the maintenance of premodern customs or a rigorous, vigorous drive toward national modernization—both things that people in Japan have ostensibly lost through materialism and indolence.[27] This nostalgia is a bit different from, say, the idea of the "noble savage" that has occasionally shaped well-meaning but patronizing American and European accounts of colonized Others: the good-hearted, uneducated but naturally wise Africans, Native Americans, and so on.[28] But this nostalgia is unmistakable in everything from NGOs' brochures about their development work in Asia to the tears and smiles in Fukasaku's film *We Can't Change the World,* discussed in chapter 1. And it is at least as much here as it is in the anger directed by leftists toward the Japanese government for assisting the United States in an astonishingly brutal war against poor Asians seeking independence from colonial rule that we must locate the Viet-Duc episode, not just in the work of the activists involved but also in the myriad ways that people across the political spectrum analyzed, discussed, and described the depth of their feelings about the boys and their struggles.

Mapping Asia in Orange

Most of the consequences to human health of dioxin exposure—cancers, abnormalities *in utero,* nerve damage—can appear randomly, and the high price of blood and tissue tests to determine dioxin levels makes them virtually prohibitive. People are therefore understood to be victims of Agent Orange, the chemical defoliant used by the United States during the Vietnam War to deprive communist adversaries of forest cover, based not only on symptoms but also in part on maps. For example, colored maps show where the heaviest use of the dioxin during Operation Ranch Hand ostensibly occurred, but these are at best imprecise instruments, with US air crews often forced to contend with enemy fire or uncertain topography that would complicate their reports of where the chemical ended up once released from the planes.[29] One might, as the US government has, determine "hot spots" in Vietnam where the dioxin was stored and where health consequences were expected to be particularly severe, using these as guides for the circumstances under which Vietnamese with disabilities or health problems might be understood to be victims. Or one might, as has done regarding the US military personnel who could have been affected, judge virtually all of Vietnam to be a danger zone, as the Department of Veterans Affairs makes clear.[30] The tens of thousands of Americans claiming to be victims are judged by the US government with criteria entirely different from the ones used for the three to four million Vietnamese making similar appeals. I once heard a relatively sympathetic US diplomat say that virtually every Vietnamese child afflicted by a birth defect was immediately described by Vietnamese as an Agent Orange victim, regardless of other potential causes; he did not address the relatively capacious diagnoses of US veterans. Victimhood is therefore an inherently political determination, judged not only by health consequences but also with reference to maps whose boundaries and colors reflect power and negotiation.

As a photographer during the Vietnam War, Nakamura Gorō paid special attention to the consequences of Operation Ranch Hand, the nearly decade-long program to deploy Agent Orange in forested regions used by communist guerillas. Nakamura himself did not achieve the mythical, martyred fame of the two most famous Japanese photographers of the Vietnam War. Two-time "World Press Photo of the Year" winner Sawada Kyōichi left behind a legacy of indelible portraits of the war's most grueling consequences, including "Flee to Safety," the iconic shot of a desperate mother crossing a river with her four children to escape a US bombing. In 1970, still-unidentified assailants killed Sawada execution-style, along with the UPI bureau chief Frank Frosch, as they headed south from Phnom Penh to visit a site of recent fighting. Another young photographer, Ichinose Taizō, never earned the international reputation that Sawada achieved but attracted attention from the Japanese media because of his astonishing fearlessness in getting as close as possible to danger in trying to snap photos. Aspiring to be the first photographer to take shots of Angkor Wat in the midst of the violence engulfing Cambodia, Ichinose was killed by Khmer Rouge militants in 1973 at the age of twenty-six. It was partly a phrase in one of Ichinose's revealing and engaging letters back home—"one step on a landmine, and it's all over" (*jirai o fundara sayōnara*)—that helped to cement his romantic image, particularly after his mother, having traveled to Cambodia to visit his grave, published a collection of them. The phrase then served as the title of Igarashi Shō's popular 1999 narrative film about Ichinose, starring one of Japan's best-known young actors, Asada Tadanobu; Igarashi had three years earlier directed the documentary *Sawada*.[31]

In contrast, Nakamura focused on the physical costs of the war and particularly of the chemical weapons used by the United States. His initial Vietnam photos from the final days of the war met limited interest, and Nakamura's subsequent work took him to Cambodia and then Iraq, producing photographic essays that took fond views of the people of both countries. But a subsequent trip to Vietnam in 1982 to document the lingering consequences of Agent Orange brought him in touch with a pair of conjoined twins, known to the hospital staff at the time as Ba and Bon, who resided in the Vietnam-German Democratic Republic Friendship Hospital in Hanoi, where they had already been met by Kutsuwada, the journalist whose account opens this chapter.[32] With separate heads and torsos but sharing a pelvis and three legs, the twins were ultimately given the names of the hospital itself: from the Bệnh Viện Viet Đức, the Nguyen brothers, Viet and Duc (respectively, Vietnam and Germany).

Born in 1981 in Kon Tum Province in Vietnam's central highlands, Viet and Duc were almost certainly victims of Agent Orange. Kon Tum itself was the fourth-most heavily sprayed province during the war, with 11 percent of its land area doused with more than 800,000 tons of Agent Orange.[33] The boy's mother, a farmer already in her early thirties at the time of their birth, had lived throughout the war in the area and had reportedly relied on water from a well later determined to be contaminated by dioxins from the spray. Unable to care for their sons—who shared a lower body but with two heads, necks, upper chests, and pairs of arms— their parents abandoned them at a local hospital, divorcing shortly afterward. The boys were brought to the Vietnam-East German Friendship Hospital in Hanoi shortly thereafter but would be transferred to Ho Chi Minh City's Tu Du Obstretrics Hospital, which had begun specialized care for infants and mothers affected by Agent Orange, later in 1982. Known by then as Viet and Duc, the two began to attract the attention of the Japanese media in 1983, particularly when the left-leaning *Asahi Shimbun* followed up a 1981 documentary about the effects of Agent Orange with a story occasioned by an international symposium held in Ho Chi Minh City about the health consequences of the wartime use of chemical defoliants. The story drew attention to the broader issue of Agent Orange use, but it was framed largely around the young lives of Viet and Duc, adorned with a photo of them surrounded by smiling Vietnamese physicians.[34]

Working with several activists touched by their story, Nakamura himself would play a key role in bringing Viet and Duc to considerable renown in Japan. Another central actor was Fujimoto Bunrō, a professor of education at Shiga University with interests in the rights of the disabled, who traveled on a fellowship to Vietnam in 1985. In meeting Viet and Duc at Tu Du Hospital, Fujimoto spoke with the energetic and enterprising physician Nguyen Thi Ngoc Phuong. Phuong would later say that, having worked in obstetrics since the late 1960s, she had become alarmed by the increasing incidence of birth defects at her clinic, conducting a study in 1982 that seemed to show a clear correlation between the extent of dioxin use and the number of birth defects, frequently many times higher than what one might expect in a random sample.[35] Although her suspicions had been long-standing, the study itself followed the increasing prevalence of news accounts and lawsuits in the United States by former military service members against the US government, claiming damage from exposure to Agent Orange while in Vietnam.

Indeed, the 1983 symposium—with the Americans representing the largest contingent of physicians but accompanied by scientists from the Soviet Union, Japan, and elsewhere—was a mark of the increasing global attention to Agent Orange, even as the Vietnamese government itself was surprisingly reticent on the topic. As Tine Gammeltoft notes, in part because of concerns about potential reputational harm to Vietnamese agricultural exports as well as the desire to cultivate ties with the United States, Hanoi was reluctant for years to make the Agent Orange issue a public one. Earlier Vietnamese news accounts had noted the possible connections between the herbicide's use and the incidence of congenital disorders and disabilities, but until the early 2000s these remained at the level of personal concern and debate rather than national or officially sanctioned discourse.[36]

And so Phuong's ability to attract international attention and support was likely key in her longer-term efforts to secure aid for Agent Orange victims; it was certainly essential in the case of Viet and Duc. Nakamura had worked to secure permission from the Vietnamese government to return to the country to photograph the consequences of Agent Orange, a goal he reportedly had had since seeing a child wandering through a devastated and obviously poisoned mangrove forest in Cape Ca Mau in 1976. By 1981, he had amassed a personal library of nearly eight thousand photos, including a number of Ba and Bon. Shortly thereafter, he even traveled to the United States to meet with concerned veterans' and physicians' groups, and in 1983 the respected, popular publishing house Iwanami released his photographic essay book *Mothers Were Exposed to Agent Orange: The Lingering Scars of Dioxin*.[37] Phuong may have confronted a tight-lipped Vietnamese government on the Agent Orange issue, but she found a rising tide of concern among the Japanese she met.

Fujimoto later expressed surprise at the forthrightness with which Phuong asked him, during his 1985 trip to the hospital, to have Japan provide a wheelchair for Viet and Duc, and he presented the story as a moral mission for Japan both to help the disabled as well as to support victims of war violence.[38] This would have been the expected stance for Fujimoto, who, in 1981, had cowritten the Japanese book *War and the Disabled: Testimony from Vietnam.*[39] When interviewed by the *Asahi Shimbun,* he emphasized his desire to provide a bit of mobility to the mostly bedridden Vietnamese twins. After returning to Japan, Fujimoto requested the help of his former student, Kawahara Masami, a pioneer for the rights of the disabled who had only a few years earlier become Japan's first wheelchair-bound public librarian. Working with others in Fukui Prefecture's disabled rights community, Kawahara introduced Fujimoto to Yamaguchi Masahiro, a quadriplegic with experience in designing wheelchairs. Together they created the "The Group Hoping for Viet and Duc's Development" (*Beto-chan Doku-chan no hattatsu o negau kai,* but abbreviated below, and conventionally, as the Negau Kai),[40] quickly raising a million yen (about US $4,000 in 1985) to build the chair for Viet and Duc and to send anticancer drugs to Vietnam for broader use in children's care.

When Dr. Phuong visited Japan later in 1985 both to express thanks for the wheelchair from the Negau Kai and to appeal for further assistance to Vietnamese dioxin victims, her presence was sufficiently important that Asahi television booked her for an appearance on its sensationally popular new program, *News Station.*[41] Phuong detailed concerns facing Viet and Duc in the larger context of dioxins, making sure that she connected the problem that Vietnam was facing with potential risks in Japan. In a coauthored 2010 report in the nonprofit medical journal *Inochi to kurashi* (Life and living), Fujimoto would recall that Phuong had, on the show, skillfully reported not only on the problems for Viet and Duc but also on the risks that dioxins produced through petrochemical production and use might pose to Japanese.[42]

Asians with Speed

Throughout 1985 and into early 1986, Japanese newspapers and television programs continued occasional stories on Viet and Duc, the brave doctor working to protect them and other dioxin victims, and the Japanese network of activists for the rights of the disabled who had established the Negau Kai. And then, in late May 1986, Tu Du Hospital reported that Viet—often described as the more chipper and upbeat of the twins—had begun to run a serious fever, falling into critical condition and imperiling Duc's life as well. As *Asahi* journalist Kutsuwada Takafumi wrote in a long report on June 13, by June 10 a pediatric blood-pressure monitor donated by the Negau Kai clacked away rapidly, showing the boys to be in great distress. Viet's temperature held stable at 39°C (102°F) while Duc's had gone to 38°C (100°F).[43] With public attention growing, Prime Minister Nakasone Yasuhiro became personally involved, announcing to the journalists on the prime minister's beat that he would dispatch Japanese doctors and specialized equipment to Ho Chi Minh City to care for the boys and determine the next best steps.[44]

Nakasone himself may have been moved by the boys' plight, but his announcement can hardly be separated from the political climate at the time. With an election looming in less than a month, the prime minister eagerly sought to burnish his credentials as a decisive, speedy, effective but compassionate leader, not the dictator so often described by his opponents in the Japan Socialist Party. Indeed, in a televised speech on June 29, just a few days before the election, Nakasone, with typically laughable bluster, explained his decision:

I think we can call my government is run the Nakasone Way (*Nakasone-ryū*). The first point is that it's a government that's easy to understand. The second is we've got the ability to do things quickly (*supiido*). In this era of high-speed information, the Japanese have become the people with the greatest information and knowledge anywhere in the world. So we've been working to take the initiative in responding to citizens' concerns. I've gotten rid of the way it used to be: something comes up from a department manager, up to an agency manager, then to a cabinet member, and then up to the prime minister to get his signature, then back down. Now when there's something important, I call straight from the prime minister's office, I talk to the vice minister, or the section head, or the cabinet minister, and I find out what's going on and what needs to be done.

Just recently, there was the problem with the Vietnamese twins, Viet and Duc. Everyone else was wringing their hands and wasting time (*urouro shiteotta*). I said right away, dispatch some doctors from the Japanese Red Cross. I had the Ministry of Transport prepare the plane, I got government money ready to go. The Foreign Ministry got in touch immediately with the Vietnamese government to get the visas set. The Japan Red Cross doctors left from Haneda the next day, and they've already returned, haven't they? We should all be praying for the recovery of Viet and Duc. That's natural for us as Asians and as human beings. But this also is the era when we need a prime minister with capability and speed.[45]

Although Nakasone had crafted the image of capable and speedy leader, it does seem likely that the LDP's dominant performance in 1986 reflected the declining fortunes of opposition parties such as the Socialists rather than deep enthusiasm about the ruling party.[46] Whether in an effort to eke out a final few votes or to remind his audience that he was no dictator but rather a caring and compassionate leader, Nakasone signaled the public visibility of Viet and Duc as well as at least one of the political meanings that their illness might have.

Within a week, the Japanese Red Cross had succeeded in persuading the Vietnamese government to send the boys to Japan, where they were greeted with great fanfare at Narita Airport on June 19 and then transferred to Tokyo on June 20. Nakasone once again played a key role, authorizing the use of the Japan Airlines DC-8 normally operating as the prime minister's plane because of the Red Cross's determination that the boys would likely not survive aboard a long commercial flight. The early reports in Japan suggested that the Japanese Red Cross was planning to separate the boys, but grave concern rose about the public relations consequences that would befall the organization if one of the boys, probably Viet, were to die, given the difficulty of dividing their internal organs in a manner that could ensure a healthy life for both. Japanese doctors could do the actual work, wrote physician and nonfiction author Miwa Kazuo in *Bungei Shunjū,* Japan's most popular magazine. What they could not do, however, was to take responsibility for the potentially catastrophic and even fatal outcome.[47]

Accompanying the boys were three women: Dr. Phuong as the key hospital leader and liaison to Japan's Red Cross, their attending physician Dr. Phat (Nguyen Son Thi Phat), and Nurse Muoi (Nguyen Thi Muoi), who was often described as the surrogate mother who took key emotional care of the boys. In subsequent weeks the Japanese newspapers and television programs focused on Duc's recovery—as the illness had left Viet weakened and with significant brain damage—as well as on the exposure

of the doctors to life in Japan. For her part, Phuong was already a relatively seasoned traveler and, whether intentionally or not, highly effective
in playing to public sympathies in Japan, emphasizing both the global
risk that dioxins posed as well as her gratitude to Japan's generosity with
its sophisticated and technologically advanced medical care.[48] In Miwa's
account, Muoi took the chance to have some fun as well, shopping in
Shibuya and even learning how to wear the kind of cosmetics that would
have been unavailable in war- and recession-ravaged Ho Chi Minh City.[49]

In a moment that left her Japanese and Vietnamese colleagues flabber-
gasted, Dr. Phat undermined some of the ease of the narrative surrounding
the maternal Vietnamese figures caring for the boys with the help of their
sympathetic and adept Japanese counterparts. Having announced that she
was planning to take a bus tour of Tokyo, Dr. Phat instead traveled to the
US Embassy in Tokyo, where she was met by her husband, a South Vietnamese ship captain who had fled the country in 1975, resettling in New
Orleans.[50] US Representative Lindy Boggs had responded to a request
from Phat's husband's attorney after the husband reportedly learned of
her trip to Japan in a Vietnamese-language newspaper.[51] After she was
allowed to flee to the United States, the Japanese Red Cross reacted with
some panic, keeping its comments to a minimum except to say that it
had not known of or aided her plan to defect. Recognizing the risks to its
relations with both the United States and Vietnam, the Japanese government did not lodge any formal protest, although it worked assiduously to
reassure Vietnam that it was not part of a plan to embarrass the country.
Phuong then briefly returned to Vietnam, and the Japanese Red Cross
made a formal request to the Vietnamese Red Cross to send another doctor. Phuong returned on August 12 with her close colleague, Dr. Ta Thi
Chung, who would remain through the end of the boys' stay.[52]

The brief English-language account of Phat's travel to the United
States—not officially called a defection by the Japanese government,
although Japanese newspapers used the word *bōmei,* referring to political
asylum or defection—carried with it an important piece of information
that was discussed only lightly in the Japanese press. Likely in a sympathetic effort to reduce the perception of cruelty potentially associated with
an attending physician's decision to abandon conjoined twins undergoing
medical treatment, the United Press International story indicated that Viet
had fallen into a coma and was not expected to recover. This appears to

have been incorrect, for Japanese papers mentioned that Viet was drink-
ing and eating. But they shied away from what would be signaled subtly
in later accounts: that Viet's struggle with encephalitis had left his brain
badly damaged. Instead, the news accounts dwelled primarily on the success of Duc's treatment, his enthusiasm, and the fact that both boys were
alive. When they returned to Vietnam at the end of October, the *Yomiuri* reported that Duc sobbed about leaving Japan but that Viet smiled
broadly (*nikkori*); an *Asahi* roundup several months later referred to both
boys doing well (*genki*).[53]

Unavoidable Decisions, Impossible Sequels

These representations signaled how the Japanese media would cover the
next major interactions between Japan and Vietnam over Viet and Duc's
lives. After all, there were myriad moral lessons that the boys' conjoined
bodies and perilous health might have conveyed. To be sure, Japanese advocates for the rights of the disabled, particularly the Negau Kai's members, emphasized the importance of treating those with disabilities with
dignity, care, and respect. Advocates of environmental justice drew connections between Viet and Duc's dire circumstances and the terrible fates
of victims of Minamata Disease, the broad term referring to the ailments
associated with mercury poisoning from industrial pollution of Japan's
oceans.[54] For others, Viet and Duc's condition primarily reflected the cal-
lous brutality of US military power.[55] For many leftists, of course, these
causes were largely bound up with one another, the same way that activists in the late 1960s could hold protests that simultaneously decried the
Vietnam War, promoted the rights of the disenfranchised, and criticized
heartless companies for putting profits ahead of people's health. But the
overriding narrative—the one emerging in part from these Japanese activists, from the appeals of a Vietnamese medical researcher trying to ensure
continued attention to a public health catastrophe, and particularly from
news media eager to tell a good story—became one of a qualified triumph,
one produced by a combination of technical skill and deep humanism that
allowed Japan to save the lives of these two unfortunate boys.

Throughout 1987 and into early 1988, Phuong made repeated appeals
for help from Japan, both in terms of continued financial support for Agent

Orange victims, including the many in Tu Du Hospital, as well as in trying to secure a commitment from the Japanese Red Cross to separate the two boys surgically. This surgery—already the subject of discussion in 1986—faced a number of severe constraints. Vietnamese doctors expressed confidence that they did not need to rely on Japan—that they could handle the surgery themselves in Vietnam. The Japanese Red Cross, though certain that the operation would be a success if handled in Japan, worried about what would happen with the boys' return to Vietnam and also struggled with the prospect that Viet himself would not survive. Even as it became clear that Viet's continuing health problems were likely to imperil Duc if they were not separated, Japanese doctors argued with their Vietnamese counterparts about the priorities of the surgery. Vietnamese physicians emphasized the importance of saving Duc by "cutting away" (*kirisuteru*), a term that Miwa repeatedly uses, fully aware of the harsh implications; it can mean not only "cut away" but also "cut down" or "abandon." And this is in the context of an article that criticizes the Japanese Red Cross for its unwillingness to make the difficult decisions. Indeed, the Vietnamese doctors seem gritty and tough in Miwa's account because they had ostensibly grappled with the ethical issues and determined that Viet would have to die so that Duc could survive.[56] In the end, Miwa writes, Phuong agreed with the Japanese doctors and pushed for the surgery to save both.[57]

The doctors dispatched by the Japanese Red Cross to advise and to observe the surgery played an ancillary role, although Japan was the source of virtually all of the high-tech surgical tools and medical equipment that the nearly thirty Vietnamese doctors and nurses would use in the surgery itself. For their part, the Japanese doctors kept a low profile, serving as liaisons for the Japanese journalists dispatched to cover the surgery. Anesthesiologist Araki Yōji, for example, advised one Vietnamese doctor, during a rehearsal on a special medical doll for separation surgeries, on how to insert a catheter under the collarbone for intravenous anesthesia, but that appears to have been done only at the request of the Vietnamese physician. Even so, the dispatch of the Japanese doctors and the role of Japanese medical equipment figured prominently in virtually all of the news coverage surrounding the thirteen-hour surgery.

It ended successfully, up to a point. Viet and Duc's internal organs were sufficiently distributable to keep both of them alive, even if only one of them—Duc—would retain most of his normal bodily functions. Although

Viet and Duc were themselves discussed only sparingly in Vietnam, the surgery itself appears to have been of great interest to the country's mass media. Much of this likely reflected less their victimization at the hands of the United States through Agent Orange and more the emphasis on the skill, dedication, and kindness of the Vietnamese surgical team that successfully completed the operation. Japanese television news programs and newspapers covered the run-up to the surgery extensively and were even more comprehensive, in sometimes extraordinary and surprising detail, during the surgery's aftermath. The *Yomiuri*'s coverage extended to Dr. Phuong's press conference after the surgery, emphasizing that she had to wipe away the tears while smiling, saying the boys had come through the surgery successfully and that their temperatures had started to fall to normal levels.[58] Much as it had since first reporting on Viet and Duc several years earlier, the *Asahi* kept a spotlight on Duc's words and actions. In one story, Duc was restless the morning after the surgery, crying and telling doctors that his leg hurt, although the article did not say whether he was talking about the leg he still had or the leg that had gone to Viet.[59] The *Asahi* followed up the next day with a story about how a frightened and disoriented Duc begged to be allowed to go back to the specially equipped room where he and Viet had spent most of their lives. He asked at one point "Where's Viet?" and the nurse pointed him to a bed four meters away—the farthest away he had ever been from his brother.[60] Although the *Asahi* and other newspapers addressed the issue in only a circumspect manner, Viet himself had fallen into a coma from which he would never recover.

Over the next few years, the Negau Kai continued to follow up with news releases and reports, and Japanese news outlets did occasional features to update audiences about Duc's progress. There was, however, relatively little to say about Viet, other than that he remained on life support. While Dr. Phuong continued her international outreach efforts to secure funding and support for Agent Orange victims, Japanese attention to the issue declined unmistakably after the fever pitch of 1988, when the Viet-Duc case was routinely recognized as one of the top ten stories of the year. Duc's survival had, in a sense, provided an end to the story, so subsequent articles about him fleshed out the "happily ever after" details of his life rather than highlighting the continuing atrocity of Agent Orange and its legacies.

The hope not to continue the story but rather to draft a sequel may have led to the *Mainichi Shimbun*'s decision to cover in 1991 the birth of a new set of conjoined twins who subsequently lived at Tu Du Hospital. Bin-chan and Tan-chan, as the girls were called in the Japanese press, were not the first conjoined twins born in Vietnam after Viet and Duc; two other pairs of boys—the already-separated four-year-olds Son (described as taciturn and quiet) and Faa (excitable, even pushy) and nine-month-olds Hau and Zan—already resided in the hospital. Bin-chan and Tan-chan had already caught the attention of the other boys, with Faa reportedly grabbing the hem of a doctor's white coat and saying "I'm going to make Bin-chan and Tan-chan my girlfriends, so separate them already!" In an interview with the *Mainichi,* Dr. Phuong explained that she was anxious to separate the twins; Bin-chan had been healthy, but the purple spots on Tan-chan's skin from birth suggested congenital heart problems that had left her weak, potentially endangering Bin-chan as well. Asked for a comment to the *Mainichi's* Japanese readers, Phuong said, "In Vietnam, there is an extremely large number of children who, because of the consequences of Agent Orange, are stillborn or die shortly after birth. In particular, there were seven pairs of conjoined twins born in our hospital over the past year; five of them have already died. I just want to save Bin and Tan. Everyone in Japan, please help us again."[61]

Over the following three weeks, the *Mainichi* publicized a campaign to save the unfortunate five-month-old girls: the hasty, informal creation in Osaka of the "Group to Save Bin-chan and Tan-chan" (*Bin-chan, Tan-chan o sukūkai*), headed officially by the writer Tokunaga Shin'ichirō but primarily run by Yamamoto Naoya, a dentist from Shiga Prefecture (where Negau Kai founder Fujimoto Bunrō was teaching) who had earlier been active in raising funds for Viet and Duc's surgery.[62] In a three-part series, the *Mainichi* then detailed the lives of the girls, their care at Tu Du Hospital, the effort to determine whether Agent Orange was (as it was strongly suggested) the cause of their condition, and the fears of their mother, who could not easily care for them in her poor village. Each article ended with the contact and donation information for the Sukūkai, which held its formal inaugural meeting on April 23, 1991, in Shiga; among the group's advisors were Inaba Minoru, governor of Shiga Prefecture, and Hirono Hiroshi, chairman of Shiga Bank.[63]

That very day, the girls' condition took a turn for the worse. With Phuong herself later thanking Japan for its support and saying that the separation surgery that the Sukūkai was about to finance would have saved their lives, the hospital's director informed the media that Bin and Tan had, on April 23, suddenly begun to vomit up the fluids they were being fed and struggled with their breathing. Rushed to the hospital's intensive-care unit, Bin-chan and Tan-chan survived for nearly two weeks while doctors did everything they could to keep them alive. In the end, on May 8 they suffered a heart attack and passed away; by the time the news was conveyed in the *Mainichi* on May 10, the girls' body had already been returned to their parents, and they had been buried in Ho Chi Minh City.[64] The Sukūkai and the *Mainichi* were denied the even qualifiedly happy ending of the Viet-Duc case, although they continued to raise money. In October 1991, Dr. Phuong visited Shiga Prefecture and was given the 881 million yen (approximately US $67,000) that the Sukūkai had collected initially for Bin and Tan, with the expectation that it would support Tu Du Hospital's continuing efforts.[65]

Denouements

Bin-chan and Tan-chan are barely remembered in Japan; although they became a cause for the *Mainichi* and a small circle of activists, even successful surgery for them would have likely attracted less attention than the pioneering operation to save Viet and Duc. But the legend of Viet and Duc would grow throughout the late 1980s and well into the 1990s. Collections of supplementary readings for Japan's social studies classes for elementary and middle schools frequently contained discussions of Viet and Duc, routinely with references to the assistance Japan had provided in their surgery, and photos of them sometimes served as the key visual materials in the brief Vietnam War sections of middle school history textbooks. The major Japanese newspapers followed up with reports each year on Duc's progress: his efforts to walk to school on the artificial leg that the Negau Kai had provided, his decision to study computers after dropping out of high school, his volunteer activities to give hope to other disabled Vietnamese children, his 2006 wedding (attended by a number of Negau Kai representatives) to another volunteer, and the birth of his twin children, Phu Si (Fuji) and Anh Dao (Sakura), a son and a daughter, respectively.

When Viet—who had never regained consciousness—passed away in 2007 from renal failure, after suffering from pneumonia and other maladies in the last year of his life, all of the main Japanese newspapers paid tribute to him and the survival of his courageous brother. One librarian from Nakano Prefecture wrote an essay in the *Asahi Shimbun*'s "Voices" section reflecting on the effect that a 1991 picture book by the children's writer Matsutani Miyoko, *Letters from Viet and Duc,* had had on her students.[66] The librarian had read the book, illustrated by Iguchi Bunshū, out loud, showing its pictures to children from second through sixth grades (usually seven to twelve years old) as the students gasped during the grim tale of the determined brothers. The essay's author quotes the book's final passage, ostensibly written or spoken by Duc, which contains at least one of the book's clear messages: "Promise never to wage war. No to Agent Orange. No to chemical weapons. That's what we ask. From Viet, my brother who can't speak, and from me—the request from both of us."[67]

It is a remarkable book, notable for the ferocity with which Matsutani specifies the cause of their malady—the US use of Agent Orange, from planes taking off from the bases it held in still-occupied Okinawa—as well as the broad and far-reaching consequences of the US use of chemical weapons, and for the deep melodrama of the text and pictures. Viet and Duc are, of course, blameless and innocent, ravaged by the outside forces of a cruel military whose reliance on bases implicated even Japan. In its brief discussion of the surgery, Matsutani focuses repeatedly on Japanese generosity—the wheelchair, the medical support, the Japan Airlines flight to Narita, even the possibly apocryphal story of Duc's use of the word *"okaasan"* (Japanese for "mother") to refer to Nurse Muoi after awakening from the separation surgery in 1988. Categorized by one educational materials firm as a story suitable for children about the consequences of war, alongside the classic anime *Grave of the Fireflies, Letters from Viet and Duc* presents the tough lives of the two boys in a quick thirty pages. The first four introduce Viet and Duc, discussing their town and their birth; the next six cover US use of Agent Orange, displaying it as a nightmare, with one of Iguchi's drawings sweeping across two pages, showing a mountain of naked, sick, dying, or dead babies, some of them conjoined much like Viet and Duc, stretching on endlessly. The next six pages report on their lives after moving to Tu Du Hospital, with the Negau Kai's wheelchair appearing about halfway into the book. As the boys travel to Japan aboard the JAL jet, "Uncles" Fujimoto and Kawahara make an appearance in the book, speaking of America's use of the Okinawan bases and referring even to the wartime famine during the Japanese occupation of

Vietnam: "As we listened to our two uncles, we came to understand why people in Japan have been so concerned about us." Matsutani covers their subsequent treatment and separation—again, with heavy reference to Japanese support—for the next eight pages, finally concluding with a smiling Duc announcing the book's message as he leans on his crutch in front of a rice paddy.

At least to the librarian writing in the *Asahi* upon Viet's death in 2007, the book's canny projection of the boys' personalities—condensing their lives into a visually graphic representation of military violence, dying babies, surgery, recuperation, and a call for peace—is a convincing success. She concludes her brief essay with a statement to the recently deceased Viet himself, a young man who had been unconscious for nineteen years and had likely developed cognitively only until age four: "Viet, please watch over your brother Duc from heaven. I've been telling your request to my beloved kids."

An opinion piece like this would likely have been ignored by the majority of *Asahi* readers or glanced at and quickly forgotten, perhaps even provoking a bit of embarrassment among more cynical subscribers at its sentimentalism. But its presence also discloses an emotional politics surrounding Viet and Duc, an emotional politics that works specifically because of the melodramatic narrative in which it sits. Even at the time of the picture book's publication, ten-year-old Duc was a more complex figure than the author could have noted, and the compressed, distilled story that the book tells is, of course, crafted to fit the messages that Matsutani aims to share with the reader. To speak of Viet's wishes or requests (*negau*) in 2007 might even be ethically troubling, given his cruelly abbreviated development and mostly coma-bound life. In a sense, however, this is beside the point: the conversation is really more about Japan's children and their moral education than it is about Viet and Duc as actual people. The brief and sentimental essay in the *Asahi* in no way distorts the book, and she misrepresents Viet and Duc's lives only in ways that were de rigueur in broader Japanese discussions about them. And it fit neatly with depictions of moral malaise in a post–bubble-era Japan had so much in common with their country—also devastated by the brutal use of non-conventional weapons by US military forces, leaving behind, among others, a trail of juvenile victims guilty of nothing more than trying to grow up—that it might be understood as the other Vietnam: the Vietnam that lost its war and won (in a manner) its peace, but that had subsequently lost its way.[68] Japan now faces the moral imperative to assist its unfortunate Asian neighbors whose economic and technical development lags behind Japan's, even as they maintain a cultural core of essential decency that is on the verge of collapse in Japan.

What Viet and Duc Taught Us

It is therefore commendable that the essays in the book *What Viet and Duc Taught Us* are as free as they are of the kind of faux naïveté that the title implies.[69] After all, the trope that one learns the most valuable lessons of all from the colonized, the weak, the vulnerable, the disadvantaged, the mentally infirm, the sick, the dying, and so forth is a fairly tiresome one.[70] It also has the uncomfortable consequence of disguising, in a self-flattering way, the power relations between the writer and those about whom he or she writes.[71] The book, published in 2009, more than twenty years after the separation surgery, brings together a number of the key players in the original Negau Kai and Tu Du Hospital, celebrating the success of the operation, of Duc's life, and, most significantly, of the ties between them. Viet, having died two years earlier, is only a memory, and the interview with an apologetic Duc is brief and relatively uninformative; he remembers his various rehabilitation trips in and out of Japan, speaks with pride of his marriage and his wife's love, and expresses his hope to do what he can for Vietnam's disabled community. Duc then thanks the interviewer and says he is sorry for having to keep the conversation short because of other time commitments.[72]

In the book's final essay, Fujimoto reflects on one of Dr. Phuong's comments to him: "The Negau-kai's activities have been priceless" (*Anata-tachi [Negau-kai] no katsudō wa okane ni kaerarenai koto desu*). Reflecting on this pricelessness—or the inability to translate the activities into money—Fujimoto talks about the growth of the community of Japanese and Vietnamese working together not just for Viet and Duc but as part of a larger goal to protect children around the world who have been disabled and victimized by war.[73] The book features brief discussions of the lessons learned by Vietnamese medical practitioners from the 1988 surgery and about broader research on the relationship between dioxins and congenital abnormalities, and its final section—on a relatively pre-dictable note—focuses on the Negau Kai's own development, especially reflecting on the moral virtue and support of Dr. Phuong. But the conclud-ing lessons—about the need to help children who are victims of war and about the use of nonconventional weapons—are hardly ones that were learned through the process; they are virtually identical to the goals that the Negau Kai's founders had had nearly twenty-five years earlier. This does not make them liars, of course; it only underscores that the narrative arc of learning and received wisdom masks a subtler set of changes. These had affected Japan just as surely as Vietnam's own economic transforma-tion in the twenty years before 2009 had altered the terrain for Duc and his caretakers.

Economic growth can be depicted in myriad ways, from an upward trend on a graph to a longer, episodic recounting that places the focus on individuals and their decisions. This chapter has focused on a certain kind of national narrative that makes sense of postwar Japanese growth as both a story of national agency and as a moral imperative in a threaten-ing world. By focusing on the story of Nguyen Viet and Nguyen Duc, it draws on a story tailor-made for sentimentality and melodramatic effect, but it also calls attention to the ways in which these modes fit all too easily within a national story of innocence and virtue surviving war and violence. And, most importantly, despite the obvious politics behind the emergence of Viet and Duc as figures in Japanese debate, they were sus-ceptible to imagination across political divides, from antiwar leftists to Prime Minister Nakasone's emphasis on decisive, conservative leadership and on Asian camaraderie.

When Fujimoto and other Negau Kai members visited Ho Chi Minh City in 2013 to celebrate the twenty-fifth anniversary of the successful surgery, they were met by an international crowd of about 250 people, entertained in part by a songs performed by Vietnamese singer Nguyen Phi Hung and Japanese singer Yoshie Ruth Linton, who had collaborated on a tribute song to Duc written by Japanese schoolteacher Uchimoto Takashi. As Linton, a minor bilingual star in Japan, told the *Tuoi Tre News* service, "Everybody in Japan knows that Duc is married and has twins of his own. Many Japanese recognize Duc as a symbol of Vietnam. But I did not know that there are people in VN who are still affected by Agent Orange today."[74] This is perhaps an exaggeration; after all, unlike during the 1990s and early 2000s, the story of Viet and Duc is barely mentioned in formal school curricula today and is no longer part of the associated supplementary materials that are commonly used across the country. Although Duc makes occasional appearances on television in Japan and members of the Negau Kai still hold infrequent seminars, he is a household name only for people in their late twenties and above, and would likely be known to younger Japanese only if they have specific interests in Vietnam or in antimilitarist causes. More interesting is the fact that for Linton, Duc's life and continued success are clearly better known than is the possibility of other lingering consequences of Agent Orange. At least when Duc shows up in Japan or on television these days, it is almost invariably because of the opportunity to remark on the happy changes in his life—his marriage, the birth of his twins, their names' homage to Japan—and to reflect fondly on Japanese and Vietnamese friendship or to consider the hope that he can continue to bring to the disabled.

And ultimately, this is what remains in much of the discussion of Viet and Duc in Japan. Though resolutely sentimental, these newer accounts of Duc's return trip to Japan rarely focus on US military power, the use of chemical weapons, or the ravages of war, even if these are understood by some viewers to be in the background. They instead tell in emotional terms a story that is largely about Japan, about the country that tried to use its scientific and technical capacity, as well as its innate if sometimes suppressed decency, to try to rescue two sick boys. The accounts of course provide a testament to Duc's determination and kindness, but with the awareness that these features were enabled by Japan's having stepped in to save him when he needed it because that's only natural for Asians, and for humans.

4

COOL OPTIMISM

When the renowned political scientist Joseph Nye introduced his now-famous concept "soft power," he was insisting on the prematurity of reports of US decline. By the late 1980s—with the struggling manufacturing base and the seemingly inexorable rise of commercial powerhouses such as Japan and West Germany—faith in American dominance had dimmed considerably, even as Ronald Reagan's sunny optimism had ostensibly rescued the country from Jimmy Carter's malaise and the despondent legacies of the Vietnam War. The problem was not the Soviet Union, visibly hobbled by calcified leadership, economic mismanagement, and the disastrous consequences of the Afghanistan war and the Chernobyl nuclear disaster. It was instead the dynamism of other parts of the globe—particularly those under US military protection—that seemed likely to displace US economic leadership. Throughout this era, top scholars such as Charles Kindleberger, Robert Keohane, and Robert Gilpin focused extensively on "hegemonic stability theory," the view that a major power like the United States would pay disproportionate costs for the

Figure 4.1. Prime Minister Abe Shinzō removing his Super Mario costume at the closing games of the 2016 Summer Olympics in Rio de Janeiro

Source: The Mainichi Newspapers

maintenance of an open trading system that provided even greater benefits to other states. Paul Kennedy's sprawling and widely read popular history *The Rise and Fall of the Great Powers* nearly positioned America, then paying for a global military presence that preserved an international order advantageous to its competitors as well, to go the way of the Habsburgs and the British empire. Through retrospectively predictable miscalculation, the United States had, according to these influential observers, made itself vulnerable to the kinds of overcommitments to an old economic order that left it comparatively uncompetitive in the next.

This popular and academic concern with national decline prefigured, of course, Japan's later anxieties about the burst of the 1980s bubble and the lost decades that followed, and it is not entirely coincidental. After all, Japan loomed large in US images of national decline: the technologically advanced, economically nationalistic country whose power remained an "enigma"[1] and could fill the prodigious imagination of novelist Michael Crichton, whose novel *Rising Sun* (1992) depicted a Japan nearly as menacing as the dinosaurs in his 1990 book, *Jurassic Park*. International relations scholars themselves contributed to the impression of Japan as the beneficiary of American misjudgments, with Richard Rosecrance's 1986 book *The Rise of the Trading State* and Hanns Maull's widely cited 1990 article on "civilian powers" both routinely appearing on political science syllabi.[2] It is easy in retrospect to view these as misjudgments but important as well to remember the popular and intellectual pervasiveness of a story of US decline and Japanese ascent: a story that was deeply meaningful in both countries.

Nye, first in a 1990 article and then in his ominously titled 1991 book *Bound to Lead*, argued that the United States would avoid the predicted fate in part because of its rich endowment of a resource he called "soft power," the power to persuade rather than the power to coerce. For Nye, the issue was not just about the United States; it was instead about the nature of power in a radically changing global system. And so "soft power" would be a driving force in the future, and for the time being, only the United States had it in abundance. For Nye, part of this appeal derived from US cultural and commercial influences overseas, especially when they in some way encoded American values of democracy, liberalism, and tolerance. This resembled Yale political scientist Bruce Russett's earlier contention that US popular culture—the global role of blue jeans, rock and roll, and the like—provided the United States with power resources that were blurry and yet very real.[3] Nye specifically argued that Japan would not be able to compete with US power because it, unlike the United States, had limited military clout, had little control over global communications, and accepted few immigrants, an important feature of US power that not only convinced outsiders of America's benign intentions but also allowed easier cross-border pooling of ideas, good will, and common sense. For Nye, Japan was "deficient" in "global ideological appeal."[4] In the face of Japan's emergence as a potential economic challenger to US hegemony, recognizing soft power was a way to recalibrate the expectation of US decline.

Nye's solution has long outlasted the initial problem. Even after the United States rebounded to become unquestionably the world's only superpower, was christened a "hyperpower,"[5] and seemed to stand astride the globe as a colossus, the idea of "soft power" snowballed, continuing to animate domestic debates while finding itself increasingly embedded in the foreign policy proposals and initiatives of many of the countries against which US soft power was supposed to have worked. This development has attracted critical scholarly attention, including the recognition that soft power is unintelligible without some consideration of emotion or affect. After all, the power to persuade was not based primarily on superior US logic and deployment of evidence, or persuasiveness in the sense of an academic article; it was instead something akin to attractiveness, with other people liking the United States or its values and therefore accepting its foreign policy proposals because of their emotional connection to their source.[6] And so the rapid uptick in the early 2000s in Japanese interest in soft power, a resource that some influential observers in Japan had previously argued would prove to be unattainable, bears scrutiny for what it might tell us about Japanese conceptions of the country's regional and global roles.

Although "soft power" remains a buzzword in Japanese international relations debates, particularly with regard to digital content industries and public diplomacy, its heyday was in the early 2000s, when a consensus began to emerge among myriad commentators and writers around the expectation that recession-struck Japan was about to turn a corner in terms of global status.[7] In the latter half of the decade, scholars and writers sometimes celebrated Japan's transnational success in popular culture[8] and frequently analyzed it dispassionately to point out its effects and limits.[9] Some then turned against the whole idea of "Cool Japan," in part because of the gap between government enthusiasm over the concept and the ossified distribution systems and inadequate marketing that would limit its appeal to the hardest-core fans.[10] One of the elements that makes Ian Condry's 2006 book *Hip-Hop Japan* so successful and important is his imaginative treatment of cultural globalization in a manner that highlights the difficulty of ascribing artistic products to individual nations while also respecting the imminent creativity of the artists.[11]

The most sustained and thoughtful work on the government's handling of "Cool Japan," Daniel White's 2011 dissertation for Rice University's Department of Anthropology, assesses the complex ways in which affective connections to national status and to pop culture commodities are transformed, through the organs of policy itself, into emotional concerns and declarations. White's analysis covers a wide array of governmental and semigovernmental strategies, including the development of Japan's "cute ambassador" programs in the 2000s. Shrewdly drawing from cultural theories of affect and emotion and from the sometimes bewildering, sometimes poignant efforts of Japanese bureaucrats to promote national status, he leaves little doubt that claims about soft power are designed at least as much to provide local emotional legitimacy as to analyze a country's resources in terms of friends and foes alike.[12]

This chapter tackles the "soft power" debates of the early 2000s, using literary theorist Lauren Berlant's conception of "cruel optimism" to offer clues that tie the emotional elements of soft power debates to a larger national narrative about Japan and its global status. In doing so, it links debates about international relations to obvious and transparent national narratives, focusing on their consequences for policy. The chapter's goal is not to drive another nail into the analytical coffin of "Cool Japan" but rather to show how a national narrative not only infuses views of a country's past but also shapes visceral and pervasive judgments of its future. After all, the Japan that became cool was the one that was in the process of shedding its uncool roots, even those ostensibly responsible for much of its vaunted postwar success. And it was because of this coolness, and the soft power it would provide, that Japan's global status would return to its rightful place: a country not just respected but also loved.

Japanese Popular Culture in Asia

How influential had Japanese popular culture become internationally in the early-2000s heyday of "Cool Japan"? Because of the diversity of the industries involved—music, magazines, films, broadcast television, video games, and cellular phone content, to name but a few—no one has yet compiled a comprehensive statistical account, let alone provided a compelling way to disentangle Japanese cultural products from the many transnational flows emanating from other Asian nations, the United States, and Europe.[13] Even the Japanese government has thus far been stymied in its efforts to determine precisely how large the trade in cultural goods has become. As a consequence, the information available is primarily illustrative and anecdotal, and usually slanted in a direction designed either to indicate that "cool" Japan dominates the region or that "passé" Japan has already been eclipsed by other sources of cultural power in the region.

For example, popular music was one arena in which Japanese artists clearly broke ground during the 1990s.[14] Although the popular Japanese acts in the United States and Europe were usually alternative groups such as Shonen Knife, which had devoted cult but not mass followings in Japan, Asian markets rapidly embraced "J-pop" singers. In 1996 the trio Dreams Come True managed to sell 100,000 copies of its album *Love Unlimited* in Taiwan, where, like South Korea, Japanese popular music had actually faced legal restrictions for decades.[15] In 1998 Singapore began a new FM station dedicated to J-pop (though mainly aimed at the city-state's Japanese expatriates), and by 2000 the girl group Puffy (known in the US market as "Puffy Ami-Yumi" because of copyright concerns involving rap impresario Sean "Puffy" Combs) sold 200,000 albums in Asia.[16] Already extremely successful in Taiwan and somewhat so in Hong Kong, the Japanese music industry was clearly delighted in 2000 when the South Korean government lifted a restriction against the sale of Japanese pop there, provided that the lyrics were not in Japanese,[17] which presaged further liberalizing moves in 2003.[18] Music industry experts, however, quickly realized that Korean popular music—which more seamlessly blends hiphop influences and relies on authentically multilingual band members—would overtake J-pop in Asia.[19]

As they have for many of the past thirty years, Japanese video games faced mixed success in the Asia-Pacific region. Although Nintendo had become the global video game champion, originally riding arcade games such as *Super Mario Brothers* to success, it has faced intense competition in the crucially important home video console market. The Sony Playstation and Playstation2 (also Japanese) performed far ahead of competing console lines (such as Nintendo's GameCube and the Microsoft X-Box, America's main entry in the market), but sales were limited in Asia because of Sony's concerns with the probability of software piracy.[20] The money in video games usually comes not from the consoles—often sold at a loss—but rather from specific software lines or game franchises, so the threat of license and copyright violation is especially daunting to a fast-moving industry working on razor-thin margins.[21] Moreover, the video game software was far from exclusively Japanese, with American firms Electronic Arts and Activision and France's Ubisoft playing important roles. Even where the hardware was available, the threat of software piracy was large enough to have restricted software distribution, so sales in Thailand, Malaysia, Singapore, Hong Kong, and Taiwan remained limited.[22] Moreover, console games represented an expensive market even before the rise of streaming and mobile content ate into the dominance that Playstations, GameCubes, and Xboxes had briefly enjoyed. That also limited the appeal of Japan's leading console systems in most Asian nations, privileging less expensive online gaming in which Japan was competing with software developers elsewhere.[23]

At times, Japan's live-action television programs have been extraordinarily popular in Asia. Japanese television dramas have played to large audiences in Southeast Asia, notably in Singapore and Thailand, but they left an especially large impression on China, Taiwan, and Hong Kong. Particularly in the mid-1990s, Japan's limited-run dramas (which usually continue for approximately ten to twelve episodes, as opposed to US programs, which generally go off the air only after wearing out their welcome) impressed Asian viewers with their high production values, the accessible beauty of their young casts, and the putative realism of their narratives.[24] Like J-pop, these dramas would largely be overtaken by Korean programs in the 2000s.

And so the undoubted champion in Japan's pop culture team around the world, especially in Asia, has long been anime. Although US animated films continue to dominate the American box office, television revenues in the United States and around the Pacific Rim have painted a strikingly different picture. With *Pokémon, Sailor Moon, Dragon Ball Z,* and *Digimon,* Japanese animation creators had achieved extraordinary global success by the 1990s in part because of their ability to adapt their programs for overseas markets. By some estimates, Japan was the source of 60 percent of the world's animated television programming by the early 2000s, and annual sales of anime-related licensed goods (action figures, trading cards, etc.) were estimated in 2003 to be roughly $17 billion.[25] Although anime has been extraordinarily popular throughout Asia, licensed goods sales were, by the early 2000s, especially heavy in the United States and Japan. Bandai, one of the leading licensed-goods manufacturers, wrote in 2002 that "our business activities in Asia center on the production of toys in Hong Kong, Thailand and elsewhere. . . . [These products are] destined for the parent company in Japan and overseas sales subsidiaries."[26] Of course, on the streets of Shanghai or Hong Kong, one could easily buy dolls and action figures modeled after Japanese anime characters, but these unlicensed goods resulted in no proceeds for Bandai and the other Japanese firms.

The changing composition of film cast and crew may be the best symbol of newly integrated entertainment markets in the Asia-Pacific. The earlier primacy of Hong Kong films in the region, especially with the long-term success of stars such as Jackie Chan and Andy Lau, long made the territory the regional industry capital, but Japanese and Korean firms have also clearly seen the possibilities afforded by joint productions featuring multinational casts. Director Wong Kar-Wai's use of half-Japanese, half-Taiwanese Kaneshiro Takeshi in his *Chunking Express* and *Fallen Angels* certainly improved their marketability in Tokyo, especially with moments like the *Chunking Express* scene in which the multilingual charmer attempts to pick a woman up by using two Chinese dialects along with Japanese and English. Wong's 2004 science fiction film *2046* includes a performance by Japanese superstar Kimura Takuya alongside pan-Asian superstars such as Tony Leung and Zhang Ziyi. Kimura's bandmate from the group SMAP, Kusanagi Tsuyoshi, learned Korean specifically to break into the Korean television and film market, and he appeared in a Korean-language Japanese film, *Hotel Venus,* based on his popular television program, *Chonan Kan.*[27] And the Korean action film *2009 Lost Memories* posits an alternate future in which Japan completely dominates Asia, but even in this brazenly nationalistic film we see Japanese star Nakamura

Tōru as one of the film's leads, which became a crucial marketing element for Tokyo theaters. Here, straightforward box-office considerations have pushed directors to reach across borders to attract recognizable talent, producers to find acceptable cross-border themes, and stars to learn new languages to help them stay on top.

During Japan's Cool Japan craze, the widely acknowledged zenith of the country's pop culture success overseas was the 2002 Academy Award victory for Miyazaki Hayao's *Spirited Away*. Having earned more than $150 million at the Japanese box office, it became the top-grossing film in Japanese history, beating the record previously held by *Titanic*.[28] *Spirited Away* had a successful run in Asia, especially with more than a million tickets sold in South Korea, and ultimately earned more than $260 million in global ticket sales.[29] Even more widely reported in Japan, however, was the film's extraordinary critical acclaim, symbolized by its winning the Academy Award for Best Animated Feature. Even so, in the United States its $10 million in revenues was easily outdistanced by those of its competitors for the Oscar: *Ice Age* ($176 million) and *Lilo & Stitch* ($145 million).[30] Of course, box-office receipts and television ratings do not necessarily tell us much about influence in popular culture. As has been widely noted, many popular Japanese dramas and other commodities are popular as black-market, pirated discs, suggesting that the measurements themselves may be wildly imprecise.[31] Pop culture markets, moreover, are extraordinarily ineffective at measuring the effect, let alone quality, of a given creative effort.

My point here is simply that Japan was and remains extremely important, though never hegemonic, in Asian popular culture, at least as far as the conflicting data allow one to determine. But one might have been forgiven for reading a great deal into the success of anime, video games, and J-pop, particularly in the late 1990s and early 2000s, in that moment when anime attracted substantial Western attention and K-pop was still a mostly national phenomenon. Significantly, the popularity of Japan's cultural products was internationally noted in a moment that Japanese seemingly had little else to cheer about. If Japanese entertainment industries really were remaking Asia and the world, they would have represented a ray of hope in an otherwise bleak landscape of national collapse. Japan's overall cultural weight from the era was open to debate, but Japanese excitement about it was understandable.

The Craze about the Japanese Popular Culture Craze

Until the Cool Japan wave hit, most of the theorizing about Japanese popular culture and entertainment came from researchers concerned with Japanese leisure practices that might shed light on everyday structures regarding gender, class, sexuality, and power.[32] Japanese intellectuals and opinion magazines began to focus more assiduously on the spread of the country's popular culture in the 1990s. At the height of the *Power Rangers* craze, a 1994 issue of *Gaikō Fōramu* (Diplomatic Forum), then published by the Ministry of Foreign Affairs, included an article on the increasing popularity of Japanese popular culture and the country's place as a leader of a "new Asian civilization."[33] In a 1997 paper, Saya Shiraishi examined the cultural meanings of the popular anime *Doraemon*, which was shown throughout Southeast Asia.[34] And in a special collection on Japanese culture in a globalizing era, the left-leaning opinion monthly *Sekai* included studies of Japan's consumer society and its effects on artistic creativity, Japanese cultural products and their indigenization by Asian consumers, and Chinese audiences' use of Japanese television programs and magazines to learn about life outside of China.[35] In these articles the focus was not on Japanese influence per se but rather on patterns of globalization that can alter both the efforts of artists and the experiences of the audiences.

The *Sekai* issue, however, also includes a fascinating and instructive conversation between musician Kina Shōkichi (sometimes described to English-speaking audiences as an Okinawan Bob Marley because of his musical talent, his political messages, and his ability to blend popular music with "authentic" sounds from an exotic island) and the Korean-Japanese activist and commentator Shin Sugok. Covering gender relations, ethnic conflict, sexual fetishes for mothers (*mazakon*) and young girls (*rorikon*, although they do not use the term), Kina and Shin address the possibility that Japan's post-bubble economic funk will open up space for new diversity, creativity, and openness. Shin in particular stresses that the collapse of traditional authority structures in the post-bubble era may open up space for alternative voices that have implicitly been left out of long-standing rhetoric about what Japanese culture is.[36]

Though expressing this in terms harsher than many subsequent commentators would use, Shin nicely captures a developing sense among scholars and observers that Japanese popular culture has become exciting, fast-paced, and active specifically because the obliteration of "traditional" structures has somehow opened the floodgates for pent-up creative urges. And yet the main consumers of these urges were, until their sudden elevation in the midst of the Cool Japan craze, the least likely heroes for Japan: the *otaku* (nerds). Journalist Nakamori Akio has been credited with creating the term, which generally refers to hard-core anime and manga fans with few social skills and even fewer professional and personal prospects. In 1989 the term took on a sinister new meaning with the arrest of child molester and murderer Miyazaki Tsutomu in Kobe, where police found that he owned a vast number of pornographic comics and videos.[37] The term, however, has become more widespread, losing some of its stigma along the way, particularly with the publication of Azuma Hiroshi's justly famed cultural critique *Otaku*.[38]

By all accounts, Japan's current cultural vitality would have been unimaginable without the *otaku*, the term's earlier pejorative connotations notwithstanding. The painter Murakami Takashi, perhaps the most important spokesperson for the contemporary aesthetic that fuels Japanese popular culture, famously allied himself with the *otaku*. Building an artistic movement based on his "superflat" conception, Murakami has argued that Japanese art is simultaneously two-dimensional and lacking in perspective, similar to Japanese visual traditions (flat), and also compressed, crowded, and devoid of meaning (superflat). Murakami's sculptures reflect this view with caricatured versions of Japanese pop culture icons, and his own *otaku*-staffed studio has famously blurred the line between high art and commercialized icons.[39] Just as he appears to be critical of an overly commercialized society that compresses meaning through the proliferation of mass-produced junk, he also embraces the contemporary aesthetic that it generates. The superflat conception is important not because it is in any sense self-evidently true but rather because it briefly became a unifying theme among many in Japan's contemporary arts business.[40]

The Japan depicted in these accounts is a dissonant, postmodern mess, yet all the more appealing for it. Shin's view of the breakdown of traditional authority implicitly lies at the center because of the self-conscious way in which marginalized groups—*otaku,* ostentatiously self-sexualized schoolgirls, foreigners—play a role. And it calls attention to a central aspect of the Cool Japan discussions: that the postwar Japan of state-industry collaboration for national growth, of idealized salarymen and their multigeneration families living in harmonious homes raising the next generation of loyal contributors to the shared fruits of Japanese development, had fallen like Icarus. In its ashes was a New Japan, a collection of free-spirited artists and creators who would have struggled in the salaryman landscape but were now celebrated for their iconoclastic vision and refusal to follow the established path. To an extent, of course, this general proposition dramatically overstates social change in Japan, just as earlier views of orderly, white-collar Japan badly missed how marginalized groups handled life in a society that ideally would not have them. But this celebration of Japan's seemingly anarchic popular culture appeared to be possible only because of wide consensus that there was something topsy-turvy in 1990s Japan. The losers were winning, and they were changing Japan along the way.

It was into this environment that journalist Douglas McGray stepped in 2001, working on a grant from the Japan Society. As a researcher in Tokyo, McGray spent time with the popular arts community, interviewing key figures (including Yamaguchi Yuko, designer of Sanrio's "Hello Kitty") and trying to understand how conservative, stodgy, and ultimately depressed Japan was responsible for vibrant and popular culture products embraced by consumers around Asia. Often overstating the extent of Japan's domination of Asian markets (after all, the success of one or two singers in Taiwan does not make for a regional J-pop boom, particularly when compared to K-pop's success), McGray argued in *Foreign Policy* that Japan was likely to remain powerful and important because it was a lifestyle leader, able to generate consumption and social patterns elsewhere because of its local artistic creativity. In his famous formulation, Japan would achieve a kind of soft power because of its "Gross National Cool."[41]

Clearly aiming to seize upon a trend that was catching the eye of its local readers, *Time* magazine's Asian edition published a special issue with the cover "Cool Japan." Referring frequently to McGray's thesis about post-bubble Japan's position as the cultural touchstone for the rest of Asia, *Time*'s feature story emphasized that Japan's facility in popular culture would be part of a larger shift toward service industries, thereby offsetting the hollowing out of Japan's manufacturing base and some of its less competitive sectors.[42] In shorter pieces, *Time*'s writers provided glowing vignettes and studies of the creative forces behind Japan's transition:

construction magnate Mori Minoru, filmmaker Kore-eda Hirokazu, and Minister of State for Economic and Fiscal Policy Takenaka Heizō. Collectively, the *Time* articles address Japanese change, making punk bands, anime, skyscrapers, and neoliberal economics part of the same general trend toward Japanese rejuvenation. And all of it is "cool."

Although Japanese scholars of international relations doubtless knew of "soft power" shortly after Nye coined the term in the late 1980s, few used it with regard to Japan until McGray's article appeared. Only America, in the eyes of the few Japanese observers interested in discussing it, had soft power. In 2001, before becoming minister of state for economic and fiscal policy, Takenaka—then a professor at Keio University— edited a volume on the possible development of "soft power" for Japan. Takenaka's introduction deals with soft power cautiously, arguing that for historical and linguistic reasons, the United States has soft power resources that would likely remain elusive for Japan. But he also suggests that Japanese economic reform can pave the way toward a more vibrant economy that will once again shape other countries' plans and expectations.[43] Other authors in the collection address more straightforwardly the issue of popular culture and soft power. Kamiya Matake of National Defense University takes seriously Nye's judgment regarding the importance of shared values, not just the spread of American commodities; he argues that *Pokémon* and other Japanese anime exports will not lead to greater soft power. Instead, he locates Japan's likely soft power in its ability to reform its economy and then take a more active and open role in global politics.[44] The renowned anthropologist Aoki Tamotsu writes nearly with despair about the uselessness of pop culture in promoting soft power; even though European children watch *Pokémon,* Japanese studies centers are shrinking, and Japan seems not to be in vogue as a topic or a country.[45] The book, in retrospect, provides little optimism, particularly when compared with McGray's article only a year or so later.

And so the popularization of the term owes far more to McGray than to Takenaka and colleagues, partly because of McGray's cleverness with his "Gross National Cool" phrasing but largely because he is American. Indeed, vocal approval from Americans seems to have been extraordinarily important to current Japanese discussions of the role of their popular culture, far beyond any measurable economic impact. The *Spirited Away* phenomenon—which coincided with McGray's piece—captures this perfectly. Although the movie's American and even global box-office receipts were relatively modest, its Academy Award victory (which followed unanimous and rich critical acclaim) was widely used in Japanese policy discourse to suggest that Japan has arrived. Combined with the staggering popularity of *Pokémon* and other anime in the West, Miyazaki's film generated growing interest in Japanese policy circles. Indeed, the Digital Contents White Paper, an annual report published by the METI-affiliated Dejitaru Kontentsu Kyōkai, uses *Spirited Away*'s transnational success as the first and most important example of the changing appreciation for Japanese popular culture.[46] And "Gross National Cool" captured the Japanese elite imagination in a way that few other recent American articles have. In November 2003, Japan's leading business newspaper, the *Nikkei Shimbun,* even cosponsored a major symposium featuring McGray and titled "Cool Japan: Japan's Cultural Power." As *Time*'s special issue noted, the term "Gross National Cool" was known to virtually every bureaucrat in Japan, with "soft power" usually accompanying their comments.

Culture Policies as "Content" and Power

As a policy idea, improving soft power through cultural promotion empowered certain policy organizations to take steps they otherwise might not have, and also introduced a new potential criterion for evaluating policy success. This is not to say that the drive for soft power was solely or even primarily responsible for creating new policies; instead, it offered new opportunities and rationales for engaging in initiatives that many policy makers had already intended to pursue. After all, government strategies for cultural exchange, information technologies, and tourism hardly began with McGray's article. As early as 1995, the Culture Agency (*Bunkachō*) created a working group on multimedia and then subsequently produced a 1997 report on "new media arts" for the twenty-first century.[47] But the sudden excitement about Japan's "Gross National Cool" provided options for state engagement with recreation and entertainment industries, in some ways allowing administrators to put disquieting (and even frightening) forms of social and economic change to national purpose.

This would hardly be the first time. In the 1980s, with the rapid increase in the value of the yen and subsequent decrease in the cost of overseas tours, administrators in the Ministry of Transport (later absorbed into the Ministry of Land, Infrastructure, and Transport [MLIT]) had projected that Japanese outbound tourism would likely double in only a few years. In some ways, this might have been a terribly undesirable turn of events. After all, the increase in outbound tourism clearly came at some expense to the domestic tourism market, over which the ministry had jurisdiction; Hawaii's gain would be Ishikawa Prefecture's loss. The demographics were also worrisome; with Japanese business and family travel increasing only marginally, much of the outbound travel action came from groups of women—most disconcertingly, unmarried women—traveling overseas. In spite of occasional public outcry about the threat of AIDS and the rumor that Japanese women were traveling to Bali for sex, clever Tourism Bureau members recognized that this change in leisure patterns could just as easily be interpreted as Japan's willingness to redistribute the economic gains from its massive trade surplus, thus promoting international understanding, economic fairness, and open borders all at the same time. Therefore, in 1986 they created the "Ten Million Program," which "aimed" at doubling Japanese outbound tourism to levels that the administrators assumed it would hit with or without their encouragement. By doing so, they were able to justify more access to the national budget and the establishment of new institutions over which they had jurisdiction, two common goals of Japanese policy organizations.[48]

The Gross National Cool/Soft Power initiatives shared with the Ten Million Program an eagerness to embrace social change, put it to national use, and support existing policy priorities. Clearly, I do not mean to suggest that Japanese ministries are incapable of change any more than I would argue that the collapse of the bubble acted as a light switch, automatically changing Japan from an economic dynamo to a bedridden victim. But institutions are important specifically because they define what people take for granted and therefore how they will understand new information, their environment, and their goals.[49] Derek Hall has argued that the large-scale drive toward economic "liberalization" in Japan is not in fact a retreat from institutionalized economic nationalism; instead, liberalization is defended and apparently understood in nationalist terms.[50] Similarly, government officials working with popular culture and "digital contents" were trying to do what they had always done: promote the development of industrial forces that can serve national goals.

Tourism once again provides an excellent example. Partly as an effort to demonstrate his support for local regions badly hurt by Japan's economic recession, and several years before the tourism boom Japan has enjoyed since roughly 2010, Prime Minister Koizumi in 2002 announced the establishment of the Tourism Policy Advisory Council. The goal of the group was to develop new ideas for attracting foreign tourists to Japan, policies that would likely be attractive to MLIT Tourism Bureau members aiming to maintain budgetary interest in their management of the nation's recreational travel infrastructure. Of course, with the continued high cost of travel to Japan, terrorism-related reductions in international air travel, and occasional Asian shocks such as the SARS crisis, the council almost certainly recognized that a rapid or even medium-term increase in tourism to Japan was extraordinarily unlikely. And so its final report emphasized not the economic returns to Japan of tourism but rather the political returns of increased exchange. Indeed, it explicitly linked cultural exchange, soft power, and the creation of "cultural security" (*bunka anzen hoshō*). It also cited McGray to point out that Japan's Gross National Cool had become part of the country's appeal.[51]

Similarly, the Ministry of Foreign Affairs (MOFA) also began to incorporate "soft power" into its lingo, although it remained cautious about any suggestion that Japan was trying to exercise power over its neighbors. In a 2002 speech to the Vancouver Board of Trade, Foreign Minister Yoriko Kawaguchi emphasized that Canada and Japan both share an idea of "soft power" in that they prefer to exercise their international authority through peaceful means.[52] In an emblematic 2003 report, the Japan Foundation, closely related to MOFA, stressed the importance of cultural and educational exchange programs for Japan's diplomacy because of their contributions to the nation's "soft power." For a time, this language nearly supplanted earlier emphases on "mutual understanding." Citing McGray, the Japan Foundation referred to "Gross National Cool" and suggested that Japan's cultivation of its cultural resources could improve its "national image" and thereby strengthen its global hand. The report focused heavily on the role that "soft power" plays in a changing world, culminating in recommendations for MOFA and Japan Foundation activity that were still consistent with existing priorities, not new ones.[53]

Japan's economic policy makers also seized on "soft power" as a crucial wedge for funding and supporting their efforts to promote Japan's "content industries," a term that refers largely to online content and could in essence incorporate new films, videos, games, published writing, and music. Because the money in information technology now appears to lie largely in the content itself and not necessarily in the infrastructure used to transmit it, there can be significant rewards for firms, individual artists, and perhaps even governments able to sell people what they want or perhaps influence what they want. The old Ministry of Posts and Telecommunications began to commission reports on information technologies in 1995, as did its research affiliate, the Posts and Telecommunications Research Institute.[54] Although these focused primarily on the types of infrastructure involved, they presaged an era in which the government would start to consider the importance of government intervention in the creation and not just existence of information or entertainment content.

Alongside the Ministry of Public Management, Home Affairs, and Posts and Telecommunications, the organization most responsible for conceptualizing Gross National Cool became the Ministry of Economics, Trade, and Industry (METI). Although long dominated by an interest in manufacturing industries, the ministry began by the late 1990s to devote considerable attention to information industries. To some degree, the ministry's interest in defining virtually all artistic work as "content" involved a bit of historical revisionism; the METI-affiliated Digital Content Association published a timeline of digital content tracing the development of film in the late nineteenth century, music recordings in the 1920s, and the like.[55] Especially by 2002 and 2003, METI took an impressively ambitious approach to the issue, establishing working groups on comprehensive and specific aspects of media content governance, all aimed at generating recommendations for the ministry to generate long-term creativity in Japan, protect Japanese intellectual property rights in Asia, cross-fertilize different media industries, and so on.[56] As with its general industrial mission, METI aimed at ensuring that Japanese content creators and providers—anime, J-pop, film studios, game developers, toy producers, and virtually any other entertainment industry capable of catching global attention—would remain competitive over the long term. To that end, its study groups inquired widely about the nature of entertainment after the Internet revolution.

More remarkable than METI's new ambitions was the broad governmental acceptance of the "Gross National Cool" core: Japan had become hip and fashionable specifically because it had changed into something different. And so the Digital Content Working Group, part of a government advisory council, asked in 2003 about what kinds of firms would be needed in the future: large entertainment firms capable of professionally capturing the global market or small firms of near-amateurs who have ideas that rapidly catch fire? Would the market be driven by hip trendsetters or by the reclusive *otaku*, whose obsessiveness speaks to a particular character's or program's appeal? Should the government be focused on necessity (*pan*, or bread) or on the entertainment of its citizens (*sākasu*, or circus)?[57] In other words, and mirroring the commentary of cultural critics such as Shin Sugok, uncomfortable social changes (e.g., *otaku* empowerment) had become central to Japan, not just to its national cool but also to its economic resurgence. And so the question became how government industrial policy, very nearly the perfect symbol of pre–Cool Japan to many observers, could harness the power of developments attributed largely to a Japan in which ministries no longer call the shots.

Japan is far from the only country in which those in power have sought to co-opt the appeal of marginalized, or self-marginalizing, critical figures. After all, in its public celebration of social change that its owners would likely have opposed in an earlier era, the *Nikkei Shimbun*'s 2003 ad campaign—"Women have changed. Now how about men?" featuring a beautiful, self-confident, *Nikkei*-reading professional woman smiling, with a sheepish young man watching her from behind[58]—was no ghastlier than US corporate sponsorship of successive Woodstock concerts in the late 1990s or than Ronald Reagan's bizarre use of Bruce Springsteen's "Born in the USA" at campaign events a decade earlier. But this was not a corporation acting as the disinterested face of global capitalism, pulling at whatever icons could sell newspapers or soda to middle-aged consumers trying desperately to deny their surrender to The System, nor was it a politician already adept at deploying the language of the Left against itself. Instead, state actors in Japan seemed to accept that the creative forces they were seeking to employ could exist only in a system that did not aim to control or use them. Cool Japan existed because Uncool Japan collapsed; now Cool Japan would need to show that it was, after all, still Japan.

The Cruelty of Coolness

The semiofficial magazine *Gaikō Fōramu*'s special 2003 issue included nearly a dozen articles focused on Japanese soft power and the country's popular culture success overseas. Four of the articles were, in essence, short testimonials by anime-loving or J-pop–loving professionals in Thailand, China, Russia, and Australia, and with one longer article by the Guatemalan ambassador to Japan, who weighed in with a piece about the enduring popularity of Akira Kurosawa films.[59] And in May 2003, *Chūō Kōron*, a leading mainstream opinion journal, had a special collection on the same general topic, including a translation of McGray's article, an essay by Keio University law professor Tadokoro Masayuki about Japan's soft power, and a conversation between American scholar Susan Napier and anime director Okada Toshio described as a "showdown between Japanese and American anime *otaku*" (*nichibei otaku taiketsu*).[60]

The use of the word *otaku* to describe the authors in a leading journal is instructive in that it signaled that the marginalized had entered the mainstream by dint of Japan's shift in national status. The *Chūō Kōron* and *Gaikō Fōramu* issues share something with *Time*'s special coverage: an understanding that "cool" Japan has emerged from the rapid and often disorienting social changes that were conventionally depicted as having been unleashed on Japan through demographic transformation and economic decline. And they provide reassurance about what these changes will mean. The articles paint a picture of a Japan in transition, though marked by important cultural legacies from the past. "Uncool Japan"— presumably the Japan of lifetime employment, examination hell, rigid gender differentiation, and obsessive deference to authority—would have been unable to have this kind of cultural effect on the rest of Asia because it simply could not have produced this kind of vibrant, diverse, and yet distinctive entertainment environment. In this view, Japan had experienced a phoenix-like rebirth from the self-inflicted wounds of rapid modernization; combined with its unique traditional culture, this had generated a new cultural milieu that is simultaneously viewed as surprising and yet somehow inevitable. But the hope went even further: because the world— particularly the Asia-Pacific—was catching on, with even the Americans rejecting their own mass-produced pop culture in favor of Japan's zanier alternatives, Japan could stand to benefit politically, provided that it could figure out how to make the most of an auspicious moment.

The appeal of soft power was understandable—and very broad. For Japanese liberals, "soft power" has represented a way for nonmilitary Japan to have an effect on global politics. Journalist-turned-politician Nagatsuma Akira, for example, has positioned soft power as the appropriate expression of Japan's international contributions, eschewing military engagement as far as possible.[61] For mainstream or more conservative observers, "soft power" could help Japan be seen as more "trustworthy," meaning that the global spread of Japanese popular culture could increase international friendship and trust. In this framework, "soft power" and support for the arts become a component of "public diplomacy," thereby helping Japan make more effective use of its "hard power."[62] Indeed, Japan's expansion of its global security role during this era (e.g., the deployment of MSDF ships to the Indian Ocean in support of US military activities in Afghanistan) would have been impossible without government efforts to build trust with its Asian neighbors.[63] Because of its impressive elasticity, "soft power" appealed equally, though very differently, in Japanese policy—and to lawmakers of virtually all stripes.[64] Moreover, "soft power" may have represented to concerned Japanese what it had earlier to concerned Americans: that reports of their country's demise were premature.

This means that "Gross National Cool" and "soft power" were certainly politically consequential, though perhaps not in the way that the terms' users might suppose. If we think of "soft power" not as a category of power resources, but rather as an idea—a component of a cultural and ideographical structure of governance—it might affect a country's policy even if the country does not really possess it in any meaningful way or, worse, if it does not really exist at all. Of course, whether Japan has (or had) soft power is almost certainly impossible to tell and is not in itself germane to policy. After all, the term "soft power" became popular in the United States not only because of Nye's writing talent and his important position in international relations theory but also because it sat well with Americans' views of themselves. Because US culture and values are constitutive of Americans, it is practically impossible for Americans to determine effectively whether their values are really shared or not. The same is likely true for Japanese.

One of my favorite things about living in Japan is my daily ability to chat with Japanese friends, colleagues, and acquaintances about life here and overseas. Aside from being good practice for my Japanese, it also affords me the opportunity to try to understand the world as Japanese see it—phenomenology on the cheap. There is, of course, a certain amount of temporary intellectual dishonesty involved; during the time I speak with a Japanese person about some issue, I am likely to take that person's views as somehow representative of a larger community: Japanese women, Japanese conservatives, or, in moments of complete laziness, all Japanese. But when we speak about the United States and my counterpart says something with which I disagree, my tendency is not to accept the comment as possibly valid or as representative of something useful or important; it is quite simply wrong because I as an American understand my country, and he or she as a Japanese does not. Of course, as a researcher I struggle with this profoundly stupid impulse, but its existence speaks to a larger concern: other countries' (or, rather, people's) views of one's own country have no independent merit except insofar as they correspond to something we believe. In other words, when we speak about how other countries see us, we are almost certainly talking about how we see ourselves and using other nations as a kind of mirror to express our own pride, insecurity, anger, or sadness. Americans like myself are probably the worst judges of our own soft power because we cannot separate our cultural effects elsewhere from our own deeply ingrained views of ourselves.

Indeed, little noticed in the critical response to Nye was the extraordinary level of coincidence between the way *Bound to Lead*'s other countries viewed America and American values and the way that educated American liberals understood America and American values. And so freedom, liberalism, openness, and tolerance of other cultures became the sources of America's soft power; they were the reasons that others admired the United States and were, conveniently enough, also the aspects of America of which Nye and his readers were proudest. Indeed, although the books aim in different directions and support quite divergent political agendas, Nye's view of American soft power bears more than a passing similarity to Francis Fukuyama's oft-noted *The End of History*. Although Fukuyama aimed primarily at developing a theoretical argument about liberal democracy's triumph over communism and fascism, his book has been used to provide a more hard-edged, conservative version of the universally desirable values that Nye recognizes in his own nation. Where Nye argued that these would earn America friends, Fukuyama maintained that time had run out for alternative ways of understanding the role of the state: to quote the anime-influenced film *The Matrix*, "It is the sound of inevitability."

To be fair, Nye's later refinements of his "soft power" claims focused on the need for multilateralism in US foreign policy, and he soon downplayed the role of cultural influence. But this reflects different debates held at different times.[65] American "hard power" seemed, at least by the early 2000s, beyond any dispute, so there was little reason to focus on the cultural component of superpower status. Indeed, Nye's emphasis on "smart power" (combining soft power and hard power resources for national advantage, or what was once called "diplomacy" in archaic English) indicated that America could not achieve long-term security by alienating all of its allies. The claim certainly resembled his earlier point about the changing nature of power in the post–Cold War system. But the revised argument had teeth for different reasons: unlike soft power, smart power was not the compensation for a country with diminished hard power resources; it instead called for responsible governance for a country that should have been thinking in the long term. Soft power's instability and conceptual trajectory made this seems less like an argument for the strength of American cultural and political institutions and more like a plea for humility.

For this reason, the rapid increase in attention in Japan to soft power and Japan's cultural weight elsewhere probably has less value as a tool for evaluating Japan's regional importance than it does as a heuristic device for grasping how Japanese policy makers viewed their regional and global roles at the midpoint of Japan's two lost decades.[66] And the motifs discussed above—contemporary Japan's rise from the ashes of economic recession, the continuity between rebellious Japan's pop culture and earlier cultural traditions, and the political weight afforded by the wide acceptance of Japanese entertainment icons—were essential elements of the debate because of the way they reconfigured a larger national narrative in which Japan's rise as a peaceful, manufacturing/trading powerhouse had been thwarted. Japan's future global status would depend not on its "Japan-as-number-one" or bubble-era trajectory toward economic dominance but to something else, something new, something beautiful about the country in the eye of the beholder. Whether one wanted a nonmilitary and generous Japan or an assertive yet trusted Japan, the prescription was similar. Japan would need to support the spread of its popular culture overseas in order for other countries to see what post-bubble Japan really was: a changed country, a country of originality and even individuality, a country that remembers its traditions even as it boldly meets the challenges of modernity. It was a country that would not hurt a fly.

Lauren Berlant's *Cruel Optimism* provides an opportunity to rethink soft power within a larger set of modalities of contemporary international politics. Berlant, having made major contributions to affect theory because of her renowned "national sentimentality" trilogy, argues that a specific, perhaps even addictive, kind of buoyancy has become a dominant motif of life in advanced industrial countries, or at least in the United States.[67] Widely cited and debated, Berlant's elegant definition holds that "a relation of cruel optimism exists when something you desire is actually an obstacle to your flourishing." This might have allowed a glib, condescending treatment of self-sabotaging poor and working-class Republican voters, watching television programs and films about the impossibly wealthy and holding self-destructively to an American Dream that is less likely to come true for them than would be being struck by lightning immediately after winning a Powerball lottery. Berlant's justly famed work, however, admirably focuses as much on the keenly felt illusion of political agency, even among avowed political critics and activists, as it does on the merciless grind facing those aiming for a better financial future. After all, rogue performance art aimed at bringing the national security and surveillance state to heel is likely no less heartbreakingly delusional than are websites and magazines showing Jay-Z and Beyonce's home, as if most of the viewers are likely to find themselves there someday and therefore need to know the layout.

Berlant's contribution provides an alternative way to read soft power's emotional power. Like happiness, like well-being, soft power has become its own cottage industry, with marketing researchers weighing in on "national brands" and policy makers from Beijing to Brussels[68] aiming to understand how to achieve or to maintain it. The stated goals are both commercial—helping one's own producers—and political, and their pervasiveness speaks to something that goes beyond the poignant insecurity of Americans and Japanese. Indeed, soft power's conceptual ubiquity, despite the absence of clear evidence that it exists or matters, suggests that governments and citizens get something important from its invocation; they receive validation of their global status as an attractive nation, one that is liked and respected. Indeed, even if one rejects the idea of status as an ordering concept in international relations, as does David Lake in a thoughtful discussion differentiating status from hierarchy, its frequent invocation and its inseparability from people's beliefs suggest that it may be a crucial matter for domestic political debate and consumption.[69] The problem—as the United States has experienced in different ways in the whiplash Bush-Obama-Trump eras, and as Japan experiences through the periodic and widely reported critiques of its handling of wartime history issues—is that the world seldom fully cooperates, rarely loving a country as much as the rhetoric of soft power might indicate. Although public diplomacy issues framed around "soft power" may not in themselves be harmful, they reflect a desire that is in the end nearly certain to be betrayed: to be valued globally as one values oneself. And the frequently disappointing search for that validation suggests that nothing can make Japan (like the United States, South Korea, Germany, and Brazil) stably and universally beloved or persuasive. Soft power's durability as a topic of conversation says more about the cruel unattainability of the future status a country is supposed to achieve than about its actual relevance to the substance of international relations.

What Kind of Power?

The unattainability of the future has often been diagnosed by Japanese officials as the result of the failures of their policies or of the products they aim to hawk overseas. As cultural studies scholar Kōichi Iwabuchi notes, Japanese popular culture overseas often carries a *mukokuseki* quality, meaning that its national origin cannot easily be determined. With anime characters, stories, names, and titles designed for transnational audiences, Japaneseness has somehow been bled out of them. Iwabuchi, however, notes that in addition to the way in which *mukokuseki* actually becomes a signifier of Japanese origin, there are actually a number of Japanese entertainment products—bands, television dramas, etc.—that actually carry a clear Japanese "odor."[70] Obviously aiming to link the products and the country that produces them, Japanese policy makers, particularly in MOFA, have promoted the idea of the "Japan brand." The goal here is to improve "public diplomacy" by making other people more aware of Japan's contributions to global culture, design, and entertainment.[71] Unless people overseas know that Japanese artists created *Sailor Moon,* how can it confer "soft power" on the Japanese government?

Iwabuchi, though trying to show that Japanese popular culture has become part of a fragmented process of globalization, concedes that in certain cases, Taiwanese audiences have consciously identified themselves more closely with Japanese dramas and films than they have with Hollywood fare, which seems both more fantastic and more foreign.[72] Using interviews with Chinese audiences in five different cities, Nakano Yoshiko and Wu Yongmei offer a similar finding. Yet they also reject the notion that this has become some kind of simple and unproblematic "cultural proximity," to use Iwabuchi's language. Instead, Nakano and Wu argue, this fascination arises from the yearnings of the new bourgeois classes in China and their dreams for a wealthier and more open lifestyle just around the corner.[73] In this view, Japan acts as a combination of a crystal ball and a mirror: it is one version of the future that the modernizing economies of Asia hope to achieve.

Well before Japan became the pop culture maverick that it purportedly is, it already served as a kind of cultural touchstone for its neighbors in Asia. Indeed, for many in 1960s Taiwan, South Korea, and elsewhere, Japan's technological achievements served as representatives of what they might themselves enjoy in their lifetimes if they worked hard enough and had enough good fortune. Set in 1962 Hong Kong, Wong Kar-Wai's masterpiece *In the Mood for Love* brilliantly evokes his characters' class positions, as well as the setting of his story, through clever references to the commodities they can purchase. When Mrs. Chan's husband returns from a business trip to Japan with an automatic rice cooker, it immediately becomes the talk of the apartment building, not because it is Japanese and exotic but rather because it is convenient and modern. Japan is ahead, and it serves as a symbol of what other Asians, even the Shanghainese community in Hong Kong, might accomplish.[74] Many Japanese products overseas—whether they are Matsushita rice cookers in 1960s Taiwan or *Tokyo Love Story* in 1990s China—gain at least part and perhaps most of their meaning from their representation of modernity.

In the 1960s and 1970s, Japanese also looked abroad to find relevant examples of how their lifestyles might improve, although their models came primarily from the United States and Western Europe. To a degree, this tendency became a target of government policy as well. In a methodological discussion in their massive 1974 report titled *Yoka Sōran*

(Overview of leisure), published by the MITI (METI's predecessor) Leisure Development Office, advisory committee members explained that their research on appropriate leisure and lifestyle changes included a number of comparative case studies but that only the ones from advanced industrial nations (i.e., Western Europe and North America) would be relevant:

> The various subcommittees focused on 15 countries from North America, Western Europe, the communist countries, and four other regions. But if one examines the structure of leisure in these different countries, one sees great diversity from the advanced countries that have already entered an era of a new leisure civilization (*atarashii yoka bunmei no jidai*) to the lesser developed countries that still have no fixed understanding of what "leisure" means.[75]

This report, one of two major MITI-sponsored leisure studies at the time, became the intellectual cornerstone of government policies designed specifically to align Japanese recreation and entertainment industries with those of the United States and Europe.

This tendency to see the future through the current conditions of other nations continued well into the 1990s. The Leisure Development Cent er, a special foundation funded by MITI to provide policy-relevant research on recreation-related industries, used a combination of domestic research surveys and comparative studies to provide the necessary information on Japan's best approach. When I asked one official why the researchers focused on the United States and Europe rather than on, for example, Korea, Zimbabwe, or Brazil, he seemed stunned by the question and responded (very slowly, probably because he believed at this point that I had asked my question incorrectly or that I simply was not very bright), "because those are the advanced industrial nations." There was simply no alternative. The Western nations were valuable examples not because one liked or trusted them but rather because they were ahead.[76]

In one line of argument, Japan might benefit by playing exactly this modern role, particularly in Asia, specifically because it has successfully negotiated between the demands of economic and political development, on the one hand, and the maintenance of a distinctive culture, on the other.[77] If countries aspire to be what Japan is, perhaps that could confer a kind of soft power—an ability to persuade or to attract rather than to coerce. But although the relevant sources from the 1970s through the 1990s suggest that Western Europe and especially the United States provided Japan with a crucial guidepost for how the country would need to develop, there is neither gratitude nor admiration expressed in these documents. Instead, there is simple acceptance that this is the way things will be. To be sure, the United States likely benefited from this ambivalent relationship in a number of ways, but it is unclear that its leaders understood or even could have understood how to use it. And it is unclear that the place of Japanese development in other countries' narratives about their own has ever made it easier for the Japanese government—independent of the conventional hard power inducements and threats—to persuade them to behave in the way that Tokyo would wish. Much clearer, and more easily demonstrated, is the role that transnational consumption of Japanese products played when it fit into a proposed happy ending, even displayed weekly on the national broadcaster NHK's program *Cool Japan* with its panels of foreigners praising some aspect of Japan's cultural distinctiveness, for a national story that had, at least for a time, seemed to have gone off the rails.[78]

The affective dimensions of "soft power" are essential to any thoughtful approach to the subject, but the emotions involved—for all their vibrancy, all their imminence—are less visible, less easily depicted than is the story of Japanese decline for which "soft power" can act as an intellectual, Harvard-validated deus ex machina. Despite the insistence of former diplomats and a number of foreign policy intellectuals, most political scientists have dismissed the idea of soft power as a meaningful resource, or measure of resources, in international politics. Their skepticism may reflect an inherent allergy to the word *soft* and may also bespeak an unattractive commitment to the quantifiable. But the problems associated with studying emotion and affect themselves—as noted in chapter 1—suggest the value of an alternative view of why soft power continues to haunt debates about diplomacy. If soft power matters, it matters at least as much because of what it demands from people's feelings about themselves and their nations as because of any justifiable confidence in its transnational importance. But these feelings themselves can be made intelligible only because of the stories that officials and compatriots tell one another about their countries—about their struggles and goals, and about what they must ultimately mean to themselves and to a welcoming world. In the next chapter we will consider more directly how those who tell stories repeatedly shape them to produce the desired emotional effects.

STAGING *THE EMPIRE OF LIGHT*

The Japanese theater scene is littered with companies and groups whose initial success proved more fleeting than their creators might have imagined. Some of this was simple timing. The small theater "boom" of the late 1980s preceded by just a few years the pop of the Japanese economic bubble, putting economic pressure on audiences and theater owners alike. Yet this boom coincided with and reinforced a cultural moment that emphasized creativity, individuality, and differentiation, the very qualities celebrated by critics of Japan's economic miracle (with its gray-suited salarymen and blue-uniformed factory workers). At the moment in the mid-1980s that many of their classmates were still moving into Japan's major banks and ministries, preparing for lives as wealthy business figures able to wave the equivalent of $100 bills to summon taxis from nightclub districts, a small number of Japan's best and brightest were following their muses toward careers in creative arts. As the succeeding economic crisis (not to mention the rise of video games, home video, and other forms of individualized entertainment)

Figure 5.1. Caramel Box's *The Empire of Light,* 2009 production
Source: © Kazunori Ito / CARAMELBOX

dampened the outlook for their business-oriented classmates, the founders of small theater companies had to adapt to a changing economic environment, one that might still reward the kinds of stories they wanted to tell, but less reliably. When Japan's recession deepened from the 1990s through the 2000s, high-level, sustained success was available only to a small number of companies, such as Mitani Kōki's Tokyo Sunshine Boys. Many others were dissolved completely, their actors and writers moving into other companies or out of the theater scene altogether. And a few survived, connecting their creative visions to savvy marketing plans.

This is the story, in two senses of the word, of one of the survivors. Caramel Box—occasionally derided by theater critics for the sweetness and sentimentality of many of its plays—might have been one of the casualties of the struggling economic scene in Japan. Instead, the company, which was born in the mid-1980s at Waseda University, thrived during the 1990s and even into the early 2000s, and has maintained a steady place on the Tokyo and touring theater scenes since then. Its strategies have involved cultivating a strong relationship with its fans through savvy public relations and branding efforts. But Caramel Box has also survived by reliably giving its fans what they say—often in the postshow questionnaires that have been used by the company for decades—they want. Caramel Box's plays, even when adapted from different source material, are routinely structured around emotional payoffs that resolve anxiety and loneliness over prior choices by connecting them to a hopeful future in which protagonists are able to reestablish their social connections in part because of a recognition of the innocent decency of their decisions.

The Tokyo-based Caramel Box is unlikely to find its way into an episode of NHK's *Cool Japan*—the semiofficial catalogue of Japan's internationally appealing cultural products—anytime soon. Unlike classical Japanese theater styles such as Kabuki or Nōh, the sentimental, gently humorous plays of Caramel Box require of their contemporary audiences no special training or connoisseurship, and they would not likely stand out to foreign audiences as emblematically Japanese, except for the fact that the plays are entirely in Japanese, with a Japanese cast and crew, played in front of an entirely Japanese audience. Performing for a moderately sized, highly loyal, predominantly female fan base, Caramel Box eschews coolness in favor of skillfully, reassuringly delivered comfort. Its plays avoid the avant-garde aesthetics and strategies of many of the country's most prestigious groups, and its dedicated fan base knows that a Caramel Box show will produce laughter and tears, with warm-hearted humor infusing stories that invariably lead to an emotionally charged but reaffirming climax, followed by curtain calls in which the actors playfully banter with one another. Japan's theater scholars have largely ignored Caramel Box, and the company's leaders are well aware of the critiques that have occasionally been directed at it. The company has, however, survived and sometimes thrived by delivering reliably sentimental entertainment to its fans for decades.

My goal in this chapter is thus not to rehabilitate the image of Caramel Box among theater critics, although I myself enjoy its plays a great deal and would gladly defend them. It is rather to suggest that these plays offer an opportunity to consider relationships between narrative and emotion, and particularly the meanings and consequences of melodramatic representation. My argument in this book—that research on politics and emotion should focus on representation and therefore draw from logics of narrative rather than theories of emotion itself—demands attention to the ways in which experience and history can be structured as stories with necessary and predictable emotional beats. In this chapter I consider this through an examination of the explicitly and deliberately nonpolitical work of Caramel Box. In previous chapters we examined how the stuff of politics is often narrated in ways that seem to be about something other than politics—about how we feel something together rather than how we fight or struggle with one another. This chapter situates one Caramel Box play, 2010's *The Empire of Light,* in a larger context of Japanese postwar theater, showing that its structure and emphasis reflect a notion of what the audience is supposed to feel and when it is supposed to feel it, shifting the source material to make this happen. By calling attention to this structured production of emotion and to the demands on the theater company responsible for structuring it, this chapter points out that the ways of coming to grips with one's past and an emphasis on social reintegration provide one avenue for hope in Japan, an avenue that becomes wider and more obviously political in chapter 6.

Reading Politics in Japanese Theater

Caramel Box's plays are avowedly apolitical; one will not find reference in them to prevailing debates about Japan's armed forces, social justice, or economic inequality. But the group's formation reflects something important about the politics of Japan's 1980s, and the group's durability through repeated and reassuring dramaturgical structures offers something revealing about the politics of post-bubble Japan as well. The mid to late 1980s, when Caramel Box was formed and began its string of success, is too often dismissed as simply the "high bubble" era, when grotesque materialism simultaneously warped Japanese cultural values and inspired risky speculation that badly damaged the economy. If anything, the cultural zeitgeist, particularly of Japan's major cities at the time, also valorized explorations of personal creativity and individuality, with much of this positioned as a modern and even sophisticated response to the overemphasis on corporate cultures and collective sacrifice for Japan's economic development. One of the most immediately noticeable aspects of a Caramel Box performance is that the audience is overwhelmingly female. This is a fact not lost to anyone at the company, which also keeps good records from post-performance questionnaires in which fans typically note their age and occupations as well. Having largely come of age with Caramel Box itself, many fans are middle-aged and from the professional

"OL" (office lady) class: the audience is hardly representative of a uniform sensibility among Japanese people or of Japanese women. But its simultaneous marginalization in debates about Japanese politics and its centrality to patterns of work and consumption in post-bubble Japan make it especially useful for considering how hidden but important aspects of emotional representation work. As Akiko Takeyama has astutely observed, public rhetoric about hope since the late 1980s in Japan has simultaneously trumpeted individual choice and creativity for women while also leaving many in economically precarious positions that only heighten the mismatch between life course expectations and real opportunities.[1] Caramel Box protagonists, particularly their career choices, frequently reflect this continued insistence on individual creativity and self-worth, but never in the sense of an angered youth struggling against a cruel political or economic system, the kinds of issues that might have animated more explicitly political theater in the 1960s and 1970s. They instead must confront a largely well-meaning, orderly community from which their decisions have created an occasionally painful distance.

This is not to say that a study of theater must always engage the political but that the usual absence of theater in studies of the political is bewildering. Even the metaphors suggest that we ought to be engaging theater more systematically, more thoroughly. Leaders emerge on the national, political, or diplomatic *stage*. Politicians and their advisors aim to shape *narratives* for an *audience*. News profiles invite us to go *backstage* with political figures, especially important when we believe their message to be too *scripted*, too *rehearsed*. These are not the only metaphors that matter, but the pervasiveness of the comparisons suggests how deeply the idea of theater—of a show performed live by actors undertaking roles in front of viewers, in a story with a beginning, middle, and end—is embedded in our descriptions of politics. A candidate can hit a home run at a debate, but the election is unlikely to be called a ballpark. A leader can plant the seeds of a future policy, even harvest the outcome, without anyone referring to the whole endeavor as a farm.

For centuries, however, the relationships have been far more than purely metaphorical. Indeed, in the absence of other forms of mass culture, theater was long viewed as the site of political action, contestation, and propaganda. Struggles over power and legitimacy famously shaped Shakespeare's work, of course, not to mention that of his contemporaries and successors. Whether in early-eighteenth-century Parisian playhouses or in Mao's China,[2] leaders have recognized the revolutionary potential of theater, particularly through a kind of contract for the suspension of disbelief between collective audiences and the crew and cast of plays. One of the myriad pleasures of Barry Unsworth's superb 1995 novel *Morality Play* is his rethinking of the paths through which traveling players might have engaged contemporary political phenomena, particularly his recognition that theater—as a live, repeated medium—has the opportunity to adjust, to take the pulse of the audience, to rethink itself, even as its shows are frequently locked into genre expectations.[3]

Theatrical form, genre, and casting can themselves have political meanings and implications. Scholars of Japan's remarkably vibrant and durable theater traditions have, of course, long considered the political, or potentially political, content of the work; concerns about theater were central to the development of modern Japan's arts scene. In the politically tumultuous decades following the Meiji Restoration, Kawakami Otojirō, an activist in the unsuccessful People's Rights Movement, began to write antigovernment plays laced with melodrama and exaggerated sentimentality, although by the time of Japan's successes in the Sino-Japanese and Russo-Japanese Wars, he made the financially and politically rewarding decision to write and produce patriotic celebrations of the wars' heroes. These *shinpa* (new school) plays were marked by combinations of highly stylized performances associated with Kabuki (which was eclipsed in popularity by *shinpa* for roughly a decade), as well as their use of *onnagata* (male actors performing female roles), but with music and story practices associated with European and American theater. Indeed, a number of Western novels and plays were adapted by *shinpa* groups for performances in Japan. Given the chance to tour Europe with his company, Kawakami shrewdly had his wife, Sadayakko, a trained geisha, learn the female roles, understanding from his own experience studying in France that talented actresses were celebrated; Sadayakko's death scenes in various plays were reportedly so dramatic and convincing that she earned favorable comparisons to the greats of the European stage, such as Sarah Bernhardt and Ellen Terry.[4]

Though relatively short-lived as a theatrical form, *shinpa*'s consequences were extensive. With Japan's increasingly powerful role in China, as well as Japan's role in "translating" modern/Western practices for the ostensibly backward peoples of Asia, *shinpa* powerfully shaped theatrical practices in early-twentieth-century China.[5] *Shinpa* also served as the source of a genre in early Japanese cinema, with the melodramatic stories becoming a kind of "template" for the silent "ballad films" (*kōta eiga*) of the early twentieth century.[6] With the turn toward militarism, however, the Japanese government increasingly encouraged the performance and consumption of Kabuki plays that lionized authority, loyalty, and martial valor.

During America's postwar occupation of Japan, the Supreme Command for the Asia-Pacific (SCAP) worked quickly to eradicate the ostensibly militaristic, feudal, antidemocratic content of Japan's earlier theater traditions, quickly banning performances of a substantial number of Japan's most popular Kabuki plays. Distinguished scholar of Japanese theater James Brandon shows that SCAP even mandated the creation of new, "democratic" Kabuki that generally avoided direct reference to the United States and emphasized instead the inculcation of antihierarchical values and moral judgments among their characters.[7] The immense popularity of theater in Occupation-era Tokyo meant that entertainment production giants such as Tōhō and Shōchiku worked assiduously to rebuild venues in the city's devastated landscape, with department stores and other institutions stepping in to develop smaller sites capable of displaying Kabuki and other popular theater forms.[8]

Among these were the Western-style plays in the *shingeki* style.[9] Literally meaning "new theater," *shingeki* are variously depicted as modern or Western, even sometimes as directly "importing" Western theatrical practices. This has meant something akin to the kind of naturalism or realism—with action driven by the psychological or emotional states of characters, whose dialogue generally represents not just interaction but also their emotional worlds—that is viewed as central to modern or popular European or American theater, from Ibsen through Shaw, Miller through Wilson.[10] Indeed, *shingeki*'s most renowned pioneer, the director Osanai Kaoru, viewed them through the lens of Japan's modernizing needs and the limitations of *shinpa*'s hybridity in drawing Japanese theater into the twentieth century.[11]

Where the highly formalized performances of Kabuki and particularly Nōh had crafted aesthetic experiences meant in part to be transformative, or at least a rupture from the audience's world, an emphasis on realism or naturalism—particularly through *shingeki*'s rejection of earlier stylizations—became central to a durable mode of Japanese theater.[12] Realism, of course, is about more than having characters with real-sounding names behaving in ways that seem to correspond to life outside the theater doors. It is heavily mediated and culturally contingent; one need only watch the 1938 film James Cagney gangster film *Angels with Dirty Faces*, praised at the time by the *New York Times* for its "realistic point of view," to recognize that was once judged to be realistic seems now driven by affectations of performance, camera use, story, and the like, suggesting that a similar fate may ultimately befall "realistic" television programs such as *The Wire* or films like *Saving Private Ryan*.[13] In his analysis of nineteenth-century realist novelists such as Dickens and Flaubert, Peter Brooks notes that these innovators developed a new form of serious literary play, crafting worlds in which their invented characters were meant to resemble their readers in myriad ways: "One premise of this serious play is that it includes dolls that are supposed to look and act like people—characters who ought to be recognizable in terms of not only dress and appearance but also social function and, beyond that, motive, psychology."[14]

If *shingeki* encapsulated a quietly political shift for Japanese theater in the 1940s and 1950s, the sometimes confrontational, frequently surrealistic style of avant-garde theater in the 1960s aimed at something more jarring and direct. Partly for this reason, the *angura* (underground) or *shōgekijō* (small/amateur theater) companies that developed in the 1960s, many of them led by renowned artists such as Terayama Shūji or Betsuyaku Minoru, have long been regarded as essential elements of the era's political upheavals. As Masahito Takayashiki writes in his analysis of Betsuyaku's works, the limitations of language as a tool for individual expression and the emphasis on bodily communication became central themes for many of the era's artists, some of them having participated extensively in protest movements in the 1960s.[15] Though not taking direct part in 1960s protest movements, Terayama became an icon for countercultural and politically engaged figures because of his radical media and genre experiments, such as his fake radio documentary, *Adult Hunting*, which, like Orson Welles's famous *War of the Worlds* broadcast, induced a small amount of local hysteria, in this case about a fictional group of revolutionary children murdering adults.[16] His later work would cut not only across media but also between performer and audience, such as his packed

1970 "funeral" for Rikiishi, a fictional boxing prodigy killed in the highly popular manga series *Ashita no Jō* (Tomorrow's Joe).[17]

Japan's avant-garde, experimental, and countercultural theater movements thus became crucial touchstones for the radicalism of the 1960s, with artists pushing against genre and stylistic expectations in ways that coincided with the political and social ruptures of the era. By the 1980s and 1990s, the theater scene's shift from that era's experimentations encouraged some scholars to focus largely on the remaining companies that routinely crafted challenging pieces of art rather than on the larger if now declining number of companies engaged primarily in apolitical mass entertainment.[18] For some critics, the trajectory of Japanese contemporary theater has been disquieting, particularly as socially provocative or incendiary theater has been replaced increasingly by melodramatic or comic plays designed to keep audiences coming through the door for a bit of escapism.[19] These works are often comfortable and engaging, driven to maximize ticket sales and repeat performances, but their sentimental and reassuring qualities, combined with the essence of live performance that cannot be digitally reproduced and distributed with ease, have likely together limited their global impact and ensured their complete absence from the "Cool Japan" initiatives of chapter 4.

By conflating the politics of theater with explicitly political theater—with playwrights, directors, and companies aiming self-consciously to use their craft to enter public debates about authority, governance, justice, and power—we miss the opportunity to consider how these public debates are shaped by or susceptible to the same kinds of forces that animate theater itself, the very concern of many Japanese artists before the 1960s. Myriad opinion pieces and academic articles have been written about the politics of popular US television shows, such as *24*'s depiction of torture sessions that nearly always provide actionable intelligence to the show's protagonist, or *The Wire*'s critical stance toward the consequences of the "War on Drugs." But we might also consider how a procedural crime program such as *NCIS* routinely valorizes military service and loyalty, how romantic comedies erase class and educational differences to suggest that only the heart matters, or how even the occasionally rowdy humor of *The Simpsons* typically resolves episodes through the shared love of the family. All of these reference and reinforce certain institutions that have political functions, even if the directors and writers simply want to entertain audiences and resolve stories in comfortable or comforting ways.

In his seminal 1979 article "Reification and Utopia in Mass Culture," the Marxist literary critic Frederic Jameson urges critical attention to mass entertainment and its representation of class relations that are inherently political. Focusing on *Jaws* and the first two *Godfather* films, Jameson challenges views that popular entertainment functions or is designed crudely to "manipulate" viewers into accepting subordinate class positions. He instead reads into these films central themes of a better America for audiences of the 1970s. For Coppola's first two *Godfather* films, he suggests that the Mafia's visible corruption (separating it from the legitimacy of real, big business) is tempered or thrown into relief by the demands and requirements of that most virtuous of American institutions, the family. For Spielberg's *Jaws,* and paying special attention to crucial plot changes from the Peter Benchley novel on which the movie is based, this means the cooperation of technologically adept modern men (Roy Scheider's Chief Brody and Richard Dreyfuss's marine biologist Hooper) to defeat a relentless force of nature, the great white that had taken the life of the aged, demented craftsman Quint. To achieve this, Spielberg's film eliminates the class resentment and the sexual relationship between Brody's wife and Hooper, instead providing a utopian image of skilled, egalitarian cooperation that deliberately mirrors American political values. Indeed, the real world rarely gratifies people by offering the kinds of solutions we are inclined to want, leaving that duty to carefully crafted popular entertainment.[20] Who wants to see a movie in which two embittered men clash over a wife's infidelity, leaving one to die in the water and another to be saved as a wounded shark simply stops swimming? Or, worse yet and unimagined even by Benchley, in which Brody drowns Hooper in a jealous rage and then finds himself floating in the dark ocean as a fin circles lazily around him? What kind of summer blockbuster would that be?

Building on Jameson, Lauren Berlant suggests in *The Female Complaint,* one volume of her "national sentimentality" trilogy, that the affective weight of these works may come not in terms of the promised better world but rather in the imminent production of an unfinished but transformative emotional state for viewers or readers; what matters is what is felt in experiencing the art. When newer and sometimes edgier romantic films (perhaps like Todd Haynes's film *Carol,* inspired by classic films by

Douglas Sirk) update the melodramas of the past, they may lace them with the sense that the characters will not achieve anything like utopia, and instead emphasize the emotional and social value in sentimental attachment.[21] True love may be a fiction, but it is noble to yearn for it. A person's essential goodness is sentimentalized not through his or her success but rather through a continuing willingness to endure without complaint, to stick with principled desires despite the pain that these cause. These sentimental works, often derided as "women's literature" (or "chick flicks"), therefore offer the opportunity to view how larger social and political forces get communicated, if strategically, on an emotional level.

The Caramel Box Story

Like a number of other Japanese theater companies (*engekidan*), Caramel Box began its life as a student group. The group's founder and head playwright, Narui Yutaka, had been a leader of the Waseda University theater group Theater 50' (*Teatoro 50'*). Shortly after graduating, he founded Caramel Box in 1985 with two other Waseda students who were still in school—Katō Masafumi and Mashiba Azuki—and began to mount small productions at Tokyo theaters of expanded works from their Theater 50' days, including the play *Caramel Ballad,* a short riff on Charles Schultz's *Peanuts* gang: Charlie Brown, Snoopy, Lucy, and the rest. Their first production, *The Map Store and the Silver Lion* (*Chizuya to gin raion*), was staged for two nights at Tokyo's Tōgei Theater in March 1986, which also hosted a short run for their next play later that year; their other short productions appeared elsewhere in Tokyo through 1989.[22] According to an authorized history of the group, Caramel Box's big breakthrough came in 1990, when a reimagined version of the Teatoro 50' student play *Caramel Ballad,* now called *Fushigi na kurismasu no tsukurikata* (How to make a strange Christmas), played for weeks at the midsize (more than 700 seats) venue Theater Apple in Tokyo.[23]

Caramel Box's success was pronounced but not unique. In his brilliant analysis of Japan's contemporary theater scene, sociologist Satō Ikuya argues that what has been described as a "small theater boom" (*shōgekijō būmu*) in the 1980s was not only a reflection of the growing economy but also an element in further institutional development of the cultural scene of 1980s Japan. Fed in part by a wave of interest among recent college graduates who had themselves participated in or watched the performances of classmates while in school, small theater companies in Japan found that they could sustain audiences for weeks with an individual production, moving from an audience of a few hundred people or roughly a thousand for two nights to tens of thousands over a few weeks. With increased budgetary allocations for regional leisure and cultural centers in the 1980s and into the 1990s, midsize and larger theater halls were built in cities around Japan, offering more opportunities for the largely Tokyo-based theater companies to tour with their shows.[24]

Satō points out that the popularity of theater productions encouraged their inclusion in leisure development plans by regional bodies, which frequently used government funds to establish substantial performance spaces. Buoyed in part by access to larger venues and the possibility of performing a single play in different venues around the country over the course of a month or more, Japanese theater companies moved toward greater professionalization. After all, a company would have not only formal staff but also increasingly recognizable actors who could be counted on to travel with the shows and also to draw in fans who might be lured at least as much by the name of a performer as by that of the company or the playwright. One might argue that this encouraged a homogenization of theater as a cultural product, particularly as shows began to move toward the common denominators of popular entertainment rather than to genre-bending originality and provocation. But popular entertainment is a broad field, and the professionalization of theater groups also privileged those companies able to project a distinctive identity, to maintain fan loyalty, and to survive in a crowded and competitive market.

Caramel Box's early success and continued survival—it was one of the top theater groups in the 1990s and still sells out medium-size Tokyo venues for some performances while being a reliable earner in its regular tour productions elsewhere in Japan—stems largely from the integration of its onstage skills and its canny appreciation of how to deliver for its fans. At a typical Caramel Box play, the audience will enter past a series of tables selling T-shirts (around $25), DVDs of earlier plays ($50–$70), books and scripts of other plays (around $30), and assorted souvenirs associated with one show or another. Before the play, usually one or two members of the company will come on stage to remind the audience to turn off their phones and also make announcements about safety features of the theater and so forth. These announcements are usually funny and have sometimes included cast members performing an original song about turning off phones, with the performers then asking the audience to hold up their phones to show that they are indeed turned off. While a bit of a ritual, it is designed to be engaging, with the onstage company members making jokes about people's phones—back in 2011, a typical question was "Wow, is that one a 'smart phone'? Wish I had one . . ."—before thanking the audience, introducing the play's title, and then bowing.

Caramel Box's plays will usually begin with a short scene that sets up the basic tension, and about five minutes into the performance, one line will signal a key question or concern that will drive the main character and will immediately be followed by a music cue. The prerecorded song will usually be a medium-speed alternative rock number, played very loud, at which point all of the play's cast members will appear on stage to perform a coordinated dance. The dance does not neatly map onto the play's plot, and with the exception of the main character, the other cast members do not play individual roles in the dance; sometimes all the men will do one set of moves, women another, and then all move together. The main character (usually in the front and center of each dance, and frequently in a spotlight) will usually move with the others but will at one or two points in each dance be isolated from the other members, whose coordinated movements, when combined with the sudden stillness of the main role, emphasize his or her (but usually his) confusion and even loneliness. This dance operates as, in some sense, a kind of opening credit sequence, setting an emotional tone for the play and giving a sense of the scope of the cast (usually eight to ten people).

The play will usually consist of only one act and will likely take 110 minutes, something like a narrative feature film. Indeed, from the musical pieces that resemble opening and closing credits sequences to the character-driven narrative stories that transcend theatrical sets, Caramel Box plays closely resemble movies; Narui and Mashiba, like other major playwrights, have made forays into television and film in addition to radio plays. Particularly in their more comedic performances, such as the staccato entrance-exits toward the end of 1994's *Santa Claus Sang for Us,* there may actually something akin to a cinematic farce, with cross-cutting edits replaced by a stable backdrop before which different groups of characters—all supposedly in different places but at the same moment—run across the stage quickly while carrying on their own individual conversations. These are humorous specifically because the characters clearly have no idea what the other groups (who may have been speaking in front of the audience only five seconds earlier) are up to. Even their funniest plays, however, will conclude with a kind of dramatic emotional catharsis for the audience. Usually this involves some kind of acknowledgment of a previous trauma that allows the main character to reconcile powerfully with the people around him or her, many of whom will be in strongly institutionalized relationships, such as with family or classmates, as shown in the victims of an amnesia epidemic in Mashiba's 2010 play *Bye Bye, Blackbird* or the lonely writer and his comically self-aware, emotive dog in Narui's semiautobiographical and frequently restaged 1997 play, *Goodbye, Nautilus*.

After the lights go down on the main character, who has usually indicated eagerness to embark on a newly imagined and hopeful life that maintains his or her connections with others, the cast comes forward for its curtain calls. The entire cast will bow together, with perhaps a special bow for the leads, and will likely be called back for one or two more. These calls from the audience are central aspects of the Caramel Box experience because the last curtain call will be marked by a speech by one of the actors. The actor may not be the lead (in fact, frequently it is one of the smaller roles, though played by a known actor in the company) and will make some warmly self-mocking jokes about his or her embarrassment about being in front of the audience or may involve some comical enthusiasm about the rehearsal process. These often resemble inside jokes in that that they are likely to be even more amusing to fans who know the actors and have a sense, through previous performances and Caramel Box's other public relations endeavors, of their personalities and relationships. The cast member will, of course, politely thank the audience as well and will usually remind everyone of upcoming performances and ask them to spread the word. It is a ritual that Kazama Ken, a professor of theater studies who celebrates the avant-garde and political stylings of Japan's earlier theater groups, clearly finds off-putting, but he recognizes that it is an effort to make the audience feel like it is part of the show.[25] Whether or not this is the correct interpretation—although this has been my sense of it as well—it is a distinctive and indisputably successful practice, one that invariably produces big laughs from the crowd and seems to leave them in an enthusiastic mood when they exit through the lobby, where staff members sell Caramel Box goods and collect audience questionnaires at densely packed tables.

As the failure of a number of other contemporary theater groups in post-bubble Tokyo shows, Caramel Box's continued success is hardly guaranteed. In its favor, it has maintained a strong community of fans, most of whom are now in their middle thirties through early fifties, and it engages in remarkably open efforts to build new audiences, even providing discount tickets to schoolchildren; at one matinee in summer 2011, I saw an entire junior high school class in attendance. But it seems not to have built a reliably large audience segment among newer, professional, or younger adult viewers. Other theater companies—particularly the ones doing more "serious" work—are more likely to produce real "stars" whose return appearances can boost sales. Although many of Caramel Box's cast members turn up in minor roles in television and film, it has produced only one major star—Kamikawa Takaya—whose breakout hit, the NHK drama *Daichi no ko* (about Japanese war orphans in China), appeared in 1995. The remaining cast members, like the theater's organizers, rely on Caramel Box for a substantial part of their acting work but may be widely recognizable for their appearances in small roles in occasional television programs, radio plays, or commercials. And so maintaining the audience through the repetition of familiar and desired themes, the deployment of familiar faces, and the grateful acknowledgment of fans is essential to the company's sustenance.

The Empire of Light's Origins

For Caramel Box, the incorporation of science fiction or fantastic tropes— a global virus that permanently damages the minds of some, the sudden appearance of a woman who had died over twenty years earlier in the apartment of her now fully grown son, a man who can see others' lives by touching things they own—often drives the plot. But instead of moving toward a *Twilight Zone* gotcha moment, the stories usually treat these as straightforward, matter-of-fact elements, so much so that the hero or heroine—though sad or troubled—is in most ways "normal," at least insofar as their reproduction of basic routines of everyday life. They eat, work, go shopping with friends, have hobbies; they are not paranoid shut-ins, angry vagrants, or mean-spirited or troublesome. But the plays generally reveal an emptiness or uncertainty that amplifies the Everyman (or Everywoman) status of even a character with the ability to see a person's life by touching her on the arm, such as *The Empire of Light*'s Mitsunori. And for the character to be made whole, for this uncertainty to be resolved, the hidden webs of memory on which the play is premised need to be untangled.

In 2009 Caramel Box mounted one of its successful "half-time theater" shows: two short plays sandwiched around a half-hour intermission. Both were marketed as the company's takes on works by contemporary science fiction authors. Narui's *You Are in Every Landscape* is drawn from the book *Tomorrow's Memories* by Kajio Shinji.[26] *Hikari no Teikoku* (The empire of light) was written by Mashiba and Narui together and was drawn from the short story "Ōki na hikidashi" (The big drawer), one of the connected tales in a 1997 collection by the fantasy/sci-fi writer Onda Riku.[27]

Onda's collection—itself titled *The Empire of Light*—has turned out to be the first in a multivolume series about a loose "family" (which might be better understood as a tribe) who have a variety of supernatural powers that they normally suppress and hide. Having said in interviews that she was inspired by stories of the "The People" by the mid-twentieth-century American science fiction writer Zenna Henderson, Onda creates a kind of alternate Japan, one in which these special people are constantly in fear of being discovered by the authorities. Their behavior is generally benign, although the world they inhabit is a frequently violent and disorderly one. The title story of the collection comes halfway into the volume, providing the background to understand the more-contemporary stories that start and finish the volume. The story "The Empire of Light" describes the efforts of the ancient and wizened Professor Tsuru to manage a home/school for young people with special abilities in northeastern Japan during the wartime era; he tells the children that they are all part of a special family known as the Tokono. When the military Japanese government discovers the home, it tries to take the children to use their powers, but in the fight that ensues the home burns to the ground and many of the children are killed. In the remaining (and loosely connected) stories of the volume, members of the extended Tokono clan learn about their own powers while confronting a dangerous and hostile world; one of the more dramatic moments has a key character, Akiko, flashing backward and forward through time to an attack similar to the 1995 sarin gas incident on the Tokyo subway.

In an appreciative essay (*kaisetsu*) that serves as a postscript to the volume, the novelist Kumi Saori expresses some amusement at the unusual title of Onda's collection, *The Empire of Light*; she does not refer directly to *L'Empire des Lumières*, the series of paintings by Belgian surrealist René Magritte, in which sunlight becomes an almost oppressive force, threatening to reveal buildings and trees otherwise cloaked in restful darkness. Kumi emphasizes, however, that the title suggests there is almost something unendurable about the brightness of light itself. To the extent that it appears in the collection's title story, *The Empire of Light* may represent a contrast to the military empire that sought to enslave the children and the Tokono themselves. But even this is unclear, as the most obvious reference in the collection is to a prayer written by one of the key characters in the collection's wartime title story (and not referenced in "The Big Drawer," although it is in the Caramel Box play). One of the Tokono children, a shy boy named Ken, writes a prayer for his classmates and teachers:

We are the children of light.
Light can shine anywhere.
Where the sun shines, grass grows, the wind blows, and all living things can
*   breathe.*
That's true anywhere, and for anyone.
But it's not for anyone and not by anyone's grace.

We weren't forced to be alive, and we're not mistakes.
Just like with the light that shines, and then the wind that starts to blow, or
*   the flowers that bloom and spread, we're supposed to be here, and from a*
*   long time back.*
So while pressing our cheeks against the grass, letting our hair out in the
*   wind, plucking and eating fruit, and looking into the night stars and*
*   dreaming, let's stay in this world for a while.*
And then let's take one another's hands and return to the place where this
*   dazzling light was born.*[28]

It is, as Kumi says, an evocative title, but equally telling is the title of Onda's larger four-volume (and counting) project, of which *The Empire of Light* is only one part. *Tokono Monogatari* (Tokono tales) is a clear reference to *Tōno Monogatari*, the classic work by the early-twentieth-century folklorist Yanagita Kunio. As the anthropologist Marilyn Ivy has discussed in her important book *Discourses of the Vanishing*, Yanagita's collection of stories from the area around Tōno, in present-day Iwate Prefecture, sought to demonstrate the preservation of supernatural tales in the face of Japan's modernization. This project of course amplified, in comparison to the backward storytellers of Tōno, the scientific, rational successes of Japan's path toward industrial modernity.

For Onda, born and raised in Miyagi Prefecture (immediately south of Iwate—both would suffer terrible death tolls in the 2011 tsunami) before studying at Waseda University in Tokyo, the title seems more a touchstone than a deliberate critical intervention. In essence, it allows her to connect a series of science fiction stories that draw heavily from a global sci-fi vocabulary and contemporary tropes of popular literature to the well-known superstitions associated with the mountains of Tōhoku. Onda uses a conceptual language that would be familiar in a number of fantasy and horror novels or films, particularly ones that draw urban characters back into the mystical murk of Transylvania, the woods of rural England, or the *Blair Witch*–inhabited forests of Maryland: there actually is ancient knowledge in these parts that has been forgotten by or deliberately hidden from those who shuffle from cramped apartment to dreary office, stopping at convenience stores and chain restaurants before returning home to turn on the television. Onda's deft reference to Yanagita in many ways underscores Ivy's key point about the ways in which an imagined or constructed premodern world helps to make sense of the present. But her use of it in the service of a series of sci-fi melodramas ends up emphasizing the emotional and intellectual limits of a modern world that cannot imagine what it cannot grasp.

Staging Ground

Indeed, one of the reasons why Caramel Box's *The Empire of Light* is so useful for thinking about narrative politics is that it follows elements of Onda's story closely, while deviating in ways that seem built more for emotional impact than to reconcile any difficulties in staging. As Jameson noted with his analysis of the film *Jaws* and its distance from the original novel source, tracing changes made in adaptation can provide clues to a work's ideological impact. This is not to say that Caramel Box aimed to make a political or ideological statement with its entertaining show any more than Steven Spielberg wanted to turn his classic shark thriller into a resolution of US class tensions in the 1970s. But both presumably wanted their adaptations to work: to bring the stories they wanted to tell into a form that might be most effective in engaging audiences. With *Jaws* this meant skipping an extramarital affair between Brody's wife and Hooper, along with the guilt and anxiety that this produced, in favor of a streamlined buddy story that allowed them to overcome their humorously depicted differences to defeat the shark. For Caramel Box's *The Empire of Light,* this would mean the introduction of a contemporary framing device, the displacement of the novel's limited political critique, and a resolution focused on an agreement among adult characters rather than a coming-of-age discovery by a child. None of these radically alters the story, and a fan of the original would likely not feel aggrieved by the changes. But the three together fit the story into the tried-and-true shape of the emotional journey that Caramel Box habitually creates: a main character reconciles his or her past in the here and now, with understanding and acceptance allowing for a comfortable reintegration.

Caramel Box's popular retelling of "The Big Drawer" tracks the coming of age of Harada Mitsunori, a fourth-grader who has the gift of immediate and perfect recall of anything he reads. In Onda's story, although he shares this talent with his parents and his older sister, it quickly becomes clear that he has perhaps greater potential than any of them, and his precocious brilliance—he has already mastered the Hundred Tanka (*hyakunin isshu*) poems, a classical anthology—provokes the well-meaning but perilous attention of his schoolteacher, Mr. Imaeda. When walking one day with his sister Kimiko, Mitsunori spots an elderly neighbor, Dr. Ikari, with whom they have never spoken, collapsing from an apparent heart attack. Kimiko runs to get help, and Mitsunori stays with the dying man. He touches his chest and immediately sees the man's entire life play out. And so when Dr. Ikari's estranged son, a celebrated film director, comes to town, Mitsunori makes the decision to reveal to him that his father, far from ignoring his work, had seen all of his films and maintained a hidden scrapbook collecting write-ups from an adoring press. It is an emotional moment for the director, and the best Mitsunori can do to explain how he knows so much is to say "Your father told me," then quickly walk out of the house. Kimiko and Mr. Imaeda spot him, as Mitsunori struggles to deal with keeping his powers secret. His parents, alarmed at the teacher's curiosity, had already made the decision to move the family to another town, and the story concludes with Mitsunori promising his teacher "Don't worry, I won't forget you," then dreaming that what he really meant was that he had completely kept the memories of Imaeda and his classmates.[29]

In rewriting the story as the play *Hikari no Teikoku*, Mashiba and Narui confront several basic challenges. One, of course, is to keep an audience of adults absorbed in a story about a nine-year-old; presumably some are even at the play specifically to get away from their own nine-year-olds. Others include the representation of the moment when Mitsunori sees the old man's life, as well as the introduction of the Tokono and the challenges they face in living a safe life; these are left somewhat ambiguous in the story and are revealed by Onda only later in the collection, in its title story. Finally, of course, is the depiction of the story in a manner that will work for Caramel Box audiences. After all, Caramel Box provides an entertainment product, one that succeeds in large part because of its reliability. Onda's story—in some ways a good fit for the light sci-fi aspects, combined with human drama, that have marked a number of Caramel Box productions—was not written with the Caramel Box audience in mind, nor was it crafted to be told primarily through dialogue and physical action rather than third-person exposition.

In Caramel Box's original 2009 production of *Hikari no Teikoku*, the action begins in the present day, with Mitsunori (Hatanaka Tomoyuki) and Kimiko (Okauchi Mikiko) already in their twenties. They have traveled to the vacation home of Ikari Yūsuke (Ōuchi Atsuo). He does not recognize them at first but then acknowledges them as he begins to guzzle a beer that he takes from his refrigerator. Kimiko confronts Yūsuke over a screenplay he has been writing about the Tokono, which threatens to expose them. When he leaves the room to fetch the screenplay draft, having already announced he absolutely will not change his mind about making the film, Kimiko and Mitsunori argue, and Kimiko suggests obliquely that she might have to kill Yūsuke to prevent their story from being made public. When she says that Mitsunori has always been too nice, Mitsunori replies, "I was only ten years old at that time." She replies, "And I was thirteen. But that was fifteen years ago. . . ."

And then the dance begins, with the characters all dissolving in and out of lines and with Mitsunori occasionally becoming lost before being reintegrated into the group dance. After a brief pause, Mitsunori (still played by Hatanaka, now stiff-backed and emotive, a demonstratively willful kid) is in school, being mildly bullied by classmates before Ms. Imaeda steps in. The scene is played for laughs, with the cast members exaggerating the clumsiness of elementary school children in their rowdy quarrel. Mitsunori comes all too close in confiding in Ms. Imaeda, particularly as he wants praise for being able to memorize Japanese classical poetry even as he knows his parents will be angry at him. His sister reminds him of the fate of the Tokono children in the 1940s, when agents of the military government killed everyone.

When he meets the old man whose life he will "keep," the man accosts Mitsunori for having littered, grabbing his arm a bit too roughly and then promising to bandage him. Even this scene is played for laughs, with the man, named Dr. Ikari here, portrayed as a bit of a drunken codger who nevertheless recognizes that there is something unnatural about Mitsunori, quickly building an affectionate, playful relationship with the boy. When Yūsuke comes to town, seeing his father well before his death, Mitsunori stands up to the aggressive and hectoring film director, defending his father.

Like most Caramel Box plays, *The Empire of Light* is mostly a comedy involving creative people with flexible schedules. As adults, Mitsunori and Kimiko have become, respectively, a photographer and a book translator. During their scenes as children, Mitsunori and Kimiko's father is a lovable goofball, loudly demonstrating his knowledge of classical music scores, the complete works of Shakespeare, and anything else he has read to his frequently exasperated but otherwise adoring wife and children. Kimiko, even as a child, is a preternaturally adult and protective figure; she displays only a cagey and intelligent willingness to stand up to adults, not the nervous wariness she feels in the short story, particularly toward her brother's schoolteacher. Dr. Ikari is a loudmouth but hardly a fool, and the play leaves little doubt about the warmth he feels toward Mitsunori.

And Ms. Imaeda, a male schoolteacher in the story, has been written in the play to fit into one of the clear Caramel Box archetypes: that of the voluble and friendly young woman who is extremely comfortable in her own skin, despite the wacky relentlessness of her chattering.

With Dr. Ikari a major character in the play, as opposed to a revealing corpse in the story, much of the play involves the relationship between him and Mitsunori, whose loneliness and neediness are exposed primarily by the extent to which he depends on Dr. Ikari and the lengths to which he goes to maintain their friendship. Years of alcoholism have weakened the doctor, and late in the play he is confined to what turns into his deathbed, surrounded by his children. Mitsunori, defying his parents' wishes to keep away from the inquisitive doctor, touches him at the precise moment of his death, and a second dance begins. In this one, however, the loud alternative music is instrumental, and Mitsunori remains at the doctor's side as the doctor turns slowly back and forth, witnessing the other actors play out moments of his life. It is a short piece, roughly a minute in length, that ends with Mitsunori suddenly recognizing that he is in a movie theater: the one where Dr. Ikari had proudly but secretly watched Yūsuke's films.

When he reveals to Yūsuke that his father had in fact kept a scrapbook of Yūsuke's successes, Yūsuke himself has an emotional moment, realizing that his father had in fact loved him—the first of two moments when many in the audience began to sob at all three performances I have seen. The action then shifts quickly back to 2009, where Mitsunori and Kimiko are still begging Yūsuke to drop his plans to make a film about the Tokono. Yūsuke insists that it will be safe because no one will associate Mitsunori or Kimiko with this group of people with special powers. And even if they do, Japan is now a democracy, and the government would not dare to hurt them. Kimiko calls him naive, and Mitsunori says, "It's better if I show you." He grabs Yūsuke's arm, and the action shifts to the background, with loud guitar rock once again blaring as Mitsunori and Kimiko's parents suddenly appear next to one another and facing the audience, as if positioned behind the steering wheel of a car. The parents scream at each other that another car is getting closer, that they will be taken by their pursuers, that they cannot save their children. The other car continues to approach as the parents scream out the names of their children; there is the sound of a car crash, and the background goes dark and quiet (though the theater is alive with the sobs of audience members, the second such moment). Yūsuke asks who had been after them in the chase that resulted in their deaths, and Kimiko says, "We don't know, but it seems they weren't Japanese." Sensing that he has done all he can, Mitsunori smiles and leads Kimiko out, saying goodbye to Yūsuke, who dramatically rips in half the screenplay draft he has written after they step out the door. Protecting Mitsunori and Kimiko is, as it turns out, more important than telling their story on film, particularly because of Mitsunori's kindness in telling Yūsuke of his father's pride.

Sweetness and Trauma

The Empire of Light is, in a word, sweet. And indeed, this is the basic critique of Caramel Box's work: that it is too sweet. As one member of another theater company reportedly said, "*Caramel Box* plays are so sweet! . . . For anyone who can't handle the sweet stuff, or an adult who wants something bitter or spicy, *Caramel Box* is definitely not the theater group for you."[30] The critique is very much a gendered one, with the expectation that Caramel Box plays are for women who want nothing more challenging than the kinds of reassurance about the goodness of families and friends that such plays reliably provide. Kazama, the researcher who has written both on French drama and on Japan's small theater companies, argues that the "magic" (*majutsu*) of a Caramel Box show may lie in its ability to convince the audience that no matter how dramatic things might seem for characters struggling to come to grips with their slightly unnatural surroundings, the roots of tensions are really never that deep. The drama may be intense, but the real problems are simple.[31]

In his appreciative history of Caramel Box, based largely on his interviews with members of the company, Morimoto writes that this simplicity (*wakariyasusa*, or "easiness to understand") is a key virtue of the group and that there is nothing wrong with a company that pitches its performances largely to women and children (it is worth noting here that children make up only a tiny portion of an average Caramel Box audience). He quotes one cast member, Ōno Satsuki, who laughingly tells him of how other, more "serious" theater groups will occasionally sniff that Caramel Box plays are childish or are just efforts to profit by giving women exactly what they want. Morimoto turns part of the discussion on its head, arguing that other groups are more self-indulgent, considering their work to be that of self-expression to a large audience. But Caramel Box's work is designed purely to entertain. He quotes Narui: "Theater is something you express for others. Someone who can't take pleasure in providing a service (*hōshi*) for others probably doesn't have the right personality to be on stage in the first place." Morimoto takes Narui's comment in a somewhat unexpected direction, insisting that this is what makes it perfect for female audiences:

> This open-heartedness is the core of Caramel Box's appeal, and needless to say is the source of its easiness to understand. Whatever else one says, only women can give birth to children, and children are the adults of the future. The people who will build the future are women and children. Is there something wrong with plays that women and children will love and find easy to follow? And isn't that clear when you see all those people heading to the theater, and the stage and audience coming together in one "miraculous moment" (*kiseki no shunkan*)?[32]

Leaving aside the astonishing sexism of the statement, what descriptions like this of Caramel Box miss is that the plays are not only sweet. The plays' resolutions are almost invariably upbeat, and it is a special characteristic of Caramel Box productions that there is almost never a character that might be described as straightforwardly villainous. One might, of course, suggest the same about some other forms of popular entertainment: US television sitcoms or Hollywood family comedies, for example. But Caramel Box usually will not even feature the snooty, Harvard-educated romantic rival who gets his or her comeuppance or the abrasive baseball team owner who is shown up when the film's leading character, a down-on-his-luck coach just trying to win back his estranged family, successfully teaches an orangutan to play third base. Even the most problematic character in a Caramel Box production will typically be revealed to be fundamentally decent, and that revelation will usually come through a sudden confrontation with the trauma that had left him or her emotionally scarred.

Therefore, the imagination behind a Caramel Box play is not just sweet or simple but rather deeply (if comically) melodramatic. As Peter Brooks has noted, "Melodrama is a form that calls for heightened meanings, meanings made explicit through their overt manifestation and acting out. . . . [Melodramas] enact with obviousness and force essential truths about people and their relations, about ethical and psychological forces that risk remaining latent in everyday reality."[33] In its effort to craft plays that fit the expectations of its audience, Caramel Box retells the already sentimental story in a form that fits its fans' emotional demands through a return to motifs of memory, loss, and redemption, combined with the unfailing and exaggerated decency of the major characters. If Narui is correct, and giving the audience what it wants is essential to the Caramel Box approach, it is worth considering the ways in which he and Mashiba skillfully revise Onda's original story to work well for a Caramel Box audience.

After all, Caramel Box might have taken the story in a number of directions. Though not explicitly political, Onda's frequent references to the corruption and cruelty of state power, to the omnipresent possibility of violence, and to the complex relations between the Tokono and Japan itself might have offered a potential route for dramatic engagement, particularly given Kimiko's fearfulness toward her brother's schoolteacher. Similarly, Mashiba and Narui might have chosen to focus on the relationship between Yūsuke and Mitsunori; although their exchanges occupy only a few pages, they dwarf the role of the father in the original story. And the framing device could have been taken in any of a number of directions, not necessarily Mitsunori's revelation about his parents' deaths. The adaptation, however, rearranges and invents elements to fit them into the structure and style of a Caramel Box play: an introductory scene before an evocative dance number, a series of comic interactions between garrulous and well-intentioned characters, a misinformed or mistaken character whose confrontation with the past allows him to connect more powerfully with his family and his background.

And it is this promise that almost always defines the Caramel Box experience: that of a confrontation with a problematic past—fights with one's family, earlier professional and personal failures, alienation from classmates and friends—that produces an emotionally satisfying resolution, one in which the main character is made whole. If we are to assume that the happy ending is preordained because that is what audiences want, we should think as well about the almost routinized production of the crisis itself: a recognition that living one's life has entailed costs that are frequently too subtle to be engaged directly but that others would accept if only they understood the circumstances. And it is this hardly sweet recognition that makes the resolution so important. There had to be some crisis to overcome, without which the happy ending is beside the point. This is usually not because of a villain and not because of a deliberate challenge, but rather because simply in the struggle to thrive, there were sacrifices to one's dreams, to one's community, and to one's place; the Caramel Box experience is a sweet one because it represents the equivalent of being told that you are OK, that you were right (and beloved) all along.

Structured Emotionality

Since 2013, Caramel Box has held an annual "Greetings Theater" tour, performing for two or three appearances each at medium-size theaters across Japan, as one of its many initiatives designed to build new audiences. In October 2017 the company restaged *The Empire of Light* with a new cast performing a lightly extended version of the play and with one added character—Yūsuke's film producer, who pushes to make the film despite Mitsunori and Kimiko's protests—and a little more backstory, drawn from Onda's book, regarding the Tokono children. At a performance in Tokyo's Kita-Senju neighborhood that kicked off the tour, Keduka Yōsuke, the cast member playing Keiko and Mitsunori's father, took the lead in much of the extended post-performance chat with the audience. After being playfully chided by the Caramel Box producer Katō for talking for too long, Keduka faked a heart attack, seemingly dying on stage as the audio team replayed the sound of the car crash that killed his character, provoking a hearty laugh from the audience, which had largely been moved to tears when the same sound played thirty minutes earlier. And in a recorded video message, Narui, who reported he was unable to attend because he was at work on Caramel Box's next production, explained that he had chosen to adapt "The Big Drawer" for the stage because Caramel Box prefers "spooky" (*yūrei*) stories and he likes to write plays about young people. The cast handed out plastic folders as souvenirs to each of the nearly six hundred audience members present, asking them to come to additional performances in the Tokyo area or advertise the play to friends and family in the many other locations, from Hiroshima up through Niigata, at which the play would be mounted.

Caramel Box has survived ups and more recent downs in the Japanese theater scene in large part because of its canny understanding of its audience, serving them with fan goods for purchase as well as with narratives that hit reliable emotional beats. In an interview, Narui says that his plays emanate from his childhood loneliness and that in creating characters, he thinks about making people who would have been his friends. This seems like an honest admission, and one could take Caramel Box plays primarily as celebrations of friendship. Indeed, the post-play chats that break the fourth wall and lay bare the contract of suspended disbelief only highlight the sense that the group's survival has hinged on the seemingly personal bonds built between audience and company members.

But that would be to miss the repeated narrative structure, even when adaptation of another source requires some jerry-rigging to make it fit. And it would miss the politics that these plays disclose: the ways in narratives have emotional repercussions because they lead inexorably toward desired payoffs. Main characters are not simply lonely; they are lonely, isolated, or estranged in part because of their earlier choices. And they do not simply make friends or find community; they instead reintegrate because their earlier choices are understood and explained, that they were not ruinous but were instead part of a personal journey. As one wise and learned friend on the Japanese studies scene put it to me, "Salvation lies in the social," which I think accurately captures the climactic moments when the tears flow.[34] These moments remind viewers that the past cannot remain buried but that there is a linked, connected world in which the isolation and loneliness that the past might have produced need not endure: hope awaits in the form of human connection.

THE PERIPHERAL U-TURN

When disgruntled Coast Guard officer Isshiki Masaharu took the *nom de guerre* sengoku38 and uploaded a classified video of the collision between a Chinese fishing trawler and a Japanese patrol boat in November 2010, he seems to have expected the public firestorm to follow. Enraged at his government's apparent cowardice in the face of Chinese aggression, Isshiki uploaded the video specifically to embarrass the government for having released the Chinese captain without criminal charges. After being dismissed for having leaked classified information, Isshiki predictably signed a book deal for a tell-all account that would presumably attract readers sympathetic to his views of Chinese malice and of government dishonesty. His book, *For Something: Confessions of sengoku38,* published early the following spring, laid out his decision and a call for action, but of a strange sort.[1] In surprisingly mawkish and sentimental terms, Isshiki pointed to the emotional emptiness of life for young Japanese at least as clearly as he dictated a need to stand up to Chinese aggression. Young people, he argued, were aimless, underemployed, and distrustful

Figure 6.1. Kamaishi East Junior High School, summer 2012

of the government, but a renewed commitment to Japan's future might rejuvenate them. His patriotism was more than a defense of Japan against external enemies; it was a defense of Japan against its own despair.

Isshiki might have become a household name had not the 2011 Tōhoku earthquake, tsunami, and nuclear disaster crowded sengoku38 out of the national limelight only a week or so after his book appeared. His conclusion reflected the already prevalent national story—of Japan's economic miracle and rise in national status through collective effort and community solidarity, followed by materialistic individualism and the country's "lost" two decades—that was so widely told as to be nearly a cliché. It had long remained important for framing contemporary Japanese events as well as proposals for the country's future. And it would ultimately sit at the forefront of national debates about the country's global status, its path forward, and the steps necessary to return Japan to the promise it once showed. This story, whether told in the popular *Always: Sunsets on Third Street* film trilogy or in the NHK docudrama series *Project X*, or even hinted at by a singularly angry former Coast Guard member, has an unmistakably melodramatic feel, with heightened emotions and the celebration of an earlier, more communitarian, more decent Japan that succeeded in a menacing world in part because its innocence allowed the virtue of cooperation.

It was largely for this reason that the University of Tokyo's Institute of Social Science, one of the country's premier research centers on political-economic and social issues, undertook a five-year project titled *Kibōgaku*, translated officially as "The Social Sciences of Hope." Aimed at countering the consequences of Japan's long recession and the malaise that seemed to trap Japanese through much of the 1990s and 2000s, the *Kibōgaku* project went beyond an examination of what hope might be and how it might be measured, even explicitly tabling some of those concerns. Instead, the authors plunged into a detailed study of the city of Kamaishi, one of the declining towns in Japan's rural periphery. Kamaishi might have been expected to be a site of despair, losing a substantial chunk of its industrial base and watching its population decline by nearly half over the course of a few decades. If Japan's malaise has been represented to many outside of Japan as a largely urban problem—homeless elderly men on the streets, *hikikomori* youth who refuse to come out of their homes in sprawling apartment buildings, *yakuza*-affiliated loan sharks harassing the indebted of Tokyo and Osaka—it is often seen in Japan as especially dire in the countryside. And the *Kibōgaku* project leaders, acting both on tips from colleagues as well as on sheer instinct, chose Kamaishi as a counterintuitive case, one where local residents were building hope despite the serious problems that their small, diminished city has faced.

This chapter builds from the discussion thus far to show how emotion, time, and narrative intersected in a major international research project responding to the central political problem of Japan's past quarter century: the reconstruction of the promise embedded in the country's postwar economic success. In particular, it traces the efforts of a distinguished group of social scientists to apply the tools of their trade to the rejuvenation of the messy emotion of hopefulness, largely by telling a story about Kamaishi that would fit within a larger narrative about Japan, but one ending with the glimpse of a cooperative, uncontentious future in which young Japanese might be rewarded for their optimism and pull the rest of their country with them. The project would involve not just a reexamination of the past but also the valorization of those people returning from time spent in Japan's urban centers—Tokyo, mostly, but possibly Sendai, Osaka, Kobe, or Nagoya—to rebuild their peripheral hometowns by forging useful connections with the modern, prosperous center.

The scholars' subsequent response to an epochal catastrophe in their research site, as well as the unexpected political prominence of some of their efforts, suggests the durability of hope, though not in the mawkish "hope never dies" sense. Instead, modern democracy traffics in hope, in a narrative that ends with a better and more prosperous future for all; indeed, modern democracy even encourages people, including socially conscious scholars, to imagine and reproduce this better future that somehow transcends or escapes the cruel divisions of today. For all its fuzziness, hope might be most precise emotional expression of democratic politics: one in which the messy, contested struggle of today makes sense because it heralds a more cooperative, more peaceful, more satisfying future for all. In this sense, hope offers a future beyond politics. In the case of *Kibōgaku*, Kamaishi, and contemporary Japan, this allows a glimpse into the ways in which emotionally complex local circumstances can be embedded, even by those most sympathetic to them, in a larger, official story: one that makes a melodrama of the reclamation of national innocence as an essential part of the country's better future. Hope itself nearly encapsulates an apolitical world of cooperation and collective effort rather than competition and division, and it makes sense as a national emotional prescription because it so closely fits the structure of national narratives, the ones premised on collective struggle toward a self-evidently better future for all rather than the mess of actual, everyday emotion. It should be small wonder that scholars would study how to arrive there, both before and particularly after a disaster so great that its survivors might have been forgiven for giving up on hope entirely.

Hope as Social Science

Despite its frequency in political discourse, there is as yet little in the way of a social science to understand how hope might be achieved. Hope is instead understood, and sometimes mocked, as a rhetorical ploy by a political candidate whose empty promises about the future bespeak an inability to deal with the real, the now.[2] The best recent academic study of hope in the United States, Hirokazu Miyazaki's *The Method of Hope*, critically interrogates it as part of a larger anthropological meditation on temporality and action, building from social theory to investigate how the past and the future are deployed in the present.[3] No top universities or programs have devoted resources to the promotion or generation of hope, which might seem natural, given its amorphous and seemingly nonscientific nature—until one considers Harvard's decades-long project on "happiness"[4] or Stanford's Center for Compassion and Altruism Research and Education.[5] Indeed, "positive psychology" has become such an ardently defended stream of social and behavioral research in the United States that the absence of a project specifically on hope seems more surprising than it does natural.[6] After all, to his critics, *The Audacity of Happiness* or *The Audacity of Compassion* would have seemed no less idealistic and imprecise than the book title that Barack Obama actually chose.

Like positive psychology, the "social sciences of hope" immediately demanded a proactive defense. Right from the outset, the creators of the *Kibōgaku* project wrote openly of both the imperative and the challenge of writing about hope from a social scientific perspective. Although the project team was led jointly by political theorist Uno Shigeki and the economic historian Nakamura Naofumi, its most ardent and vocal proponent was their University of Tokyo Institute of Social Science colleague, the labor sociologist Genda Yūji. Genda had made an international name for himself by becoming, over the course of roughly a decade, one of the most widely read and influential voices in studies of Japan's youth employment system. With outsourcing, declining fortunes for many of Japan's major firms, and particularly dire circumstances facing small manufacturers and subcontractors, Japan had seen its ostensibly harmonious and healthy employment system deteriorate since the early 1990s. Top college graduates who had had the luxury of choosing between myriad offers from key manufacturing or financial firms now sweated out their job searches in the hopes of finding promising if not immediately lucrative careers. Junior college or high school graduates who would previously have been able to enter predictable pathways into stable and sometimes nearly guaranteed long-term employment were increasingly forced to take short-term or part-time jobs, or contract positions whose low wages were unlikely to be accompanied, as most regular employment had been, by the near certainty of long-term employment.

And there had been little end in sight, with most analysts recognizing that Japan's salad days were behind it and suggesting that there was little to be gained by trying to resuscitate postwar Japan's employment system as it had previously functioned: with a good job for most and with a substantial percentage of Japanese families led by (usually male) breadwinners able to protect their economic interests and prospects over the long term. Instead, younger workers would need to adapt—through education, training, entrepreneurship, and risk taking—to a new and more flexible system that would offer opportunities but also uncertainty, a generation that might see that first job after completing school as just that: a first job, not the last one.

Genda burst into the academic publishing market with careful but uncommonly sympathetic studies that avoided some of the angry finger-pointing by older scholars working in the Marxist traditions that have long shaped economics and labor studies in postwar Japan. Although he identified problems facing a generation of "freeters" (part-timers, a neologism drawn from the English "free" and German "arbeiter") and NEET (Not in Employment, Education, or Training) because of the declining number of new jobs offered by major employers since the 1990s, Genda was equally concerned about the consequences to young people of their constantly being blamed for their sloth, lack of ambition, and somewhat casual morals.[7] For Genda, the spectacular rise since the 1990s in the number of Japanese-language books with "hope" in their titles, most of them bemoaning its absence or offering to provide it, was indicative of a national mood, particularly among the young, that marked and reflected the dismal employment scene. The problem was not just the absence of jobs and certainly not the behavior—such as living in their parents' homes or withdrawing from social life (*hikikomori*)—of young people reacting to these economic changes but rather the difficulty that all of it had imposed on them to imagine a better future for themselves.

Genda would help to make "hope" something of a brand for the Institute of Social Science. Written in the earliest days of the five-year project, Genda's book *Kibōgaku* (with chapters by several coauthors) was built from an Internet survey that cast a wide net, reflecting on whether the respondents, mostly in urban areas and in their twenties and thirties, expressed social and economic hope, matching their responses against a wide variety of factors, including age, their previous hopes, their expectations for building a family, the numbers of friends they listed, and so forth. More of a showman than your average labor economist, Genda even included a series of photos of himself using a form of sign language to spell out the English sentence "Hope is a wish for something to come true by action" in his popularly written book *Kibō no tsukurikata* (How to create hope).[8] And when the institute published a four-volume set as the *Kibōgaku* project's magnum opus, it was enthusiastically blurbed by novelist Murakami Ryū, one of Japan's most popular writers of the past forty years.[9] The respect is evidently mutual. In his earlier summary of the project, Genda had claimed that the project was partly built on the message of Murakami's 2000 novel *Kibō no kuni no ekusodasu* (Exodus of the country of hope), about a mass defection of 800,000 students from Japan's junior high schools, inspired by one teenager who had set off on an anti-landmine expedition to Pakistan; they ultimately form a network that challenges global capitalism and Japanese political authority. As Murakami himself later did in a post-tsunami commentary in the *New York Times,* Genda points to a famous line in the novel: "We have everything in this country. Really, we've got just about anything one could want. The one thing we don't have is hope."

Crucially, all of these books go far beyond self-help entreaties, aiming to cement hope as a genuine topic for social science research. Genda himself goes so far as to argue that the social sciences, particularly economics, are premised on an implicit and unstated understanding of hope: if one considers hope to be a combination of desire and purpose, it is the source of consumption, investment, marriage, and the myriad choices that economics takes as research objects. Because economics makes sense only because of time and our plans for and use of it, hope is already an essential if unanalyzed factor in the field.[10] Central to all of this is the peculiar combination of time and agency embedded in the authors' idea of hope: it is about one's ability to act in a manner consistent with one's future goals. In a move that occasionally dovetails with Kant's third antimony—in essence, the logical conundrum for deterministic causal analysis that also allows for free will and for spontaneity—coeditor and political theorist Uno Shigeki points out the limits of predictive social research drawn on data from the past. There is, of course, always uncertainty about how the future will develop, and we should expect people to create meaning out of this uncertainty. Hope itself emerges from this uncertainty between what the available current evidence might suggest and the possibility that, through our action or that of others, things might turn out better than expected.[11] Building more from social than political theory—particularly philosophers Ernst Bloch and Washida Kiyokazu, as well as from invited chapters from *Kibōgaku* project participants such as sociologist Richard Swedberg and Miyazaki, the author of *The Method of Hope*—Uno thus locates hope as a challenge to social science not only because of the amorphousness of its emotional meaning but mostly because it signifies the limits of what social science can meaningfully tell us. It is now time, in this reading, to think with social science but beyond the limits that time imposes upon it. As the coeditor of two of the four volumes, Uno argues that the salience of "hope" as a theme in Japan as well as overseas (specifically citing Obama's *The Audacity of Hope*) raises the question about how people can believe in a better future when social life has been replaced by individualization and atomization. For Uno, a Tocquevillian scholar whose research has focused largely on how individualization has rendered more difficult the kind of cooperation and community-mindedness on which successful democracy ostensibly rests, the social science of hope represents an opportunity to analyze the ways in which potentially isolated individuals can imagine a better future through re-understanding how to work with the needs of others in mind, not just themselves.[12] Salvation, in this sense, lies in the social.

Locating Decline

Myriad Japanese books such as Ōyama Shirō's *A Man with No Talents* sit alongside popular anime such as Kon Satoshi's *Tokyo Godfathers* and internationally acclaimed films such as Kore-eda Hirokazu's *Nobody Knows* to show Tokyo, Osaka, and other major cities as representations of economic misfortunate and social disconnection. Whether one considers the homeless tent cities of the major metropolitan areas, the specter of domestic dysfunction in the form of abuse or *hikikomori* (retreat and isolation) in large and anonymous housing projects, or the predatory loan companies menacing impoverished and unemployed older men in grimy downtown environments, the images we face of Japan's economic decline are often urban ones. Given that more than half of Japan's population lives in one of three massive metropolitan areas—the greater Tokyo region,

Osaka and its environs, and Nagoya—with millions more in major cities such as Fukuoka, Sendai, and Sapporo, almost any social or economic problem that plagues Japan will rear its ugly head with dense ferocity in its cities. Indeed, the NEET and freeter phenomena have been examined in English primarily as urban problems, with only occasional attention to their implications in smaller cities or rural regions.

In the Japanese news, however, the country's rural areas—as well as the small cities that dot them—inevitably seem to be in particularly dire straits.[13] Facing not only most of the national problems that afflict the major cities but also rapid depopulation and the graying of those left behind, Japan's *shichōson* (hamlets, villages, towns) have been targets of intense and only marginally successful governmental rehabilitation efforts for decades. For this reason, the declining fiscal health of the national budget imposes especially pronounced consequences on those smaller towns, particularly those dependent on agriculture, that have become, in the much-quoted words of Michael Donnelly, "wards of the state."[14] Indeed, with the centralization of much of Japan's financial, industrial, political, and educational power in a few metropolitan districts (particularly Tokyo and Osaka), smaller cities and rural regions in Japan have been threatened not just with economic malaise but also with potential disappearance altogether. This has been a perennial concern of the Japanese government, but the 2000s have made a virtual cottage industry of sentimental news stories that focus on the literal handful of students—sometimes four, sometimes five—graduating as the last class of ninth-graders from some junior high school that is about to close because the town has run out of children.

This is hardly a secret outside of Japan, but rarely do the foreign media convey how the country's increasingly wobbly internal demographic and economic structure—with a seemingly irreversible tilt toward the metropolis—is as much of a feature in cultural and social debate as are the topics that tend to dominate the foreign news: Japan's slow growth, struggles over the country's wartime responsibility, or the rights of women. When it is told, the story, as anthropologists such as Marilyn Ivy and Jennifer Robertson have noted, is one of nostalgia and loss: the rural Japan that is the source of Japanese tradition constantly faces the threat of disappearance through the country's development, modernization, and urbanization.[15]

Kibōgaku rethinks this story by examining, largely through politically progressive lenses, the declining steel town Kamaishi, whose history of conflict, growth, and decline may have created conditions for the pursuit of a hopeful future. The mid-nineteen-century construction of a blast furnace because of the discovery of magnetite iron ore in the mountains nearby set the small city on the path of early industrialization, followed by substantial public and private investment to establish Kamaishi as a steelmaking city capitalizing on the availability of coal from Hokkaido and later, through Japan's imperial expansion, from Manchuria.[16] It was not a fully harmonious development, with labor unrest growing particularly in 1919 over working hours and conditions, strengthening both the internal cohesiveness of Kamaishi's labor unions as well their credibility in making demands.[17] A devastating 1896 tsunami and catastrophic aerial bombardment by the United States in 1945 would together scar the city but, by some accounts, also provide it with a history of resilience, or of overcoming calamity.

Kamaishi's early postwar politics was also born of conflict, with local disputes reflecting some of the national tensions facing Japan after the toppling of the militarist government. Its three-term mayor, Suzuki Tōmin, returned to his childhood home of Iwate Prefecture after his controversial and illustrious career as a journalist whose anti-Nazi sentiments had once led to his expulsion from prewar Germany. In a brief period of early postwar national prominence, Suzuki led a newspaper workers' strike that culminated with the ouster of the *Yomiuri* newspaper's nationalistic president, Shōriki Matsutarō.[18] After his removal from the *Yomiuri* by pro-US forces worried about the country's shift to the left, Suzuki returned to Iwate and ran for mayor of a rebuilding Kamaishi. In a chapter that outlines Suzuki's contributions as mayor, Uno emphasizes his commitment to transparency and public communication, explained by his background as an antiauthoritarian journalist, as well as to the city's fiscal and developmental independence. Although the city could not achieve the fiscal independence that Suzuki had wanted, relying instead on the national government for postwar reconstruction funds, Uno argues that the effort inscribed a certain "self-help" ethos into the city government that, combined with the construction of infrastructure and shared public space, strengthened Kamaishi's cohesiveness and identity.[19]

Although Nippon Steel's Kamaishi plant thrived in the early postwar era, the company's infrastructural diversification would make Kamaishi decreasingly relevant to the company's fortunes. Kamaishi thus became a case study of Japanese industrial decline.[20] By the 1970s and 1980s, the Japanese steel industry faced waves of economic turmoil: the higher fuel prices resulting from global oil crises, intense competition from upstart Korean manufacturers, and the challenges associated with the 1986 Plaza Accord and the almost instantaneous doubling of the value of the yen and the cost of its exports. With consolidation and rationalization in the steel industry, Nippon Steel made the decision in 1988 to shutter the Kamaishi plant, moving production to its more modern facilities elsewhere in Japan.[21] Kamaishi was the logical site for Nippon Steel to close a plant, given both the difficulty of expanding or modernizing a facility built in a narrow cranny of the sawtooth Sanriku coast as well as its distance from the postwar industrial heartland of central Honshu.[22] In part through the efforts of the local steelworkers' union and the appeals and efforts of the local government, Nippon Steel displayed some reluctance to dramatically harm its own reputation by departing altogether, leaving behind both a wire-making factory and a commitment to provide support for local efforts to attract and build new businesses. Indeed, although employment continued to decline, the city avoided the complete collapse that the mill's closing might have meant in part because public-private ventures, some unsuccessful in the longer term, helped to sustain a number of the jobs and families that had previously relied upon Nippon Steel.[23]

As Nakamura Naofumi notes in a summary of *Kibōgaku* in the English-language volume *Japan's Shrinking Regions in the 21st Century*, these institutional and historical developments in Kamaishi left three legacies important for the construction of hope: networks (professional, personal, administrative) within and outside of Kamaishi, an ability to connect individual to community hopes, and a strong local identity, the one that Uno had partly attributed to Suzuki's leadership.[24] Indeed, much of the rest of the *Kibōgaku* project works as the aspirational outcome of the project's initial forays into Kamaishi's conflict-ridden past. The Kamaishi of the 2000s is a struggling community, one not riven by deep economic, social, or political divisions, but ideally unified by a sense of common purpose to overcome the economic consequences of deindustrialization. Particularly in the subsequent chapters—carefully researched and effectively presented—we see the occasional struggle in the impulses behind the *Kibōgaku* project: the social scientific goal of laying bare the causes of current circumstances versus the social, ethical goal of using Kamai-shi as an example of how to build hope. Kase Kazutoshi's contribution on the local fishing industry provides an unsparing glimpse of the local politics that once made the fishing industry the poor and largely disorganized counterpart of the thriving steel industry while emphasizing as well its crucial current role in providing alternative opportunities for self-employment to the unmoored victims of corporate downsizing. In a different vein, Ōhori Ken's chapter hints at tensions between town officials with declining resources on hand and local entrepreneurs and small-business owners, many of them on the younger side, seeking support for the development of ecotourism among other priorities.

This is, of course, a progressive vision, one that sits easily alongside the attention that Japan's citizen groups have attracted among foreign and domestic researchers alike. Political scientists have focused on them largely because of the way they constitute Japan's "civil society," the Tocquevillian term that Robert Putnam famously used to evaluate the quality of democracy in Italy and the United States.[25] Much of the research on Japan's NGO sector builds from the premise that a robust civil society is essential to the success and health of a democracy. These NGOs, though not the kinds of civic organizations Putnam had in mind in his research on the associational sectors in Italy and the United States, have been instrumental in the distribution of welfare benefits within Japan and the handling of development assistance overseas.[26] It invokes the idea of citizens who, through discussion and diligence, keep the ship of state on a steady course while working together generously to solve common problems and to tend to the needs of the less fortunate.

It is not, however, a radical vision, which in some ways marks it historically. When the Institute of Social Science was established in 1947, it was shaped largely by the kinds of Marxist scholars who were at the heart of the Japanese social science of the era. Not revolutionaries, the scholars were instead scientists, focused on trying to understand the fundamental laws governing human behavior and social change, as Marx himself had been. The institute's mandate to carry out domestic and comparative research that might assist Japan's postwar development shaped a series of critical, scholarly projects aimed at amassing extraordinary amounts of data while fitting them into relatively cohesive narratives about political, economic, and social transformation. And for much of this history, there seemed to be alternatives for political and social organization—socialism, social democracy, and so forth—that might maintain the cherished freedoms associated with Japan's postwar democracy while also eliminating some of the cruelties and insecurity associated with its market economy, particularly after it soured in the 1990s. As one of the Institute's senior faculty, Hirowatari Seigō, writes in volume 1 of the *Kibōgaku* series, the project differed in style from earlier five-year projects, which had focused on grand themes like "fascism and democracy," "the welfare state," "contemporary Japanese society," and even "the 20th century system."[27] *Kibōgaku* involved the effort to think beyond the end to capitalism that earlier studies had in some ways taken for granted, considering instead how people might try to build a better life for themselves in an "era without utopias" (*yūtopia no nai jidai*).[28]

Modesty becomes the *Kibōgaku* authors. Although the title itself, as well as the seemingly religious cover photo of the sun peeking out from behind the clouds over the ocean, marks the book project as exceptionally ambitious, the authors recognize that the precise configurations necessary to rebuild hope in Japan will not match Kamaishi's. Their emphasis on local identity and on intraregional and interregional networks boils down in part to the need for a sense of community (necessary for turning personal hope into collective hope) and for the social and economic ties that are necessary to discover and act on opportunities while not closing the town or its workers off to others. In a short book summing up *Kibōgaku*'s implications, Genda, the labor sociologist, even draws on Mark Granovetter's classic 1973 sociological paper "The Strength of Weak Ties," which emphasizes that overlapping elements of closer-knit friendship circles can provide essential opportunities for information exchange and community formation.[29] Genda's point is not that all hope is lost if people cannot identify weak ties between their own groups and others but rather that young people in Japan facing a challenging employment market should be open to mobilizing broad ties across areas to build opportunities for themselves and their communities, including through innovative and entrepreneurial collaborations with local governments. It is through these connections—salvation in the social—that Kamaishi's opportunities will develop, kindling the city's hope itself.

Feeling the U-Turn

One of Japan's most widely discussed demographic trends, the "U-turn," makes a late but sustained and important entry in the *Kibōgaku* series. The Kamaishi material is located mostly in volumes 2 and 3, with volume 3 turning toward final chapters that draw heavily on a social survey of the city. Unsurprisingly to anyone familiar with rural demography in Japan, the survey includes questions that tease out respondents' participation in the "U-turn," the widely noted Japanese variant of "reverse migration," or people moving (back) from city to countryside. Indeed, while reverse migration is well-known in demography, the phrase "U-turn" is used almost exclusively in studies of Japan (or in reference to those studies), and its near-ubiquity in Japanese-language research suggests just how pervasive is the image of people who, having spent time in the metropolis, return to their rural hometowns for marriage, to take over the family business, or to care for elderly family.[30] Its relevance would have been immediately apparent to the researchers themselves as many of their interlocutors in Kamaishi's city government had themselves gone to college in the prefectural capital, Morioka, or even in Sendai or Tokyo, some beginning their careers in major cities before returning to their coastal town.

Particularly because of the importance of "weak ties" in Genda's analysis, the U-turn itself is viewed as a clear asset for Kamaishi, despite the complexity in these individual stories and in the data the survey provides. Sociologist Ishikura Yoshihiro's chapter on Kamaishi's U-turners captures a wide array of goals of those returning home, including a long plan to take over a family business upon one's parents' retirement or death, marriage to a resident, or relocation with one's family to a more spacious environment. In laying out their circumstances—most return single and then live at home with their parents for a time—Ishikura provides a somewhat gritty sense of what it means for people who had sought to build lives outside of a declining area to return, usually within a decade.[31]

In her chapter on the "life course" of the city's migrants and returnees, sociologist Nishino Yoshimi pays special attention to survey results which show that Kamaishi's U-turners evince somewhat more hope about the future than do those who have lived all their lives in the city. The numbers are too small for her to make fully reliable claims, as she knows, and she recognizes as well what an odd finding this might seem to be; after all, many U-turners appear in Kamaishi after having failed to build lives elsewhere.[32] Rather than dwell on the possibility that hopeful answers suggest a bit of rationalization regarding their futures, she instead suggests that the city's spot as a "safety net" that catches the unfortunate and holds them with loving families, groups of friends, and a beautiful natural environment can entice them into loving and extolling the virtues of the city's quiet charms and comforts. This would, she suggests, help to generate hope for Kamaishi itself. Working with the same findings, Ishikura suggests as well that more U-turners might be attracted if the sources of the city's pride were located not so much in the past—its steel-town glory days, its rugby team's absurdly long streak as national champions in the 1980s, and the like—as in the present and future. If the past serves as a source of pride, it should be in the work of earlier generations fighting in difficult times to build a better future for themselves and their city, just as young people today might.

As the *Kibōgaku* researchers are aware, these debates over the U-turn and its meaning often take place in major urban areas in scholarly and nonacademic environments alike. And they are tinged by the omnipresent threats of urban condescension toward the bumpkins of the countryside or of nostalgic romanticism regarding the periphery's charms, lost to the selfish, materialistic professionals and office drones of Tokyo. The U-turn's function in the project is to provide a sociologically grounded avenue for transformation of labor environments because of the "weak ties" linking some younger residents to counterparts elsewhere in Japan, allowing for the spread of knowledge, skills, and opportunities. But it also speaks to the complex forms of resentment, aspiration, guilt, satisfaction, disappointment, and wonder that accompany transformative journeys from one place to another. These too are legion in Japanese popular culture, particularly in stories of those who lose and find themselves by making the kind of U-turn that the *Kibōgaku* authors see as hopeful for Kamaishi.

The renowned playwright, actor, and screenwriter Kudō Kankurō tweaks these stories in his remarkably successful 2013 morning drama, *Ama-chan*. The fifteen-minute episodes of a typical morning drama series are shown six days each week on NHK, Japan's national broadcaster, and each six-month-long series focuses on the travails of a heroine either struggling to pursue her professional/artistic dream (for most contemporary series) or to support her husband and family in theirs (for most of the historical ones). They typically provide a bit of reassuring entertainment on a daily basis for viewers (overwhelmingly women for most series), and they are major stepping-stones for young stars as well as reliable and respectable paychecks for established older actors in supporting roles.

Kudō, known for his oddball humor as well as for his background in rural Miyagi Prefecture, sets his story in the prefecture just north of Miyagi, Iwate—home to the real Kamaishi. The story is primarily about Aki, the good-hearted but none-too-bright daughter of Haruko, a native of the fictional town of Minami Sanriku, who had famously and destructively left her hometown for Tokyo eighteen years earlier, on the very day a new train line connected it to the outside world. When Haruko's marriage to a kind but distracted taxi driver becomes too stifling and as Aki struggles to fit into her high school's conformist culture, Haruko bolts back to Iwate with Aki, moving in with her mother (the redoubtable Miyamoto Nobuko, known to international audiences for her lead performances in films such as *Tampopo* and *A Taxing Woman*). Surprisingly, Aki becomes a local tourist draw as by far the youngest and most comically inept *Amasan* (sea urchin diver) in town.

The program is remarkable for a number of reasons and was widely praised at the time by critics, although it was not the ratings winner that several of its more openly nostalgic successors have since been. Kudō's cheekiness comes across partly in the show's gentle mockery of Japan's pop idol culture even as he casts Koizumi Kyōko, one of the top idols of the 1980s, as Aki's mother. In her surprisingly peppery performance, Koizumi becomes something of a mouthpiece for Kudō himself, primarily in her disdain not for the tedium of small-town life or for those who enjoy it (though this had clearly motivated her character eighteen years earlier) but rather for the insecurity that small-towners frequently display about the superior wealth and sophistication of those in the cities.[33] The circumstances surrounding Haruko's departure, return, and life in between are far too idiosyncratic to be taken as meaningfully symbolic of the U-turn, just as are the kookiness of Minami Sanriku's locals (played by some of Japan's best comic actors) and the clueless self-absorption of Aki herself, although perhaps her diffidence and general stupidity make her a pretty good stand-in for an average teenager. But Haruko is a recognizable figure to NHK's large audience because the U-turn she undertakes and her fraught and complex emotions around it (in addition to those of everyone around her) are omnipresent reference points of contemporary Japanese culture. Everyone senses that the U-turn is not simply a relocation for professional reasons, a choice one makes after a calculator tells them where the cost/benefit analysis is most favorable; as with "city girl/boy returns home after many years" elsewhere, it is an opportunity for regret, for failed aspirations, for new love, for reconnection with one's roots, for family closeness, for despair, and even for hope.

Before the Miracle

Kudō cleverly turns one of the motifs of "morning dramas"—dates as intertitles—against the program's goofy charm. Because morning dramas frequently follow the process of the heroine's maturation, the dates show the passage of time, alerting the audience to the number of months or years passing between crucial parts of the story. *Ama-chan* also uses them to signal the flashbacks to 1988, when Haruko fled her town during the inaugural run on the new train line that was ostensibly going to turn Minami Sanriku from a sleepy backwater into a modern cosmopolis—and, coincidentally, when the real-life Nippon Steel was negotiating how heavily to drop the hammer on the Kamaishi plant. But the intertitles become more frequent and insistent as the story moves from 2008 through 2009 and into 2010, with the story cutting between Aki's return to Tokyo as an aspiring idol and the people of Minami Sanriku going on with their lives. However, the effect of the intertitles is by this time less to convey the months that Aki has spent in training as a singer and dancer and more to instill in the audience a sense of gut-wrenching dread, as the dates become a drumbeat, particularly as they count off individual days in 2011. Viewers are all too aware that the story is based in coastal Iwate in this time because the March 11 tsunami is going to rip through the fictional town, perhaps taking some of the show's characters with it.

Ama-chan is too canny to fall into easy predictability with the death of a key character or two whose loss might become the sentimental glue for its final month on the air. The disaster—the multistory rush of water engulfing entire cities, channeled through the narrow valleys of the saw-tooth coastline and leveling neighborhoods so far from the ocean that there was not even the smell of saltwater before the tsunami—is instead displaced. We see it from inside of a tunnel, as Aki's friend is aboard a train heading out of Minami Sanriku, feeling the earthquake and then watching from a distance, seeing what is left of her hometown. The closest the show comes to direct depiction is through a series of still photos of the model city in the train station's office as it is overwhelmed by little plastic waves.

The tsunami hit Kamaishi—like the fictional town, a coastal city with a station connecting it via infrequent, two-car trains to the cities and bullet train lines inland—roughly thirty-five minutes after the earthquake itself, breaching the recently completed seawall that had been lauded as the world's deepest breakwater. It swept in alongside the coast, cutting northwest and then southwest along the valley around the Kasshigawa River, bringing a thirty-foot-tall wall of water toward offices, homes, schools, and other buildings so far from the ocean that people would not necessarily have recognized they were indeed in a coastal flooding zone despite frequent reminders by the local and national authorities. That distance cost many their lives, as people allowed their own memories of previous earthquakes and the remoteness of the ocean to lead them to remain at home or to climb onto their own upper floors rather than to escape to the highest evacuation shelters in the mountains immediately surrounding the city.

The uncertainty also drove difficult and immensely painful calculations for many people. The general expectation was that the city would have roughly an hour before the tsunami would hit, more time than it actually had. Many had to guess whether to rush to their children's schools or trust that they would be safe with their teachers, to save elderly parents too infirm or stubborn to escape on their own, to race vulnerable fishing boats out over the tsunami to safety, or to hurry up to the top of the evacuation platforms built into the mountainsides and to trust that any loved ones would do the same. These calculations played out along Japan's northeastern coast, later producing the dark rumors of frantic drivers hitting pedestrians while rushing to save loved ones or to escape, leaving the unfortunate victims too injured to have any chance against the oncoming waves. They would in many communities leave survivors with extraordinary levels of guilt for not having saved their children, spouses, friends, or parents.

The Reversed Periphery

On the second floor of the Starbucks next to Ikebukuro's Junkudo bookstore in northwestern Tokyo, about 325 miles southwest of Kamaishi, I glanced up at the other customers as the temblor began to shake the building, looking, I guess, for cues as to what I was supposed to do and when I was supposed to do it. After perhaps six or seven seconds of some of the most violent shaking I had ever felt, I was the last one at a long, packed table of coffee drinkers to get under it, staying there and still feeling the unnerving vibrations in my legs as staff members entered and politely led us down the steps and outside. We reentered the building after several minutes to collect our belongings. I had tried in vain to call my wife, with many of the cell phone circuits jammed, but managed to get a news flash indicating that the earthquake had taken place off the coast of Miyagi, which I showed to the high school girl standing behind me as she was chatting with someone she had somehow reached on her phone, asking "Where was it? Was it inside the country?"

Over the next ninety minutes, I walked across north-central Tokyo, trying to reach the University of Tokyo, where my wife was working at the time. It took an earthquake for me to realize how little I knew of Tokyo above ground, with my navigational sense tied firmly to the colored lines of the city's extensive subway maps. I took a meandering route—guiding myself by getting from one subway station to the next—that led me past several evacuation centers, usually parks or schoolyards on high ground, with teachers corralling their students until their parents could arrive from work or from home to take them somewhere safe. The streets and sidewalks were packed but unnervingly quiet; I remember only once hearing someone in distress, a woman in a work uniform sobbing loudly and uncontrollably, with two colleagues comforting her. From what I could tell, we had narrowly dodged the Big One, the once-every-seventy-years cataclysm hanging over Tokyo like the rumbling sword of Damocles. I saw no damaged buildings and even had a moment to reflect on the marvels of Japan's earthquake-resistant engineering after experiencing the first and most violent of the aftershocks, when I was standing paralyzed underneath a highway overpass, absolutely certain that I was about to die. Even today, I am ashamed that over the next hour or so of almost giddy relief, with the Earth occasionally spasming as if God were losing the battle to contain a barely suppressed series of laughs, I had no idea (and did not even consider) that I had dodged nothing. Like Tokyo itself, I was simply peripheral to what had happened; for about two hours, longer than most, I was blissfully unaware of what was still happening.

It took a bit of searching to find my wife; the fifth floor of her building was nearly empty, and one hallway had been blocked off because it had actually cracked right between the older and newer parts of the building, the most severe physical damage I would see in Tokyo. She, like her colleagues, had evacuated and had gone downstairs to Hongo-Dori in front of the university's famed Red Gate; many aimed their cell phone cameras at it during the aftershock that had me mute with fear under the highway underpass two miles west, wondering if they would capture the exact moment when the very symbol of Japanese higher education crumbled. When I went to the main headquarters of the Institute of Social Science, I found a crowd of about twenty people—including several of the *Kibōgaku* editors and contributors—hanging out in the back lobby, watching TV and sharing cookies and coffee. Everyone knew me personally as a former staffer, frequent institute visitor, and also as my wife's partner, and as they pointed out where she was sitting, there was a good-natured "isn't this romantic, he came for his wife" vibe, although I noticed throughout the evening that there was similar and palpable relief whenever another old friend or colleague would wander in, many of us there simply because we had nowhere else to go.

The room's inhabitants were glued to the televisions, and it took me several minutes to understand what I was seeing, first the black ooze cutting across an agricultural plot in Miyagi, the boats toppling against bridges and embankments in Iwate, and as the extent of the tsunami became clearer and darkness fell outside, the increasingly startling images of fiery debris in Kesennuma and exploding gas tanks in Chiba. Most people there were, of course, particularly concerned about their friends and interlocutors in Kamaishi, where they had spent so much time over the preceding seven years. Everyone seemed relatively confident about the safety of the region's nuclear reactors, although I received a late-night e-mail from a friend who, I later learned, had by chance been at a meeting at the moment of the earthquake with several scientists. They had immediately begun to check their cell phones, determining the location of the quake and considering how bad things might get; they made ominous comments about the Fukushima Dai-Ichi reactor, so my friend colorfully warned me (unnecessarily) to stay away from the area.

In the days that followed, Princeton, where I was teaching at the time, urged me to leave Japan (generously offering to help my extended family to leave as well), as the news about the Fukushima disaster doubtless convinced a number of the university's scientists that those of us in Tokyo were at serious risk of nuclear contamination. At the university's request, I tracked down as many graduate students as I could to ensure their safety, many expressing irritation that they now had one more anxious parent to mollify. I was committed to stay, far less out of personal courage than out of family complications: cutting and running would, as usual, otherwise have been my preferred option. In the following days, my wife and I trekked across our neck of far western Tokyo, taking advantage of the rail system's power-related slowdown to explore the backstreets of the Tachikawa region, stopping at back-alley suburban coffee shops and finding the occasional drugstore that still had stocks of toilet paper, one with an exasperated clerk wondering why people were so damned greedy for it. We had to nervously check news about the water supply, particularly after a rainstorm drew contaminated water into central Tokyo's system; the city government in Kunitachi helpfully announced on its website that our source was different, that we were safe. The magnitude of the disaster was coming into view, with the daily newspapers running two-page-wide summary accounts of the day's events, this in addition to the pages and pages of stories of people looking for their husbands, wives, parents, children. And to the unnerving long-distance photos of a ghostly Fukushima Dai-Ichi plant spurting out grayish clouds that seemed ominous despite our recognition that radioactive cesium has no color.

Even reading and watching were physically draining, as we were peppered by the frequent aftershocks that could momentarily rock us into stomach-clenching fear before we had to turn back to the questions of each day: what food we could eat, what provisions we needed, whether we needed to think seriously about evacuation from Tokyo. And these of course led to a profound sense of personal guilt whenever I would put the immediacy of my reactions—discomfort, anxiety, fear—aside long enough to think of the profound, bottomless grief of those I watched on television as they discussed their loved ones, presumably crushed and drowned beneath the rubble, their bodies dragged out to sea by the receding ocean.

I remember in particular my inability to control myself from the cathartic effect of watching a television report of the last people to be safely rescued, a sixteen-year-old high school student who had been home from school that day and his eighty-year-old grandmother, both under the rubble for nine days until Self-Defense Forces (SDF) soldiers located and saved them in Ishinomaki, Miyagi. The footage included the boy's fifty-seven-year-old father sitting next to the boy's hospital bed with the teen masked and rehydrating, repeating his words on being found by the soldiers: "Thank God, you've saved us" (*tasukatte yokatta*).

Just a few months after the earthquake, one longtime resident of Tokyo reminded me that Japan would get beyond this; it was, essentially, a bad blow to the coastal region of three prefectures, and that was about it. Others, particularly those who supported nuclear power, pointed out that it was quite possible that the speedy and perilous evacuation of the zone near the Fukushima Dai-Ichi plant had likely cost more lives, particularly among elderly evacuees, than the accident itself might have; if anything, to them, the disaster demonstrated the relative safety of nuclear energy, and it was human panic that engineered casualties. All of this may well be true. But, as one friend later said to me, if one were in Tokyo throughout this period, it was easy to feel that Japan was simply going over a cliff, with no bottom in sight.

I tried to combat my own morose slide by volunteering, although going up to Tōhoku itself was unthinkable for the first month or so. Quite apart from the breakdown in transportation, the media emphasized that a number of would-be rescuers in the 1995 Kobe earthquake had required rescue themselves as they had none of the skills, knowledge, or tools that would allow them to be useful in the disaster. Alto saxophone and movie trivia were not among the specialized skills required of first responders, and I realized, with no small amount of relief, that I would be a drain on rather than an addition to needed resources. Instead, I went to the Saitama Super Arena, a soccer stadium that became a shelter for those evacuated from Futaba-machi, the now permanently contaminated town hosting the Fukushima Dai-Ichi plant. After standing in a long line all morning, as people queued to be part of the volunteer army supporting the victims, I managed to get in and was then teamed with two fourteen-year-old boys who became my bosses. Out of school because of spring break, they had become visible and seemingly ubiquitous features of the arena's volunteer circus, much of it headed by self-confident and apparently seasoned NGO veterans, with the rest of us largely following orders. The kids waved me in past the queue each of the following days that week, and I spent most of my time collecting, breaking down, and reassembling cardboard boxes as food trays with which the victims could pick up breakfast, lunch, or dinner and carry it back to their families, who were living in cardboard-petitioned sections of the arena's concrete hallways. I had gone there hoping perhaps to speak with some of the victims, to get a sense of their circumstances, with the ghastly, discreditable expectation that I might be able to write about their experiences later. Once there, however, I realized that I was walking on eggshells. The only time I spoke with evacuees directly was when I asked tentatively, in the most polite Japanese I could summon, "Does anyone need a tray?" One of the men in line—who, like his neighbors, had probably been pulled out of his home at night, then spent a week with his family on the road, and now lived alongside hundreds of other families in a concrete hallway with acoustics that could drive one mad—looked like he was barely suppressing the urge to kill me. I then asked one of the kids to take over the tray-distribution task.

I'm projecting, of course. But I myself was closer to murder than I would have predicted. I tended to get irritable about other foreigners popping into the evacuation shelter, as if I alone were the friendly *gaijin* who uniquely understood the victims' pain. This was most pronounced on Day 2, when two white musicians playing traditional Japanese instruments set up in the arena's lobby, performing for over an hour. They seemed to delight a number of volunteers and perhaps some of the victims, and I imagined grimly the accolades they likely received ("That's so great, foreigners doing classical Japanese music! Young Japanese won't play that at all!"). This innocuous performance—no different, really, than that by a Japanese college student band that had shown up earlier—left me in an irrational, barely suppressed rage.

It is not a proud memory. I myself was in a glass house, absurdly attached to my visible part in making cardboard boxes with two fourteen-year-olds who had to slow down to explain everything to me, even as there were a hundred or more able-bodied Japanese waiting in line each day to do the same thing that I was doing, only more quickly, with less drama, and probably more competently. Speaking frankly, I resented the well-meaning (and, truth be told, obviously talented and skilled) musicians' reminding me of my own emotional neediness through the disaster, and later of the difficulty of explaining to friends what the whole thing "felt" like without preposterously making myself the star of the story, as I have in this section. But their having robbed me of the emotional payoff I had wanted from volunteering also opened my eyes to the difficulties faced by many well-meaning people, including those working for the national and local governments, in crafting a satisfying conclusion for a story that generated not just misery and grief but also unfathomable dread.

And so my subsequent and more engaged reading of the *Kibōgaku* volumes in the wake of the disaster, which preceded the generous invitation of my University of Tokyo colleagues to take me along to Kamaishi in the first of my post-tsunami visits, was marked in part by my solipsistic reaction to the disaster and my eagerness to see how others might help to fashion a better ending for the catastrophe's victims. The public debates that followed about the disaster within Tokyo often referred to the city's responsibility for the nuclear disaster as the consumer of the electricity being created ominously closely to people's homes in these rural communities and included the ubiquitous reminders to "listen to local voices" even as someone in Tokyo would likely collect, translate, and publicize those voices. The debates also suggested that many were grappling with what it meant to be committed to the Tōhoku region, to understand Tokyo's fraught responsibilities toward it, and to be uncertain of how to craft a good, new ending for a story that had already been perilously close to ending badly long before the Pacific Ocean claimed thousands of lives on March 11.

Kamaishi Stories

Kamaishi lost roughly a thousand residents to the tsunami. Other towns lost more, with Miyagi Prefecture's Ishinomaki (a massive and consolidated municipality linking many smaller towns) and the much smaller Rikuzentakata, in Iwate, together accounting for nearly a third of the deaths. In Ōfunato, just sixteen miles south of Kamaishi, the narrow mouth to the city's fishing port channeled the water so tightly that the tsunami was reportedly nearly eighty feet in height. And so in the weeks that followed,

Kamaishi, despite the scale of its loss, was a bit forgotten in the international attention to the catastrophe.

It was instead recognized in Japan for more hopeful reasons. Since the mid-2000s, the highly active Disaster Preparedness Office in Kamaishi's City Hall had contracted with Katada Toshitaka, a Gunma University professor of engineering who had begun something of a crusade after the 2004 Indian Ocean tsunami to educate Japanese—especially children—to protect themselves in the event of a tsunami. With the cooperation of the city government, he carried out a survey of Kamaishi's children in December 2005, one that showed that most placed faith in authorities to rescue them in the event of a tsunami. If their homes were listed as outside of danger zones on publicly available maps, they were reassured that they would be safe. If caught between school and home at the time of a tsunami warning, they would head to one or the other rather than look immediately for high ground to which they might escape. Kamaishi's public schools, working with Katada as their advisor over the next several years, preached a kind of radical self-help to students, telling them that the real lesson from previous tsunamis was not to trust that damage would be limited, as it had been in recent decades, but rather to respond calmly but assertively to get themselves out of harm's way as quickly as possible. Indeed, after the 2010 Chile tsunami, students at Kamaishi East Junior High School went on a campaign, handing out flyers to nearby residents encouraging them to think carefully about safety and later that year undertaking a major drill with neighboring Unosumai Elementary School. Their slogan—"from people who can be saved to people who can save"—reflected a sense that their disaster preparedness might be beneficial to others. On March 1, 2010, the *Asahi Shimbun* ran an article about the city's efforts, quoting Kamaishi's Disaster Preparedness Office chief Yamada Mamoru on survey results showing that only 34 percent of people said that they planned to go to one of the city's evacuation spots in the event of a tsunami: "It's meaningless if that percentage isn't 100%. . . . It'll be great if these kids can share their awareness of disasters with adults."

The strategy seemed to bear fruit on March 11. When students standing on top of Kamaishi East Junior High School remarked to their teachers that they believed that the school's height would be insufficient to protect them from the tsunami expected to channel through the valley, several made the decision to run out and to reach the evacuation shelters on the nearby hillside. The entire school quickly evacuated, with many of the junior high students grabbing the hands of crying elementary school students who had started to walk home because of a term's-end early dismissal just before the earthquake. Running up the road toward higher ground, they passed a parking garage used as an evacuation platform, but the children judged that it was not high enough. They kept running farther up the hillside road, passing a small road cutting across the mountain, where other adults were waiting. At this point, they could see the tsunami moving farther and farther into the valley, having already demolished much of downtown Kamaishi; the kids wisely moved further up the hill, finally reaching a national highway completed only a week earlier. From there, they could see that the tsunami had breached the tops of their schools, covered the garage, and demolished the road below them. They began to walk along the mountain highway toward the city's designated shelter; several truck drivers along the way stopped to crowd them into the backs of their rigs to get them through the darkness and the cold to shelter. Their response—combined with a number of moments of good fortune, including the recently completed highway that gave them a stable platform on which to stand—saved the lives of all but two of the schools' six hundred students present that day.[34]

The "Kamaishi Miracle" rapidly became one of the top stories in the aftermath of the Tōhoku earthquake of 2011, and it is remembered as the most stirringly positive story to have emerged from the disaster. Professor Katada emerged as the sage of disaster preparation, writing articles and giving talks about the local expression *tendenko* (short for *tsunami-tendenko,* or to go separately in the event of a tsunami). For Katada, this all-too-easily-forgotten folk wisdom of the Tōhoku coast encourages people to save themselves first rather than to go into harm's way to find or to rely on others. With enough planning, preparation, and investment, it ideally operates like Adam Smith's "invisible hand" in the moment of crisis: if everyone trusts that others will also follow the practice, more lives will be saved. It of course raises ethical questions about self-reliance and self-protection rather than a focus on others, and its proponents generally argue that it is an exceptional strategy required only at an exceptional time and is more appropriate for the general public than for emergency responders.[35] But the Kamaishi Miracle seemed to show the wisdom of looking first after oneself. Japanese ethicists would continue to debate the need to plan in advance for those unable to care for themselves as well as the likelihood of survivors' guilt among those who chose to follow the strategy rather than to save their loved ones, such as those who trusted that their children would be safe at school.[36]

This is precisely what happened in the small Miyagi village of Ōgawa, the site of one of the tsunami's most grueling tragedies.[37] At the same time that the well-trained junior high students in Kamaishi were convincing their teachers to trail after them, leading their neighboring elementary school's students up the hillside and past several insufficiently high evacuation spots, the students at Ōgawa Elementary School in Miyagi Prefecture's Ishinomaki—a geographically massive municipality that had absorbed several smaller communities, including the one whose children attended the school—were waiting outside their school for their parents to pick them up. The evacuation shelters in the hillside immediately behind the school would have been high enough to save them, but the path up to them was treacherous, particularly on a snowy, cold day such as March 11. A number of parents did race to the school after the quake to pick up their children; many others did or could not, whether because they were at work or because they assumed that the school, built just one meter above sea level alongside a river eddying into the Pacific, would evacuate the kids—the kind of trust encouraged by *tendenko* proponents. Of the seventy-eight children in the schoolyard that day, seventy-four perished, alongside ten of the eleven teachers there.

As a Japanese colleague said to me, "Disasters are unfair," and it would be hard to consider a more unfair outcome of the 2011 tsunami than the deaths of almost all of the children in a community because of the inadequate planning and poor crisis management by the adults, who were, at the moment, confronted by the seeming risk of injury to the children should they try to race up an icy mountainside to safety. Over the next year, in a tsunami coda that has been discussed exhaustively by engaged writers and journalists but that rarely figures into national images of regional recovery, the community—what remained of it—descended into the kind of local debates, lawsuits, and disputes described by the novelist Russell Banks in his brilliant novel *The Sweet Hereafter*: "Significant pain isolates you anyhow, but under certain circumstances, it may be all you've got, and after great loss, you must use whatever's left, even if it isolates you from everyone else."[38] And it was the loss of those children that led not only to policy-oriented discussions of proper planning—the kind that Kamaishi would epitomize—but also to the investigations and unsatisfying legal battles that would consume parents whose children had been swept up in the cold water, battered against the debris, and found dead later by ambitious, seemingly tireless rescue and recovery teams.[39]

Indeed, the "Kamaishi Miracle" had the strange and profoundly uncomfortable consequence of displaying the town to the national media as a rare site of good news in the muddy landscape despite Kamaishi's grievous losses. Genda would later argue that he found the descriptions of the miracle to be "indelicate," largely because they ended up suggesting that it was the safety of the children—about which Kamaishi officials would express a great deal of pride—that characterized the tsunami's effects on the city, effacing the extraordinary loss there.[40] With a thousand dead, thousands of others left homeless, and the whole city facing nearly unimaginable losses, the success of a smart, well-crafted training program that accomplished what it was meant to (largely because of the bravery of the kids themselves) seemed more like the laudable results of dedicated efforts, not like a miraculous deus ex machina that could stop the waves. In a grateful aside, Genda even refers to a teacher at the junior high school who told him afterward that the *Kibōgaku* project itself had contributed to the miracle; Genda's encouragement during a school assembly of students to use oral history to understand their town's background and its local identity had led to a presentation by an elderly former employee of the steel plant. When students asked him, in conjunction with the assembly's theme, what his dream of the future was, he remarked that it was "to die still having dreams." The teacher told Genda that the remark inspired the students, implying that this too contributed to the communal sense of action and urgency that led them to make their escape.[41]

Genda's version of the story is far from self-aggrandizing; his account instead reads as a warm description which acknowledges the emotional connections that he, like his colleagues, had been fortunate to have with the town. Indeed, it appears in a collection of essays that serves as a sequel to *Kibōgaku*—telling the story of Kamaishi's reemergence, with special respect paid to those who stood their ground and did their duty in the aftermath of the town's devastation[42]—and builds stylistically from the opening and closing chapters of the original volumes, which had evocatively described the train trips to Kamaishi and the physical sensations of being there. The follow-up refers again to the analytical emphases of the original volumes—local identity, networks that extend outside of the city limits—but keeps them in the background, with only limited and tangential reference to the kinds of tensions that can arise among neighbors, officials, and residents when confronted by loss, risk, and uncertainty.

After all, the residents of Kamaishi, like other cities, experienced the full range of disasters: those whose homes had been badly damaged but not enough for full insurance compensation, those who had lost loved ones but at least found the bodies, and those whose family members had simply disappeared in the tsunami, preventing them even the consolation of a funeral. Nakamura's oral history chapter recounts a number of these experiences, providing an opportunity for those willing to share their stories of rescue, recovery, or loss.[43] But the book serves at least in part as a love letter to Kamaishi and its residents, with the authors saying explicitly that they had returned to Kamaishi after the disaster as friends rather than as researchers.

Hope as the New Normal

Prime Minister Kan Naoto's role in the aftermath of the disaster will long be debated.[44] As a longtime truculent and powerful force in the anti–Liberal Democratic Party opposition, Kan had become the second Democratic Party of Japan (DPJ) prime minister, following the fall of Hatoyama Yukio, the short-lived symbol of the transition from LDP to DPJ leadership. Kan had built his career on intense attacks on the cozy relationships among industry, Japan's bureaucracy, and the LDP, having rocketed to fame in the 1990s as a young and handsome minister of Health and Welfare who exposed and apologized for his ministry's scandalously close relations with a medical company that had distributed untreated, HIV-infected blood product to hemophiliacs. In its brief time in power, the DPJ had been both celebrated and vilified for shifting the policy process, aiming to make the country's notoriously powerful bureaucrats more responsive to political will rather than an autonomous force working closely with legislators to achieve the laws and administrative rules they wanted. Whether the DPJ's interpretation of the bureaucracy's power and value was correct was certainly open to question. But the sidelining of key bureaucratic forces and the deliberate shake-up of decision-making procedures would make it easier in the aftermath of the disaster to second-guess those decisions as factors in the government's response. After all, a nuclear meltdown resulting from a tsunami striking a power plant built in an area well-known for natural disasters would seem in retrospect to demand an unyielding, encompassing kind of public outrage from which no one could escape, Kan and his opponents alike. As many observers have noted, one might see the 3.11 disaster as the death knell for Japan's already shaky public trust in government, with Kan as an obvious candidate for removal.

Dealing with a nearly unprecedented natural disaster that quickly became a nuclear nightmare, Kan was innately distrustful of TEPCO, the operator of the Fukushima Dai-Ichi Nuclear Power Plant.[45] The company's astonishingly inept disaster planning and the crass dishonesty of its leadership frustrated him even more, leading him famously to yell at the firm and its employees that they were not to abandon the plant, which he and his advisors worried would suffer a complete and catastrophic meltdown, releasing enough radioactive material to force an evacuation of Tokyo. His initial visits to the rest of the disaster zone—aiming to reassure and answer questions from the evacuees, the newly homeless, the grieving and lost—earned him a small bit of temporary goodwill, but he seems to have missed the cornerstone of US disaster leadership: have the president visit the disaster zone in the immediate aftermath, when victims are urgently vulnerable and looking for any reassurance they can get, and keep the president away in the subsequent months when the extended promises turn out to be largely meaningless. And Kan's decreasingly successful visits to Tōhoku, culminating in a number of televised shots of angry victims shouting at him, seemed only to underscore the sense that he was a terrible prime minister in a crisis, despite the absence of any evidence that a more seasoned or more bureaucratically embedded leader would have helped the situation.

It seems to have been this dual instinct—to maintain his leadership and to keep the bureaucrats at bay—that drove Kan to make his somewhat peculiar decisions in creating and constituting the Reconstruction Design Council, a policy discussion group charged with establishing a course for the reconstruction of the areas afflicted by the disaster. Japan's *shingikai* (discussion council) system has a long history, with groups of academic specialists, public intellectuals, industry members, and citizen group leaders asked in varying combinations to weigh in, often at a ministry's initiative, on a desired legal change both to legitimize it as well as to give a focus-group–like sense of the variety of objections and concerns that might meet its introduction.[46] Kan's council—which included the governors of the three prefectures (Fukushima, Iwate, and Miyagi) most hurt by the disasters, a number of senior and respected scholars, and even a nationally famous screenwriter whose father hailed from Iwate—famously served as a rebuke, as it was visibly constituted by respected intellectuals and public figures rather than by those close to Japan's bureaucracy. Indeed, to the extent that there was coordination between the country's career officials and the council, it took place through the workings of the council's "working group" (*kentō bukai*), a larger collection of scholarly specialists working in such areas as architecture, fisheries, agriculture, welfare, and gender studies, many with deep experience and contacts with key ministries. Genda—chosen both because of his experience as a leading labor scholar concerned with youth employment as well as his ties to Kamaishi through the *Kibōgaku* project—served as one of the working group's nineteen members.

The language of *Kibōgaku* would ultimately suffuse the Reconstruction Design Council's project. Prime Minister Kan himself opened the first meeting by announcing that the March 11 disaster was the greatest crisis Japan had faced in its postwar history. In addition to determining how Japan could best help the Tōhoku region through a forward-working reconstruction effort, he asked that the council, particularly through the representation of the three prefectural governors, take special note of local voices from the disaster. After Kan concluded, Iokibe Makoto, the distinguished political scientist who served as chair of the council, made opening remarks that emphasized the fateful unity of the disaster region and the rest of the country: "What we on this Council have been asked to do is to overcome the tragic circumstances of the Great East Japan Earthquake, and to make a turn toward a Japanese society that has new hope."[47]

In other words, and in a turn that would remain consistent throughout much of the public discourse, Tōhoku's fate was connected with Japan's, a connection that makes sense both because of the omnipresent gloom of post-tsunami Tokyo and of the ways in which Tokyo tended to appropriate the regions as its own. It was notable, for example, that the informal slogan of the disaster—*Ganbare Nippon* ("Hang in There, Japan!" or perhaps "Good Luck!" or "Do Your Best!" or even "Cheer Up!," to use the translation of the book title about Viet and Duc from chapter 3)—would be visibly transformed the farther one traveled from Tokyo. On the bullet train tracks up to the north, one would quickly find "Ganbare Tōhoku" replacing "Ganbare Nippon." By the time one alighted from the train, the sign might be "Ganbare Fukushima," or "Ganbare Miyagi," or "Ganbare Iwate." When one finally arrived to visit family, to do volunteer work, to meet with local officials, or to fulfill a reconstruction contract, one would be confronted by large makeshift signs, graffiti-style, of "Ganbare Ishinomaki." Or "Ganbare Rikuzentakata." Or "Ganbare Kamaishi." Calling these acts of local resistance might be appropriate, at least insofar as many victims and local residents expressed nervous resentment about the national appropriation of their grief and anxiety even as they avidly sought the assistance that such appropriation seemed to herald. As Richard Samuels has trenchantly noted, the idea of "bonds"—*kizuna*—became an essential element of the post-disaster rhetoric, particularly as competing political forces co-opted the disaster for their own visions of national transformation, whether through radical and forward-looking reform or through a look to the past that had been lost through Japan's modernization, materialism, and acquiescence to global (or Western) influence.[48]

Despite the warm, emotive feel of the word *kizuna*, its conceptual flexibility allows it to fit within the analytical frame that the *Kibōgaku* authors had established, particularly given their emphasis on the importance of networks. For many of the economic historians involved in the volume, the networks appeared somewhat organically, the combination of family, education, and labor-related relationships that might tie members of any one community to members of another. Indeed, it was specifically Kamaishi's embeddedness in a dense institutional environment of political leaders, industrial forces, and labor activists that created the conditions allowing for hope—that had maintained pockets of wealth in the city and allowed local officials and labor leaders to push for protective concessions from Nippon Steel as it packed up and left town. Genda himself had sought to theorize these connections through reference to Granovetter's "weak ties," imagining these as porous connections allowing for flows and mobilization of information that people might use to develop and take advantage of employment opportunities.

Over the course of the two months of meetings, the council members and working group scholars struggled with the political and ethical ramifications of reconstruction planning. The biggest initial question was whether the council should deal in any meaningful way with the nuclear disaster at the Fukushima Dai-ichi plant. In the council's planning stage, the Fukushima nuclear disaster was regarded as an ongoing "crisis management" issue rather than an issue for reconstruction planning, but in the first meeting a number of voices expressed concern about sidelining the nuclear crisis and others objected to it. One speaker referred both to the nuclear disaster's centrality and to the possibility that it would simply overwhelm all other reconstruction efforts:

> In Fukushima, there were four things that caused damage: the earthquake, the tsunami, the nuclear meltdown, and reputational damage (*fuhyō*). Put those together, and it's the nuclear disaster that's at the center of this. . . . When the classification of the Fukushima accident was raised to Level 7, the same level as the Chernobyl meltdown, it shook Japan, it shook the whole world. We still don't know how extensive the damage is going to be. That's how serious a catastrophe this is. . . . I'd like to create a forum to discuss the damage from the nuclear disaster, a place where people from across the country can come together to discuss and to develop a plan for reconstruction and recovery. This is a problem that requires the help of people from across the country.[49]

Separating the Fukushima disaster from the overall council discussion, of course, seems on the one hand to be absurd on its face, as if the council's final report would be titled "The Elephant in the Room" or "Other Than That, Mrs. Lincoln, How Did You Enjoy the Play?" On the other, the years since the disaster have only amplified the view among many victims in tsunami-stricken zones far from the meltdown that their suffering, their need for reconstruction, has been forgotten, particularly with continuing global attention to the nuclear accident. Even at the time, the council's members struggled with what they clearly intended to be a positive set of recommendations that would bring consolation and optimism to those still seeking the bodies of their loved ones or wondering when they might move out of temporary housing. The Fukushima disaster raised questions that several members viewed as foundational, even metaphysical. As one council member put it,

> I think we have to write about what this disaster points to as a whole from the perspective of civilizational history. I guess this means that civilization

and nature are always in a great tension with one another, with the nuclear power problem perhaps being the most important example of this. This disaster has forced us to reflect on overriding issues, on the way Japanese society exists, the way Japanese people think about things. So as we try to prioritize our work properly, I guess it's realistic for us that we would bracket and set aside the nuclear disaster and energy policy. But if we do bracket them and keep them separate, I think we can't just follow that track in our deliberations. That is, even as we're engaging these issues in our broader discussions and trying to take a stand on what the current nuclear disaster means and what we should do about it, we also need to ensure we are paying attention to the tsunami damage and how that relates to our handling of the nuclear crisis.[50]

Over the next several months, the council's deliberations would run an uncomfortable gamut, encompassing the neoliberal reformers, including Miyagi's governor, Murai Yoshihiro, who wished for the privatization of coastal waters and the infusion of new capital to revitalize the struggling region; the urban planners who hoped to use state authority to make rational, safe, and sustainable plans for redevelopment that would incorporate the needs of local businesses, residents, NGOs, and the like; and the employment and welfare specialists, such as Genda, who were concerned primarily about the economic opportunities for those who would choose to stay in the region. That is, the discussions always risked moving into the unacceptable if necessary realm of the political, whether construed in the broader sense of public debates over leadership, justice, and governance or the narrower question of who gets what, where, when, and how.

And what risked getting lost, particularly as the discussions turned increasingly on the Japan that might have been—the Japan in which parents and teachers paid sufficient attention to the cruel history of tsunamis, the Japan in which the nuclear lessons of Hiroshima and Nagasaki had been properly absorbed, the Japan that could have once said no to the United States and its meretricious offer of atoms for peace—were the local residents. Indeed, although the members of the council themselves frequently made reference to this concern, the working group members, tasked as they were with less public and more analytical approaches, seemed acutely conscious of the dilemmas associated with the construction of a national disaster that might draw attention from the local communities victimized by the disaster. Their discussions—whether over the

consequences of the rationalization of agricultural land for Japan's "farming communities" rather than "Japanese agriculture" per se, or how the
imposition of urban planning from external actors can weaken local
cohesiveness—often took the preservation of local community, the primacy of local voices, for granted as the target of reconstruction. That is,
the discussions reflected a general if loose sense both that local communities are normatively good on their own terms and that national intervention, debated in Tokyo and described as necessary for the country as a
whole, should be first and foremost about the protection of local zones
from the consequences of external management.[51] Tokyo is, of course,
ahead, the vanguard that can assemble intellectual firepower and also
translate the wisdom of the international community for the benefit of
these regions. But the regions themselves, these bastions of a community-
oriented Japan always at risk of disappearing, were to be depicted as
essential to the government's efforts.

And so it is unsurprising that in Genda's final presentation to the working group, he closely discussed the findings of *Kibōgaku*, emphasizing
both the way in which the research program had emphasized the town's
local identity as well as the dangerous implications of seeking to reframe
the city through the lens of a national reconstruction effort:

> To the best of my ability, I've been taking the opportunity on this Working
> Group to speak concretely about employment, the economy, and things like
> that. For that reason, in the aftermath of the disaster, I've not discussed the
> important concept that has come up frequently elsewhere. That important
> concept is hope. Since the earthquake, hope has been a major buzzword. As
> you know, even in announcing the 7 Reconstruction Principles guiding the
> Council, the Council mentioned it explicitly, and with wide support: "we shall
> continue to engage in further discussions aimed at formulating a 'blueprint'
> for reconstruction that will be a source of hope for Japan in the future." Of
> course, having done research for a number of years with many colleagues on
> how to build hope, I'm grateful that it's a major part of the discussion.
>
> But one point I'd like to make is that even if the country, the prefectures
> are trying to create hope, that doesn't become hope for the residents. It's a
> tough way to say it, but hope is something that local residents have to make
> for themselves. In the countless times I've been up to Kamaishi since 2006
> and now since the disaster, one thing that has been pointed out time and
> again is that hope isn't something you can just pull off the shelf. Indeed, it's

something that has emerged from the tough experiences Kamaishi had already had before the disaster, and I think it'll remain true today. . . .

. . . For hope to thrive, people-to-people connections are extremely important. It's crucial to keep the community's connections in order to prevent residents' isolation and loneliness. It's written here in the handout for today's meeting that strong connections with these regions are extremely important, and I think we can agree that that's important for security and safety, but I think that what are really important are lighter connections (*yuruyaka na kankei*), what we know in English as "weak ties" as a sociological concept. I want to emphasize that "weak ties" are really important, in that they are gentler connections that go outside of the region, allowing for the exchange of new ideas and information that are essential for creative reconstruction.

Finally, I just want to say that people who learn the lessons and overcome challenges of the past themselves have confidence, and they are the ones who tend strongly to have hope for the future. If you think of it that way, we can watch and record the efforts of those who show the determination and drive to build new hope out of these challenges. That's what can be handed down to bring to life hope in the future.[52]

For Genda, then, Kamaishi remained a potential model of hope for the rest of the country, but only if the emotional bonds being posited by the Reconstruction Design Council's fervent emphasis on national community could be balanced with respect for the local agency that would be necessary in the region and instructive outside of it. National hope might be achieved, but not by its imposition on the disaster zone by a well-meaning council speaking for a traumatized, guilt-ridden country. It would instead rely on the social scientific drawing of lessons of rebuilding that might be translated elsewhere.

The council's final report stuck with and amplified its framing. Titled (in its official English translation) "Hope Beyond the Disaster," the report provides something of a laundry list of possible priorities for reconstruction. Controversial "special zones" that allow new (and neoliberal) property rights in coastal areas previously dominated by fisheries co-ops and other customary ownership arrangements would be mixed with an emphasis on the importance of maintaining traditional industries. International investors would be welcomed to the disaster zones even as new regulations would be required to ensure disaster resistance in the development of national land. Communities should be rebuilt, though with the understanding that not all communities—particularly those populated only by the elderly—could be rebuilt in the same way. People would be relocated as much as possible to higher ground, except where low-lying development seemed plausible or defensible. Traditional cultures should be protected, but young people and women should take a voice in ensuring that reconstructed communities include them as well. Juggling the competing views of council and working group members, as well as the panoply of demands and concerns of the disaster's victims, the report refers repeatedly if generally to hope as well as to the centrality of national-local connections:

> Our experiences of the disaster should prompt us to give conscious thought to who it is that has supported us in our lives to date, and accordingly, who it is that should be assisted in this current situation. We should heed what our conscience tells us.
>
> It is likely that we will discover what our conscience is telling us through "linkage" activities to other people and things. Linkage comes in many forms: people to people, community to community, company to company, municipalities to prefectural and national governments, local communities with other communities at home and abroad, eastern Japan with western Japan, and country to country. Whether it is large or small in scale "linkage" is the one of the activities that helps us discover the realities of "support," which in turn lights the way to a path towards reconstruction.
>
> It is just such "linkage" activities that will help the people in the disaster-affected regions to first work to achieve "harmonious coexistence" between humanity and nature, from which they can engage in "disaster reduction." . . . Such an approach will generate independent efforts to revitalize local communities and local industries. This, in turn, will elicit "hope." The capacity to live through this disaster with "hope" will become a testimony to the reconstruction process.
>
> The same can be said for other regions not directly affected by the disaster. For example, people in Tokyo should realize just how much they were supported by the Tōhoku region, and seek to repay that support in kind through various linkages. In the context of preparing for a future disaster, it will also be necessary for western Japan to move to support the Tōhoku region. This expanding series of links and support will result in an ever-growing wellspring of "hope" to be nurtured in the hearts and minds of all people.

The way in which so many people, including the members of the Self-Defense Forces, came from around the country to engage in dedicated relief activities is truly an inspirational example of linkage and mutual support being put into practice. If all the people of Japan join in ongoing efforts to support the reconstruction of the Tōhoku region, it will serve to nurture "hope" for the revitalization of Japan and make it easier for everyone to identify with. "Hope" is the seed from which "harmonious coexistence" grows, through linkage between people. This is not limited to Japan, but has the potential to spread on a global scale. Consider for a moment just how this disaster prompted an outpouring of assistance from around the world. This is something we accepted with great emotion.

Thus, just as our appreciation of "harmonious coexistence" strengthens, our heartrending thoughts of those who lost their lives in the disaster may coalesce into an understanding akin to "being at one with those who perished." By commemorating and remembering the countless lives that were lost in the instant of disaster, we will come to cherish the preciousness of our own lives.

We believe that after the destruction, we can assuredly create a firm and unwavering path to reconstruction that is filled with "hope."[53]

The Empire of Hope

One might, in a sense, judge hope in the way that Berlant describes "cruel optimism," an almost addictive, self-punishing attachment to that which is unattainable. But the report's language suggests a complementary reading as well. The authors imagine a symbiotic relationship between a devastated region and a country that seemed, to many coastal residents, as if it had generally forgotten them, that will ensure the future for both. It is an admirable concern in a way, particularly as people aimed to keep the region's struggles in focus as the odorless, omnipresent nightmare of radioactive contamination and its ghastly human consequences suffused the meeting rooms whose lights were now powered almost solely by the fossil fuels that Japan had long sought to limit through the construction of nuclear plants up north. One might also see it in the social-scientific deep dive into the institutional history of a town that was struggling to survive despite the structural transformations that had seemingly hobbled it and threatened much of the rest of the country as well. In this sense, hope might become something akin to a placeholder for something else:

perhaps worry, perhaps grief, perhaps even outrage.[54] And it was this kind of hope that people—armed with the right kind of initiative, the right attitude—might fight their way through structural decline, through anomie, and through the radioactive cloud that served as a constant reminder of what previous hopes had accomplished.

In the months and years leading up to the 2011 tsunami, Japan arguably had a need for hope. Novelist Murakami Ryū—the author of the novel mentioned in chapter 1, describing a mass exodus of teenagers because of Japan's general hopelessness—certainly thought so, as did the social scientists who created *Kibōgaku*. As the anxiety from Japan's sustained period of low economic growth, occasionally spiking with especially terrible years like 1995, morphed rapidly into the consuming grief and dread from the tsunami and nuclear disaster, so too did the calls for hope. *Kibōgaku*'s authors had picked Kamaishi as a sleepy backwater of deindustrialization to serve as the counterintuitive example of hope, the peripheral city capitalizing on local identity and weak ties to build a better future, providing lessons even to those in the center. By the time that Mikuriya Takashi, the distinguished political scientist who served as the principal author of the Reconstruction Design Council's final report, crafted the document, the need for hope seems to have been utterly pervasive and certainly urgent to those in Tokyo suddenly forced to confront the frayed stitches holding their country together. Hope suddenly seemed dependent on the periphery's ability to rebuild, even as this production of national grief and reconstruction sat uneasily with the messier and more durable consequences of mourning and devastation in the region.

Indeed, the U-turn, or even the "I-turn" (the decision of city-born people to relocate to the stricken periphery), has become seen as not just plausible but downright valorous.[55] Some of this migration has been inspired by the young volunteers, many of them previously marginally employed or semi-employed, who had become long-term residents of the volunteer centers in Tōno and elsewhere, choosing to stay in the cities where they had long worked and perhaps found meaning in their removal of debris and cleaning of salty mud from local facilities.[56] For others, such as the creators of "Ishinomaki 2.0," it was an opportunity for U-turners and I-turners alike to take advantage of the spread of information technology and individualized workplaces, encouraging people to create cosmopolitan, innovative spaces even in small, regional cities previously viewed to be virtual prisons for the creative and free-spirited.[57] These visions, of course, trade on romantic images of the peripheral disaster zones, as does the renowned nonfiction writer Kōta Ishii in his memorable and haunting book, later turned into a narrative film, about the search for bodies in Kamaishi after the tsunami. After tracing the extraordinary efforts of local doctors and Buddhist authorities to care for the remains in humane and hygienic ways, the well-born Tokyo native Kōta refers to his own trip back to the city and the ceremony officially closing Kamaishi Junior High No. 2, whose gym had served as a makeshift mortuary after the disaster. Reflecting on the broad generosity of the city's residents towards one another and other victims, Kōta concludes, "Everyone, you're so fortunate to have been born in Kamaishi."[58]

Many of the challenges facing Kamaishi and other coastal cities would, of course, have to be resolved through creative city planning (*machizukuri*), as Richard Samuels and others have noted.[59] And my point in this chapter is not to minimize the importance of these efforts or the contributions that the Japanese government can and should make to the region, or to question the value of locating hope in the ability of these cities to rebuild in humane and sustainable ways. But it is to suggest that diverse emotions—grief, horror, fear, nostalgia, concern, pride, sadness, even moments of relief and elation—associated with the 3.11 disaster are essential to any effort to capture it accurately while also potential threats to the ability to cobble together a national response that is simultaneously unifying and broadly convincing. Hope worked not because it was natural for the event and its aftermath (after all, grief or outrage could have been equally convincing) but because it was natural for what states already encourage us to do: to think of ourselves as part of a larger community whose best days lie before us if only we can overcome our divisions and struggles now. Japan's national melodramas involve a frequently reproduced story of the country's modernization and its economic vicissitudes, mapped onto a notion of the people's fundamental if occasionally wayward innocence. These melodramas, however, script neatly the roles that emotional representation can play for states and leaders responsible for moving their people beyond crises and the divisions that they can engender.

Everything Sinks

The most amusing moment at the Tokyo symposium on Japan's Gross National Cool that I attended more than a decade ago came when someone asked whether the Japanese government ought to fund more college programs on cool industries—anime, manga, pop music—to make sure that it had talented and trained artists for tomorrow. One highly successful anime producer said, "No, we need more law schools, to train us to have better lawyers so our artists get compensated when Americans steal their ideas." He got a good laugh from the audience, for he had been talking mostly about the paltry royalties paid by Hollywood studios to Japanese video game producers whenever *Resident Evil* or some similar game would become a new US film franchise. Had Suzanne Collins already written her novel *The Hunger Games,* with a conceit uncannily similar to that of Takami Kōshun's 1999 novel *Battle Royale* (turned into a superb and highly popular 2000 film by Fukasaku Kinji and scripted by his son Kenta, the director of *We Can't Change the World,* discussed in chapter 1), perhaps more people in attendance would have voted to pump funds into Japan's developing law

Figure 7.1. Governor Koike Yuriko and other leading members of the Party of Hope, October 2017

Source: The Mainichi Newspapers

school system in the hopes of developing the legal skills necessary to puncture Collins's suspicious claims of originality. Still, it would be hard to find an American film more freakishly similar, without acknowledgment, to an earlier Japanese one than the 2010 bro-comedy *Hot Tub Time Machine,* in which four middle-aged American men, with varying levels of insecurity and angst, get whisked back to the 1980s for some zany humor about the music's fashion and music, as well as the possibility, however tortured, that each might learn just a little bit about himself in the process.

Baba Yasuo's 2007 *Bubble Fiction: Boom or Bust* also featured a common household appliance—a jerry-rigged washing machine—capable of sending people back to the 1980s, with cameos and motifs designed to produce the horrified-but-somehow-nostalgic feeling that the decade has belatedly induced in the post-boomer generation.[1] Unlike *Hot Tub Time Machine,* however, the trip to 1989 is not an accident, nor is it treated primarily as an opportunity for self-discovery. Instead, the twenty-one-year-old deeply indebted freeter and hostess Tanaka Mayumi is selected by the Ministry of Finance (MOF) to head back to the era, mostly because she, unlike the bureaucrats, is small enough to fit in the laundry drum. She has two missions: to find her mother, a researcher who somehow invented the contraption and sent herself back, as well as to prevent the passage of a particularly disastrous mortgage/banking bill that had led to the collapse of Japan's bubble economy and to the social and cultural malaise that followed. Hijinks ensue, as do shenanigans and monkey business; the movie has a great deal of fun with its 1980s soundtrack and with images of money-crazed salarymen waving 10,000 yen notes to catch cabs or to reward women just for talking to them. But the film's deliberate and elaborate dopiness still allows for a remarkably canny take on generational responses to Japan's decline. Just before Shimokawaji, a handsome, rakish MOF official (the one who, grizzled and panicked in middle age, would send Mayumi back to prevent the bubble's pop), makes the decision to heed her warnings about the mortgage policy, he asks her, "Are the people in your time unhappy with their country?" Mayumi pauses and says, "I don't know. But I know that's what the future you is thinking." The next shot lingers on Shimokawaji's face for three seconds, followed by another three seconds as an extreme close-up of his eyes; this is the only such moment in the film, one that simultaneously calls attention to the depth of his dilemma and that temporarily stops the movie's jokey tone dead in its tracks.

The *Kibōgaku* organizers are all roughly my age, graduating from college in the late 1980s just as the Japanese bubble burst and as the path their country was on seemed to collapse under its feet, similar to that generation of US college students who were ready to graduate just after the 2008 financial crisis and then entered a radically different set of expectations. *Baburu e GO!* captures, in what an alcoholic might describe as a moment of clarity (much of the film is chaos and slapstick), more than the fact that younger Japanese have adapted to their environment in ways that seem almost alien to their previously optimistic, now-worried predecessors. It also suggests that Japan's postwar story and the emotional representations surrounding it have largely been constructed by those old enough to remember when the country still had promise. This is not to say that people *like* Japan's precarious situation (Mayumi is, after all, working at a hostess pub to pay off some mobsters) but rather that the emotional experience varies according to expectations, to experiences, and to anticipation. Nor does it in any way qualify the work that the *Kibōgaku* researchers did before or after the disaster in trying to diagnose Japan's social problems and to offer solutions. It instead simply suggests that their own construction of an emotional frame that surrounds these problems reflects their understanding not just of the Japan That Was but also The Japan That Was Supposed to Have Been, the one that might have encouraged the respondents to *Bungei Shunjū*'s 2011 feature question, "Is This the Japan We Wanted?" to simply answer yes, if indeed the magazine would have asked the question at all. The younger generation has been absorbed into a widely shared national narrative, but there is a difference between feeling the once-stable ground collapse and having had to scamper all along. Or at least the existence of that difference could, by 2007, be the main point of a screwball comedy whose climax involves a fight among foreign financial conspirators, corrupt Japanese bureaucrats, and a time-traveling hostess dressed as a geisha.

Everyone Visits

Regarding the collapse of the bubble and Japan's loss of hope, *Bubble Fiction* offers a solution of sorts. When he realizes that the bill will lead to bank collapses, the young Shimokawaji holds a news conference announcing that the speculation bill has been withdrawn but that bank closings and decline are inevitable and that people should be prepared; he himself will do his job and then go home to his family. The result here—a few final gags about Shimokawaji's lecherous ways and the inevitability of future pork-barrel excesses notwithstanding—is not that Japan could have followed a completely different path but rather that anticipation matters, that a different emotional investment in what Japan's success had produced and altered expectations about the future would have allowed something other than the despair that followed the bubble's pop. Despite the promise of time travel, what changes is not Japan's story itself and not its conclusion per se. It is rather Japan's emotional health, if Japanese were to commit to the things that really matter, like family and duty, rather than to the club scene and materialism that seem in retrospect to have defined the late bubble era.

For some, the 2011 triple disaster served as a moment of reckoning, for new commitments that might reframe or resolve Japan's "long postwar," largely because so many considered the 2011 events to be a disaster for the nation as a whole. This need not have been the case. The 1995 Hanshin/Awaji earthquake killed roughly 6,400, mostly in industrial Kobe, one of Japan's largest metropolitan areas. And it was politically consequential, particularly given the effect of volunteers and nonprofit organizations in stepping in to help victims; the dynamism emerging from the quake spurred the creation of Japan's Non-Profit Organization Law a few years later. But it was not a "national" disaster that spurred "Hang in There, Japan!" campaigns or a government-sponsored report saying that Japan could not be rebuilt if Kobe were not rebuilt. Some of this may have its cause in the Fukushima meltdown, but it seems plausible that even had there been a meltdown in, say, Takahama in 1995, the disaster, however terrible, would have been understood as a predominantly local one. More important would seem to be both the televised horror of the tsunami as well as the visceral, physical power of the quake in Tokyo, Japan's media and financial capital (not to mention its political center), as well as in the core of the Kanto region, where roughly a third of Japanese live. Although many victims in the North as well as their advocates around the country would later emphasize the importance of thinking first of the local consequences, it felt—was supposed to feel—to many in the Tokyo area like a Japanese disaster, not merely a Tōhoku one.

And it therefore offered the opportunity to think broadly about what this meant for Japan. As the extent of the nuclear disaster became clear, it was also a moment of soul-searching for many, particularly on the Left, who had to reflect on how much of the Japanese economic miracle had been premised on the availability of cheap electricity from nuclear power emanating from Japan's poorer coastal communities that had little financial choice but to accept them.[2] For others, it was a chance to consider how the collapse of Japanese self-esteem might be reversed through the perseverance of the disaster's victims and through the nation's recommitment to common virtues. According to the cultural critic Azuma Hiroki, the scholar noted in chapter 4 who wrote a classic book on Japan's "nerd" (*otaku*) culture, March 11 meant that the disaster itself provided the opportunity for recessionary Japan to feel proud of itself once again—to make a U-turn toward a sense of national initiative:

> I have never seen Japanese people thinking about and discussing "the public" this much. Only recently the Japanese people and the government were seen as indecisive and selfish, muddled with complaints and bickering. But now, they are boldly trying to defend the nation together, as if they are a

changed people. To borrow an expression from the younger generation here, the Japanese people seem to have completely transformed their *kyara* (character). . . . "Yeah, we can do it if we put our minds to it." "We aren't so bad as a whole nation after all." This is what many Japanese people have been feeling in the last several days, with some embarrassment.[3]

The central story framing the disaster remained that of Japan's postwar economic rise and its consequences, but March 11 at least seemed to provide the opportunity for an emotional recommitment through shared effort, frequently through pilgrimage.

The *Kibōgaku* authors, of course, traveled to and from Kamaishi for years after the disaster, checking on their respondents and friends, contributing to local efforts to rebuild, and trying to publicize the challenges and activities while also celebrating the city's successes along the way. They were not alone. NHK and other broadcasters focused on foreign volunteers to the disaster zone for many months after the tsunami, and a June 2011 episode of *Cool Japan* featured foreigners who had previously appeared as panelists on the program discussing their reactions to the devastation that they saw in their own visits.[4] By October, Caramel Box had collected donations to support its tour of free shows across Miyagi, Sendai, and Fukushima. At each stop, the company performed one of its beloved plays, Narui Yutaka's *Kenjitō Tankenki* (The expedition to Kenji Island),[5] which embeds within its whimsical structure several classic stories by Miyazawa Kenji, the revered early-twentieth-century writer who emerged, after his early death, as Tōhoku's most representative literary voice[6] and whose deathbed poem was omnipresent in the coverage of the disaster: *Ame ni mo makezu, kaze ni mo makezu* (I won't be defeated by the rain, I won't be defeated by the wind). The following month, the *Ehime Maru*—the fisheries training ship built to replace the one sent to the bottom of the Pacific by the *USS Greeneville* and its distinguished visitors—embarked on a weeklong trip to the region. The students of Uwajima Fisheries High School and those from neighboring towns had written and compiled messages of sympathy and support to the disaster's victims, and the students and staff delivered the letters (and hundreds of satsuma tangerines) directly to students from Ishinomaki Fisheries High School who met them at Ishinomaki's industrial port.[7] Nguyen Duc himself traveled from Vietnam to Ishinomaki to speak with and to inspire disabled victims of the disaster, in a summer 2012 trip broadcast by NHK as expressing "bonds across national boundaries." He told NHK, "Japan gave me the hope I needed to live. This time, I want to shout my support for the victims."[8]

All of these events were reported by the press, although they mostly bled into one another and myriad other stories about people coming together to bring comfort to the disaster's victims. After all, seemingly every celebrity, every official of note headed to Tōhoku at some point, and among researchers working on Japan, there was even some uncomfortable discussion of whether it was something of an obligation to go to volunteer, to document the suffering, to theorize about the unfairness of a disaster that could exacerbate vulnerabilities and leave a radioactive zone keeping families from their ancestral homes. I know that for many of my colleagues, as for myself, this has presented agonizing choices over how to respect the victims, to support some kind of improvement in their lives, to tell meaningful stories or present meaningful information but to avoid the kind of pornographic attachment that devastation can invite.

This book has aimed to suggest that the links among politics, emotion, and culture are messy in large part because we have become accustomed to allowing states to speak for and to represent national emotions in unproblematic ways. I do not know how all the visitors to Tōhoku felt about their visits; I am not sure I can explain how I felt when I went because I am not sure how I can articulate with any precision the complex combinations and sequences of grief, horror, amusement, professional ambition, guilt, despair, self-doubt, elation, and, yes, hope that seemed to dominate my time there. My sense from conversations with Japanese and foreign colleagues is that their combinations were individually different but no less complex than mine. They were certainly no more easily captured by the language that even well-meaning administrators and officials might have applied to their own efforts to define the ways in which Japanese felt, or were supposed to feel, about the victims, the outpouring of global support, and their own roles. The things most of us have felt have informed our analytical decisions and likely our research outcomes: what we have said, taught, and written about the disaster.

This is, in some sense, the point of "affect theory," or of paying careful attention to the circulation of feelings and sensations among participants in shared social experiences. And the reflection demanded of scholars working in this new field undermines and challenges the social scientific approach to emotion that emphasizes experimental methods and the linking of specific emotions to specific choices. I would even argue that the rigor demanded of scholars who engage in productive reflection about their own position in emotional frames matches and in some ways exceeds that of those who use experimental settings and draw from neuroscience in explaining behavior. The latter may be motivated to produce findings that can be replicated in subsequent experiments, surely one way to think of rigor. But the former seem more engaged in taking seriously the ways in which human emotion goes beyond even the most comprehensive set of Happy-Sad-Embarrassed emoticons that might appear in a Twitter feed. And yet in many ways, these imprecise representations are what we have in politics, and the logic guiding them is less the actual stuff of real feelings than of the national story—as with the *Ehime Maru* accident, Viet and Duc, and Japan's soft power—in which 3.11 is embedded.

My goal in this book has been to suggest that we can take seriously both the need for critical reflection on emotionality and the analytical need for structured analysis by focusing on the demands of prevailing social narratives. That is, we may not be able to describe perfectly how we feel at any given time, but we often understand how we are supposed to feel; these suppositions can be clarified by examining the stories in which we are embedded, the ones we routinely tell one another and ourselves. That these often end with the elevation of one's national community—whether Japanese, American, Chinese, Russian, Vietnamese, or other—to a position of international respect and even affection ought to help us to think about how official emotion matters and why.

When Prime Minister Abe traveled to Washington and made a well-received speech to the US Congress in 2015, he thanked the United States for its help in the aftermath of the 3.11 disaster as well as for its work to overcome the scars of World War II by rebuilding Japan. There was even something imperative in his language: "The finest asset the U.S. has to give to the world was hope, is hope, will be, and must always be hope." Though perhaps previously emanating only from the United States, hope was now a mutual contribution, as the United States and Japan together represented an "alliance of hope."[9] The clear subtext in the address was the Beijing-led alternative that presumably offered less hope, or even no hope at all. Much less clear was what hope actually meant, other than something good and something that obviated even the need to discuss the messy realities of politics, of a relationship in which one partner has continually fretted about its ability to make decisions. Abe himself might have launched that exact criticism of hope's fuzziness during the 2017 parliamentary elections, when Tokyo's conservative governor, Koike Yuriko, challenged the LDP leadership that had famously and unsuccessfully tried to sideline her in the 2016 gubernatorial election. Koike's new party was not exactly a clear alternative to the LDP: it agreed largely with Abe's goals for constitutional revision and a more proactive military stance, but differed on taxation issues and on restarting Japan's nuclear power program. A bit optimistically, she named it *Kibō no Tō*: the "Party of Hope." Within days of its founding, Koike banned candidates unwilling to hew to her line on constitutional revision and then decided not to run for the Diet herself, keeping her job as governor while dooming her party to immediate defeat. The decision inadvertently but predictably made *Zetsubō no Tō* (the Party of Despair) a trending hashtag on Twitter.

Japan First

Unusual among utterly terrible films, 1973's *Nihon Chinbotsu* (Japan sinks) has attracted a remarkable degree of scholarly attention and even nostalgia. Based on a plodding novel by renowned science fiction writer Komatsu Sakyō, the three-hour-long film follows an all-star cast as they struggle to deal with seismic events likely to end with Japan's utter submersion, a cinematic experience not terribly unlike (whether in its all-star cast or its glacial pace) American disaster films of the era, such as *The Poseidon Adventure* and *Earthquake!* Because of the neurotically apocalyptic plot and the struggle to save Japan from its complete obliteration, the novel and the film have been analyzed countless times for their images of national disappearance.[10]

Less often discussed, though not completely ignored, is Tsutsui Yasutaka's much more effective and concise parody, "Everything Sinks but Japan."[11] Shorn of the crypto-scientific jargon meant to make Japan's submersion seem plausible to Komatsu's readers, Tsutsui embraces the nuttiness of a world in which every other country has sunk to the bottom of the ocean, leaving their rich and powerful to flee to Japan. The story opens with Frank Sinatra, having recently tried to learn some Japanese, singing *enka* songs to earn his keep and continues through more elaborate but equally amusing tales of what Japan would do if it were suddenly and irreversibly on top of the world. The extraordinarily low-budget 2006 film version—the kind of budget that makes a "making of" featurette superfluous because there is simply nothing to wonder about in such a hasty, slapdash, but good-natured effort—plays up the mockery of Japanese nationalism. Amused Japanese bureaucrats gleefully accept Chinese and Korean entreaties that everyone just forget about the damned war. Japanese bar patrons buy drinks for Arnold Schwarzenegger and Bruce Willis (both played by pint-sized impersonators) who must resort to performing, respectively, their *Terminator* and *Die Hard* roles for the amusement of their inebriated fans. A stand-in for Tokyo's notorious then-governor Ishihara Shintarō enthusiastically plays up Japan's potential military response to a geological (or is it meteorological?) challenge. Japan is not the vulnerable nation battered by a world it cannot control but rather the newly self-confident and inexplicably fortunate survivor, the world's last hope.

Japan has long been a leader in disasters or at least in working to prevent or mitigate them. It often surprises American and European observers that even after the 2011 tsunami and nuclear disaster, researchers particularly from elsewhere in Asia still come to Japan specifically for research on and training in disaster management, which has evolved into an academic and political movement in the country. Yamada Yoshiko and Daniel Clausen view risk "as a diplomatic opportunity," one that has allowed Japan to leverage its own levels of preparedness and responsiveness—even if periodically lamented within Japan itself—to work for the nation's international benefit, particularly in demonstrating yet one more arena in which Japan can be a regional or global leader.[12] Since the 1990s, but even more so since Japan's unique experience with the March 2011 triple disaster, Japan is a leader in helping other countries prepare for and deal with their own disasters.

In 2014 Kawashima Shin, a distinguished scholar of international relations at the University of Tokyo, wrote a fascinating column as editor-in-chief of Nippon.com, a multilingual website aimed at promoting global knowledge and awareness of Japan. Run by the Nippon Communications Foundation and connected to the Sasakawa Peace Foundation, Nippon.com has continued the Sasakawa Foundation's decades-long move away from its more explicitly conservative or nationalistic roots. Kawashima's essay charts and perhaps justifies Japanese public support of international research about Japan, particularly in the midst of government concern about the effect of Japan's economic decline on global awareness of and interest in the country; it seeks to set aside predictable challenges, frequently from Japanese conservatives, that international research on Japan often has a left-wing (or, more to their point, anti-Japan) bias. It is an excellent column, one that would certainly be encouraging to that beleaguered lot of Japan specialists, particularly in the United States, who are concerned about declining enrollments, disciplinary challenges to regional studies, and the possibility that we will be left behind by our colleagues in Chinese and Korean studies. In one key passage, he writes:

> I think we should stop concentrating our international PR efforts so heavily on the field of culture, which has traditionally been stressed, and on issues in dispute, such as territorial claims and historical perceptions, which have recently become a major priority. Instead, I would suggest paying more attention to sharing information about the various social issues that Japan now faces domestically—in other words, telling the rest of the world about Japan's everyday realities. Our country is a "problem pioneer," already grappling with population aging and other issues that others will confront in the future. We should keep this fact in mind.[13]

Everything sinks, it seems, and Japan got there first, the vanguard of experience that should keep it relevant for others around the world. Even this encouraging article, this smart effort to thread a challenging political and intellectual needle, comes back to that area where Japan could be regarded as ahead, its status assured, if only others were to pay attention to it. Kawashima's column is convincing and seemingly devoid of sentimentality or glee; he simply lays out the facts as he sees them and makes a set of proposals. But it makes sense only because of a story with which Nippon.com's readers will likely be familiar: of Japan's economic miracle and its consequences for the 1980s–1990s boom in Japanese studies, as well as its subsequent stagnation, particularly in the face of dynamism elsewhere in Asia. And it reassures because Japan remains a pioneer, not just in Asia but also globally, having found itself in the kind of demographic and economic mess that is beginning to typify other countries as well. In that near-despair, there lies a kind of hope, one that draws its force quietly from a feeling about what Japan is and what it will continue to work collectively to become. And it works because it becomes the end of a story, one in which Japan is a few pages ahead of everyone else.

NOTES

1. Maybe They Will Smile Back

1. OECD figures (2013–2014), http://www.oecd.org/dac/stats/aid-at-a-glance.htm# recipients.

2. Hall's work on this topic is highly convincing in the development of certain modes of emotional expression between states. Todd H. Hall, *Emotional Diplomacy: Official Emotion on the International Stage* (Ithaca, NY: Cornell University Press, 2015).

3. There is no shortage of obvious references here, but Martin Fackler and Ian Johnson of the *New York Times* captured it in this way: "The angry emotions in China also reflect a thinly veiled animosity toward Japan that is rooted in Japan's brutal military occupation during World War II." See "Arrest in Disputed Seas Riles China and Japan," *New York Times,* September 19, 2010, A1.

4. James Fallows, "Annals of Agitprop," *Atlantic,* December 8, 2008, http://www.theatlantic.com/technology/archive/2008/12/annals-of-agitprop/9171; Jessica Chen Weiss, *Powerful Patriots: Nationalist Protest in China's Foreign Relations* (New York: Oxford University Press, 2014); Jessica Chen Weiss, "Authoritarian Signaling, Mass Audiences, and Nationalist Protest in China," *International Organization* 67, no. 1 (2013): 1–35.

5. Bethany Albertson and Shana Kushner Gadarian's award-winning book *Anxious Politics: Democratic Citizenship in a Threatening World* (Cambridge: Cambridge University Press, 2015) examines the effect of anxiety in part through experimental methods. The 2016 presidential campaign might be viewed as a further and independent elaboration of their key concern.

6. Roland Bleiker and Emma Hutchison, "Fear No More: Emotions and World Politics," *Review of International Studies* 34 (2008): 115–35.

7. See Julia A. Stern, *The Plight of Feeling: Sympathy and Dissent in the Early American Novel* (Chicago: University of Chicago Press, 1999); Sianne Ngai, *Ugly Feelings* (Cambridge, MA: Harvard University Press, 1995).

8. Benedict Anderson's *Imagined Communities* (London: Verso, 1983) is highly attuned to the emotional or affective experience of nationhood, just it is to the importance of national narrative.

9. Among important recent contributions, see the essays in Rebecca Kingston and Leonard Ferry, eds., *Bringing the Passions Back In: The Emotions in Political Philosophy* (Vancouver: University of British Columbia Press, 2007); Cheryl Hall, *The Trouble with Passion: Political Theory beyond the Reign of Reason* (Oxon, UK: Routledge, 2005); Sharon Krause, *Civil Passions: Moral Sentiment and Democratic Deliberation* (Princeton, NJ: Princeton University Press, 2008). One particularly useful and well-recognized take is Albert O. Hirschman's classic study *The Passions and the Interests: Political Arguments for Capitalism before Its Triumph,* rev. ed. (Princeton, NJ: Princeton University Press, 2013). See especially Jeremy Adelman's informative afterword.

10. See, for example, Rose McDermott, "Mutual Interests: The Case for Increasing Dialogue between Political Science and Neuroscience," *Political Research Quarterly* 62 (2009): 571–83. But the neuroscientific turn has been controversial in part because the aspirations of political scientists in using neuroscientific findings have sometimes outpaced the analytical claims that more cautious neuroscientists themselves have been willing to make. See, e.g., Jan Slaby, "Neuroscience and Politics: Do Not Hold Your Breath," *E-International Relations,* May 8, 2015, http://www.e-ir.info/2015/05/08/neuroscience-and-politics-do-not-hold-your-breath. For a more sustained critique, see Jan Slaby, Philipp Haueis, and Suparna Choudhury, "Neuroscience as Applied Hermeneutics: Towards a Critical Neuroscience of Political Theory," in *Essays on Neuroscience and Political Theory,* ed. Frank Vander Valk (New York: Routledge), 50–73.

11. For an early overview of some of experimental methods in political science, see Rose McDermott, "Experimental Methods in Political Science," *Annual Review of Political Science* 5 (2002): 31–61. On field experiments, see Macartan Humphreys and Jeremy M. Weinstein, "Field Experiments and the Political Economy of Development," *Annual Review of Political Science* 12 (2009): 367–78; and Susan D. Hyde, "Experiments in International Relations: Lab, Survey, and Field," *Annual Review of Political Science* 18 (2015): 403–24. The increasing pace of the studies based on experimental methods has led to a debate on the ethical implications. Scott Desposato considers political science's track record in dealing with the ethics of these experiments in "Ethical Challenges and Some Solutions for Field Experiments," 2014, http://www.desposato.org/ethicsfieldexperiments.pdf.

12. See Bleiker and Hutchison, "Fear No More." Jacques E. C. Hymans uses social psychological conceptions of identity and emotion to explain nuclear weapons development in his *The Psychology of Nuclear Proliferation: Identity, Emotions and Foreign Policy* (Cambridge: Cambridge University Press, 2006).

13. Kathleen Stewart, *Ordinary Affects* (Durham, NC: Duke University Press, 2007); Sara Ahmed, *The Promise of Happiness* (Durham, NC: Duke University Press, 2010); Brian Massumi, *Parables for the Virtual: Movement, Affect, Sensation* (Durham, NC: Duke University Press, 2002).

14. Eugenia Lean, *Public Passions: The Trial of Shi Jianqiao and the Rise of Popular Sympathy in Republican China* (Berkeley: University of California Press, 2007); Jun Uchida, "A Sentimental Journey: Mapping the Interior Frontier of Japanese Settlers in Colonial Korea," *Journal of Asian Studies* 70, no. 3 (2011): 706–29.

15. Jie Yang, *Unknotting the Heart: Unemployment and Therapeutic Governance in China* (Ithaca, NY: Cornell University Press, 2015); Anne Allison, *Precarious Japan* (Durham, NC: Duke University Press, 2014); Daniel White, "The Affect-Emotion Gap: Soft Power, Nation Branding, and Cultural Administration in Japan" (PhD diss., Department of Anthropology, Rice University, 2011).

16. Ruth Leys, "The Affective Turn: A Critique," *Critical Inquiry* 37, no. 3 (2011): 434–72.

17. Martha Nussbaum, *Upheavals of Thought: The Intelligence of Emotions* (Cambridge: Cambridge University Press, 2003). Bleiker and Hutchison use Nussbaum effectively in articulating their own views of emotional representation in politics, also arguing for the importance of broad national narratives. See Bleiker and Hutchison, "Fear No More."

18. *"Nippon o torimodosu,"* as made abundantly clear in a 2012 Liberal Democratic Party commercial. See https://www.youtube.com/watch?v=S5rhUHmPbZc.

19. Peter Brooks, *The Melodramatic Imagination: Balzac, Henry James, Melodrama, and the Mode of Excess* (New Haven, CT: Yale University Press, 1976).

20. Elizabeth Anker, *Orgies of Feeling: Melodrama and the Politics of Freedom* (Durham, NC: Duke University Press, 2014).

21. Rose McDermott, "The Feeling of Rationality: The Meaning of Neuroscientific Advances for Political Science," *Perspectives on Politics* 2, no. 4 (2004): 693.

22. See, e.g., Jonathan Mercer, "Feeling Like a State: Social Emotion and Identity," *International Theory* 6, no. 3 (2014): 515–35.

23. See L. H. M. Ling's discussion, with particular reference to "face-saving" and "expediency" in Arab culture. L. H. M. Ling, "Decolonizing the International: Towards Multiple Emotional Worlds," *International Theory* 6, no. 3 (2014): 579–83. She draws from Seyed Hossein Mousavian and Mohammad Ali Shabani, "How to Talk to Iran," *New York Times,* January 3, 2013.

24. Andrew Ross, *Mixed Emotions: Beyond Fear and Hatred in International Conflict* (Chicago: University of Chicago Press, 2013); Emma Hutchison, "Trauma and the Politics of Emotions: Constituting Identity, Security and Community after the Bali Bombing," *International Relations* 24, no. 1 (2010): 65–86; Emma Hutchison, *Affective Communities in World Politics: Collective Emotions after Trauma* (Cambridge: Cambridge University Press, 2016).

25. Mercer, "Feeling Like a State," 523.

26. See Ken K. Ito, *An Age of Melodrama: Family, Gender, and Social Hierarchy in the Turn-of-the-Century Japanese Novel* (Stanford, CA: Stanford University Press, 2008). For an inspired examination of the sentimental Japanese novel's early modern roots, see Jonathan E. Zwicker, *Practices of the Sentimental Imagination: Melodrama, the Novel, and the Social Imaginary in Nineteenth-Century Japan* (Cambridge, MA: Harvard University Press, 2006).

27. Sara Ahmed, *The Cultural Politics of Emotion*, 2nd ed. (Edinburgh: Edinburgh University Press, 2014), chapter 1; Serguei Oushakine, *The Patriotism of Despair: Nation, War, and Loss in Russia* (Ithaca, NY: Cornell University Press, 2009); Christina Schwenkel, "Post/Socialist Affect: Ruination and Reconstruction of the Nation in Urban Vietnam," *Cultural Anthropology* 28, no. 2 (2013): 252–77.

28. See, e.g., Funabashi Yōichi, ed., *Kenshō: Nihon no "ushinawareta 20-nen"* [Investigation: Japan's "lost twenty years"] (Tokyo: Tōyō Keizai Shinpōsha, 2015); Fukao Kyōji, *"Ushinawareta 20-nen" to Nihon Keizai: Kōzōteki gen'in to saisei e no gendōryoku no kaimei* [The "lost twenty years" and Japan's economy: The structural causes and the solutions for rebuilding productivity] (Tokyo: Nihon Keizai Shimbun Shuppansha, 2012); Tokyo University Institute of Social Science, eds., *Ushinawareta 10-nen o koete* [Overcoming the lost decade] (Tokyo: University of Tokyo Press, 2005, 2006).

29. Ryan Avent ("R. A."), "Lost Decades: The Japanese Tragedy," *Economist Free Exchange* (blog), August 3, 2012, http://www.economist.com/blogs/freeexchange/2012/08/lost-decades.

30. Tomiko Yoda, "A Roadmap to Millennial Japan," *South Atlantic Quarterly* 99, no. 4 (2000): 663–66. Yoda's capacious but succinct overview persuasively highlights the wide concern with national agency.

31. See especially Chalmers Johnson, *MITI and the Japanese Miracle: The Growth of Industrial Policy: 1925–1975* (Stanford, CA: Stanford University Press, 1982); David D. Friedman, *The Misunderstood Miracle: Industrial Development and Political Change in Japan* (Ithaca, NY: Cornell University Press, 1988); Frances Rosenbluth, *Financial Politics in Contemporary Japan* (Ithaca, NY: Cornell University Press, 1989).

32. This is one of the key insights of Sheldon Garon's *Molding Japanese Minds: The State in Everyday Life* (Princeton, NJ: Princeton University Press, 1997).

33. Carol Gluck, "The 'Long Postwar': Japan and Germany in Common and in Contrast," in *Legacies and Ambiguities: Postwar Fiction and Culture in West Germany and Japan*, ed. Ernestine Schlant and J. Thomas Rimer (Washington and Baltimore: Woodrow Wilson Center Press and Johns Hopkins University Press, 1991), 63–78.

34. For some particularly important works, see John Nathan, *Japan Unbound: A Volatile Nation's Quest for Pride and Purpose* (New York: Houghton Mifflin Harcourt, 2004); Kenneth B. Pyle, *Japan Rising: The Resurgence of Japanese Power and Purpose* (New York: Public Affairs, 2007); Alex Kerr, *Dogs and Demons: Tales from the Dark Side of Japan* (New York: Hill & Wang, 2002); Tomiko Yoda and Harry Harootunian, eds., *Japan after Japan: Social and Cultural Life from the Recessionary 1990s to the Present* (Durham, NC: Duke University Press, 2006); David Pilling, *Bending Adversity: Japan and the Art of Survival* (New York: Penguin, 2014); Fukuda Shin'ichi, *Ushinawareta 20-nen o koete* [Overcoming the lost two decades] (Tokyo: NTT Press, 2015).

35. *Always: san-chōme no yūhi*, 2005, dir. Yamazaki Takashi. For an extensive discussion of the film's representation of Japan's early postwar history, see Asaba Michiaki, *Shōwa sanjūnendai shugi : mō seichō shinai nihon* [1950s-ism: The Japan that won't grow anymore] (Tokyo: Gentōsha, 2008).

36. David Leheny, *Think Global, Fear Local: Sex, Violence, and Anxiety* (Ithaca, NY: Cornell University Press, 2006), chapter 2.

37. For a longer discussion of *Project X* as public memory, see Hiraku Shimoda, "Memorializing the Spirit of Wit and Grit in Postindustrial Japan," in *Japan since 1945: From Postwar to Post-Bubble*, ed. Christopher Gerteis and Timothy S. George (London: Bloomsbury, 2013), 242–56.

38. Mary Brinton, *Lost in Transition: Youth, Work, and Instability in Postindustrial Japan* (Cambridge: Cambridge University Press, 2011). In describing moralistic views about selfish young Japanese, Brinton points to Yamada Masahiro's depiction of "parasite singles," which he illuminates most clearly in his short book *Parasaito Shinguru no Jidai* (Tokyo: Chikuma Shinsho, 1999). She also recognizes Genda for his important accomplishments to the study of labor markets and youth.

39. The *Kibōgaku* volumes were published in Japanese by the University of Tokyo Press in 2009: see http://www.utp.or.jp/series/kibougaku.html.

40. "Kore ga watashitachi no nozonda nihon na no ka?" *Bungei Shunjū* 89, no. 4 (April 2011).

41. Peter Brooks, *Reading for the Plot: Design and Intention in Narrative* (Cambridge, MA: Harvard University Press, 1992).

42. See Rogers M. Smith, *Stories of Peoplehood: The Politics and Morals of Political Membership* (Cambridge: Cambridge University Press, 2003).

43. Frederick W. Mayer's *Narrative Politics: Stories and Collective Action* (New York: Oxford University Press, 2014) makes these connections effectively, although Katherine K. Chen's somewhat arch review of the book calls attention to the already well-developed work in sociology that Mayer largely ignores. See her review in *Social Forces* 1–2 (2015). Francesca Polletta's *It Was Like a Fever: Storytelling in Protest and Politics* (Chicago: University of Chicago Press, 2006) examines the use of narrative more systematically in the context of the civil rights movement and US racial politics. Chen herself embeds her examination of stories and social organization in her award-winning book *Enabling Creative Chaos: The Organization behind the Burning Man Event* (Chicago: University of Chicago Press, 2009); her argument specifically about narrative can be found in "Charismatizing the Routine: Storytelling for Meaning and Agency in the Burning Man Organization," *Journal of Qualitative Sociology* 35 (2012): 311–34.

44. Richard J. Samuels, "Kidnapping Politics," *Journal of East Asian Studies* (2010): 363–95.

45. Another excellent analysis is in Robin Erica Wagner-Pacifici, *The Moro Morality Play: Terrorism as Social Drama* (Chicago: University of Chicago Press, 1986), which builds from Victor Turner's theories of dramaturgy, especially in "Social Dramas and Stories about Them," *Critical Inquiry* 7, no. 1 (1980): 141–68. Turner's work on social drama and the dramaturgical structuring of action and communication, highly influential in anthropology and sociology, has been largely ignored by political scientists.

46. The literature is too extensive to list, but leading examples include Alexis Dudden, *Troubled Apologies among Japan, Korea, and the United States* (New York: Columbia University Press, 2008); Yinan He, *The Search for Reconciliation: Sino-Japanese and German-Polish Relations since World War II* (Cambridge: Cambridge University Press, 2009); and Jennifer Lind, *Sorry States: Apologies in International Politics* (Ithaca, NY: Cornell University Press, 2008).

2. Souls of the *Ehime Maru*

1. William H. Little, "A Case Study in Applied Oceanography: The Lifting and Moving of the *Ehime Maru*," *Oceanography* 15, no. 4 (2002): 33.

2. The high school's website (http://uwajimasuisan-h.esnet.ed.jp) makes only passing reference to the disaster but has a variety of information on the school's courses and curricula.

3. See *Minna no kōkō jōhō*, http://www.minkou.jp/school/600.

4. National Transportation Safety Board (NTSB), "Marine Accident Brief" (No. DCA-01-MM-022), September 29, 2005, 1–2, 25–27.

5. Scott Waddle (with Ken Abraham), *The Right Thing* (Nashville: Integrity, 2002).

6. NTSB, "Marine Accident Brief," 24.

7. Tanaka Akihiko, "2001 Jihyō: '*Ehime Maru* Jiken' to Mori Yoshirō" [2001 comment: Mori Yoshirō and "the *Ehime Maru* incident"], *Chūō Kōron*, April 2004, 35.

8. Curtis H. Martin, "The Sinking of the *Ehime Maru*: The Interaction of Culture, Security Interests and Domestic Politics in an Alliance Crisis," *Japanese Journal of Political Science* 5, no. 2 (2004): 289.

9. Kristina Drumheller and William L. Benoit, "*USS Greeneville* Collides with Japan's *Ehime Maru*: Cultural Issues in Image Repair Discourse," *Public Relations Review* 30 (2004): 177–85. See also Melvin J. Dubnick, "Accountability and Ethics: Reconsidering the Relationships," *International Journal of Organization Theory and Behavior* 6, no. 3 (2003): 409.

10. Waddle, *The Right Thing*, 152–53.

11. Richard J. Cohen, "We've Apologized Enough to Japan," *Washington Post*, February 28, 2001, A23.

12. See Chalmers Johnson, "Okinawa between the United States and Japan," Japan Policy Research Institute Occasional Paper No. 24, January 2002, http://www.jpri.org/publications/occasionalpapers/op24.html; Gavan McCormack, *Client State: Japan in the American Embrace* (London: Verso, 2007).

13. For an excellent English-language study of this case, see Linda Isako Angst, "The Sacrifice of a Schoolgirl: The 1995 Rape Case, Discourses of Power, and Women's Lives in Okinawa," *Critical Asian Studies* 33, no. 2 (2001): 243–66.

14. See Chalmers Johnson, "The 'Rape' of Okinawa," *Japan Focus* 6, no. 3 (2008).

15. For a superb examination, see Christopher Nelson, *Dancing with the Dead: Memory, Performance, and Everyday Life in Postwar Okinawa* (Durham, NC: Duke University Press, 2009).

16. Yoshida Etsuko, "Lō Anguru—*Ehime Maru* jiken to sono kazoku" [Law angle: The families of the *Ehime Maru* incident], *Hōgaku seminā*, September 2001.

17. Martin, "The Sinking," 303; NTSB, "Marine Accident Brief," 49.

18. Waddle, *The Right Thing*, 115, 119, 121, 125, 127. There were sixteen visitors in all. Eight were subsequently listed as residing in Texas, although four other couples were from Colorado, Massachusetts, Kansas, and Hawaii. See http://www.cpf.navy.mil/subsite/cpfnews/0102Greeneville17.html. It seems that fourteen of them were connected with the oil industry, and another couple included a sports journalist and his wife, which may explain Waddle's count.

19. "Report of the Court of Inquiry into the Circumstances Surrounding the Collision between *USS Greeneville* (SSN772) and Japanese M/V *Ehime Maru* That Occurred off the Coast of Oahu on February 9, 2001," from Vice Admiral John B. Nathman, Rear Admiral Paul F. Sullivan, Rear Admiral David M. Stone of the US Navy and Rear Admiral Isamu Ozawa of the Japanese Maritime Self Defense Force, April 13, 2001, 116, http://www.cpf.navy.mil/subsite/ehimemaru/legal/*GREENEVILLE*_Combined_COI_Rpt.pdf.

20. Martin, "The Sinking," 306–8.

21. Most of these revolve around issues of war responsibility but have become broader in their orientation, showing how the deployment of emotional idioms is a linchpin of contemporary diplomacy. See Todd H. Hall, "We Will Not Swallow This Bitter Fruit: Theorizing a Diplomacy of Anger," *Security Studies* 20 (2011): 521–55. On the international politics of war apologies, see Alexis Dudden, *Troubled Apologies among Japan, Korea, and the United States* (New York: Columbia University Press, 2008); Jennifer Lind, *Sorry States: Apologies in International Politics* (Ithaca, NY: Cornell University Press, 2008); Yinan He, *The Search for Reconciliation: Sino-Japanese and German-Polish Relations since World War II* (Cambridge: Cambridge University Press, 2008); Thomas U. Berger, *War Guilt, and World Politics after World War II* (Cambridge: Cambridge University Press, 2012).

22. Yoshida, "Lō Anguru—*Ehime Maru* jiken to sono kazoku."

23. George J. Tanabe, Jr., "Japanese Need Body Remains of *Ehime Maru* Victims," *Honolulu Advertiser*, February 25, 2001, http://the.honoluluadvertiser.com/2001/Feb/25/25opinion17.html.

24. Department of State Washington File, "Transcript: Ambassador Foley's Farewell Speech to Japan Press Club (Apologies Alone for *Ehime Maru* Accident Are Not Enough)," February 23, 2001, http://usinfo.org/wf-archive/2001/010223/epf501.htm.

25. Kokkai Gijiroku, *Sangi-in Gaikō Bōei Iinkai* [Minutes from the House of Councillors Committee on Foreign Affairs and Defense], February 27, 2001.

26. Kokkai, *Sangi-in Gaikō Bōei Iinkai*.

27. Kokkai.

28. Takayama Masayuki, "Ehime Maru: Nichibei 'hikaku shazai' kō" [Ehime Maru: Thoughts on American and Japanese apologies], *Shokun*, May 2001, 88.

29. Whether or not the ship's actions amounted to a "joyride" was a central discussion in the court of inquiry following the incident. Admiral Albert Konetzni, commander of the US Pacific Fleet's Submarine Force, evidently testified to the court that "It wasn't a joyride. I detest that word. It was training." See Waddle, *The Right Thing*, 184.

30. Robert C. Chaplin, "Bonds of U.S. Navy and JMSDF That Experienced [*sic*] through CNFJ Work," http://www.janafa.com/ronbun/2009-0901-1.pdf.

31. Shimizu Kōichi, "Sentai hikiage ni yoru itai shūyō to hoken" [Insurance and the accommodation of dead bodies from raised ships], *Songai Hoken Kenkyū* [Indemnity Insurance Research] 72, no. 3 (2010): 120–21.

32. Mike Allen, "Bodies from Kennedy Crash Are Found," *New York Times*, July 22, 1999.

33. For a thorough discussion, see Christina Schwenkel, *The American War in Contemporary Vietnam: Transnational Remembrance and Representation* (Bloomington: Indiana University Press, 2009).

34. Katherine Verdery, *The Political Lives of Dead Bodies: Reburial and Postsocialist Change* (New York: Columbia University Press, 1999).

35. Material related to Project Azorian, declassified in 2010, can be found in the Nuclear Vault in the National Security Archive at George Washington University. See http://www.gwu.edu/~nsarchiv/nukevault/ebb305/index.htm.

36. The CIA's YouTube feed includes an edited fourteen-minute video featuring the funeral. See https://www.youtube.com/watch?v=aJAJUJ41PBI.

37. Takayama, for example, makes explicit reference to it but mostly to point out the apparent absurdity of the expectation that the Americans might raise a ship with no strategic value, unlike the Soviet sub. Takayama, "Ehime Maru," 88.

38. Greg Baumann, "*Ehime Maru* Recovery Successful," *Faceplate* 6, no. 1 (2002): 4.

39. Little, "A Case Study," 33.

40. Matthew J. Francis et al., "Offshore Mooring Pile Design for the Recovery of the *Ehime Maru*," *Proceedings of the 13th (2003) International Offshore and Polar Engineering Conference* (Honolulu, Hawaii, May 25–30, 2003).

41. Little, "A Case Study," 33–34.

42. John A. Lewis, Jr., et al., "The Recovery and Identification of the Victims of the *Ehime Maru/USS Greeneville* Collision at Sea," *Journal of Forensic Sciences* 49, no. 3 (2004): 539.

43. See the news briefs and transcripts available on the "*Ehime Maru* Recovery" page, complete with a head logo featuring a navy diver in a faceplate, at the site of the commander of the US Navy Pacific Fleet, http://www.cpf.navy.mil/subsite/ehimemaru/index.html.

44. Bert Marsh, "SUPSALV Sends," *Faceplate* 6, no. 1 (2002): 2.

45. Baumann, "*Ehime Maru* Recovery," 5.

46. Chaplin, "Bonds of U.S. Navy and JMSDF."

47. US Pacific Fleet Public Affairs, "Ehime Maru Successfully Moved to Final Relocation Site," Story Number NNS021122–14, November 25, 2001, http://www.navy.mil/submit/display.asp?story_id=4723. Emphasis has been added, but the parenthetical description of the Mizuguchi family is from the original.

48. Julian Barnes, *Flaubert's Parrot* (New York: Vintage, 1990), 161.

49. http://www.cpf.navy.mil/subsite/cpfnews/0108recovery12.html.

50. "Embarks aboard U.S. Navy Ships," http://www.navy.mil/navydata/navy_legacy_hr.asp?id=165.

51. Hayashi Hideki, "'Meiyō' to wa nani ka: *Ehime Maru* jikō o tsūyaku to shite mitodoketa kaijōjieikan no omoi," *Seiron*, February 2003, 320. It is worth noting that by the time the article was published, the US-Japan alliance seemed to be on very solid ground, given the deployment of JMSDF ships to the Indian Ocean in support of the war in Afghanistan.

52. Hayashi, "'Meiyō' to wa nani ka," 322.

53. Hayashi, 325.

54. Hayashi, 326.

55. "Navy Agrees to Pay Ehime $11.5 Million," *Japan Times*, April 11, 2002, http://search.japantimes.co.jp/cgi-bin/np20020411a6.html; Juliana Gittler and Hana Kusumoto, "Last Two *Ehime Maru* Families OK Settlement," *Stars and Stripes*, February 22, 2003, http://www.stripes.com/news/last-two-ehime-maru-families-ok-settlement-1.1511.

56. Ikeda Naoki, "*Ehime Maru* jiken ni okeru beikaijihō to shibō songai baishō no hōteki ronten," *Hōritsu jihō* 76, no. 2 (2004): 113–17. The original language is "izoku no kokoro ni yorisō nichibei kyōdō no bengo katsudō datta."

57. Joshua Breslau, "Globalizing Disaster Trauma: Psychiatry, Science, and Culture after the Kobe Earthquake," *Ethos* 28, no. 2 (2000): 174–97; Joshua Breslau, "Cultures of Trauma: Anthropological Views of Posttraumatic Stress Disorder in International Health," *Culture, Medicine & Psychiatry* 28 (2004): 113–26; David Leheny, "Remaking Transnationalism: Japan and the Solutions to Crises," in *Japanese Aid and the Construction of Global Development: Inescapable Solutions*, ed. David Leheny and Kay B. Warren (London: Routledge, 2010), 282.

58. Yoshida, "Lō Anguru—*Ehime Maru* jiken to sono kazoku." Refers to the "Ehime Maru jiken no shinsō o kyūmei shiyō" meeting.

59. This is my best effort to translate the original Japanese, which is "Kawari hateta sugata datta ga, ito-oshiku, jibun no moto ni kaette kita to iu anshin ga atta."

60. Nawa Kiyotaka, "Itai to reikon: *Ehime Maru* jiken yori miru" [Dead bodies and souls: Examining the *Ehime Maru* case], *Taishō daigaku sōgō bukkyō kenkyūjo nenpō* [Annual of the Institute for Comprehensive Studies of Buddhism] 27 (March 2005): 114–15.

61. The quotations from Terada appear in an interview at the end of a piece by the attorney working with the victims' families. Ikeda Naoki, "Ehime de nani ga okotta ka?" [What happened in Ehime?], *Ōsaka no machi* [Osaka Town] 53 (2003), http://www.mmjp.or.jp/machi/53forWEB/page10.htm.

62. Ikeda, "Ehime de nani ga okotta ka?"

63. For a lengthy report by a Japanese diplomat who extensively praises these local networks while also emphasizing the US Navy's handling of the case, see "Kenkyū Nōto: Bei-taiheiyō gun no dōmei manejimento taisaku to shimin shakai to no renkei—*Ehime Maru* jiko to sono ato no yūkō kankei" [Research note: The connections between civil society and management of the US Naval Pacific Alliance—the *Ehime Maru* accident and friendly relations afterward], *Gaimushō chōsa geppō* [Ministry of Foreign Affairs Research Monthly] 3 (2008): 33–55.

64. Kokkai gijiroku, *Sangi-in kokusai mondai in kan suru chōsakai* [Minutes of the House of Councillors Survey Group on International Issues], March 7, 2001. I have taken the step of translating *shutaisei* as both "autonomy" and "agency." At times, Soeya seems to be emphasizing a more equal role, but at others, he emphasizes an almost metaphysical feeling among Japanese that they cannot make independent choices.

3. Cheer Up, Vietnam

1. Quoted in *Gendai shakai shiryōhen* [Collected materials on contemporary society] (Tokyo: Reibunsha, 1983): 290–91. I thank Hanai Kazuyo for having found these materials for me and also Professor Jin Sato for putting me in touch with her.

2. Christina Schwenkel, *The American War in Contemporary Vietnam: Transnational Remembrance and Representation* (Bloomington: Indiana University Press, 2009).

3. Charles K. Armstrong, "America's Korea, Korea's Vietnam," *Critical Asian Studies* 33, no. 4 (2001): 527–40.

4. A subsequent Academy Award winner, *Forrest Gump*, manages to out-*Platoon Platoon* by expressing sad but innocent bewilderment that the Vietnam War happened to America in the first place.

5. Many, however, continued to support and sponsor artists in the counterculture of the era. See William Marotti, *Money, Trains and Guillotines: Art and Revolution in 1960s Japan* (Durham, NC: Duke University Press, 2013).

6. Glenn D. Hook et al., *Japan's International Relations: Politics, Economics and Security*, 2nd ed. (London: Routledge, 2005), 103–5. For a superb English-language account of Japan's involvement in the Vietnam War, see Thomas Havens, *Fire across the Sea: The Vietnam War and Japan, 1965–1975* (Princeton, NJ: Princeton University Press, 1987).

7. See, for example, the "Haigujin" blog at http://d.hatena.ne.jp/haigujin/20100202/1265120742.

8. Simon Avenell, "From the 'People' to the 'Citizen': Tsurumi Shunsuke and the Roots of Civic Mythology in Postwar Japan," *positions: east asian cultures critique* 16, no. 3 (2008): 711–42. See also the commentaries on Avenell's "From the 'People' to the 'Citizen'" article in *positions: east asian cultures critique* 16, no. 3 (2008) by Laura Hein (743–51), J. Victor Koschmann (753–60), and Wesley Uemura-Sasaki (761–68).

9. This evocative English-language title is drawn from a line of dialogue but differs radically from the original Japanese title: *Totsunyūseyo: Asama Sanso Jiken* [Siege: The Asama Mountain Lodge incident].

10. Mark Schilling, "The Final Days of Revolutionary Struggle in Japan," *Japan Times*, March 20, 2008, https://www.japantimes.co.jp/culture/2008/03/20/films/the-final-days-of-revolutionary-struggle-in-japan/#.WfVrpkx7FPM.

11. The full Japanese title is *Jitsuroku Rengo Sekigun: Asama Sanso e no Michi* [United Red Army: The path to the Asama Mountain Lodge].

12. Kitada Akihiro, Komori Yōichi, and Narita Ryūichi, "Gaidomappu: 80–90 nendai" [Guide map: 1980s–90s], in *Sengo Nihon Sutadiizu 3 80–90 Nendai* [Postwar Japanese Studies 3: 1980s–1990s], ed. Iwasaki Minoru et al. (Tokyo: Kinokuniya Shoten, 2008), 6–42.

13. Yamashita Norihisa, "Posuto Reisen to 9.11 no Aida" [Between the post-cold war and 9/11], in *Sengo Nihon Sutadiizu 3 80–90 Nendai* [Postwar Japanese Studies 3: 1980s–1990s], ed. Iwasaki Minoru et al. (Tokyo: Kinokuniya Shoten, 2008), 43–64.

14. See, e.g., Abe Shinzō, *Utsukushii kuni e* [Toward a beautiful country] (Tokyo: Bunshun shinsho, 2006), 30–36.

15. Uno Shigeki, "Sengo Hoshushugi no Tenkanten to shite no 1979–1980: Ōhira hōkokusho—Saidoku" [1979–1980 as a turning point in postwar conservatism: Rereading the Ōhira Report], in *Sōhatsu Suru Nihon E: Posuto 'Ushinawareta 20-Nen' no Dessan* [Toward an emergent Japan: A sketch of the post-"lost decades"], ed. Andrew Gordon and Kazuhiro Takii (Tokyo: Kōbundō, 2018), 45–61. See also Akiko Takeyama, *Staged Seduction: Selling Dreams in a Tokyo Host Club* (Stanford, CA: Stanford University Press, 2016), chapter 1.

16. Fujiwara Kiichi, "Ajia no naka de no nihon no yakuwari" [Japan's role in the midst of Asia], NPO Sanka-gata Shisutemu Kenkyūkai lecture, October 3, 2007, http://www.systemken.org/2007.10.3.html.

17. Ministry of Foreign Affairs, "Japan's Official Development Assistance: Accomplishment and Progress of 50 Years," 2004, http://www.mofa.go.jp/policy/oda/cooperation/anniv50/pamphlet/progress1.html.

18. See, e.g., Alan Rix, *Japan's Economic Aid: Policymaking and Politics* (London: Croom Helm, 1980); Alan Rix, *Asia in Japan's Foreign Aid Challenge: Policy Reform and Aid Leadership* (London: Routledge, 1993); Dennis T. Yasutomo, *The Manner of Giving: Strategic Aid and Japanese Foreign Policy* (Lexington: Lexington, 1986); David M. Arase, *Buying Power: The Political Economy of Japan's Foreign Aid* (Boulder: Lynne Rienner, 1995).

19. Cited in Tsukamoto Tsuyoshi, "Waga kuni no ODA yoron no haaku to sono chōsa hōhō no ikkōsatsu" [A study of the popularity of ODA in Japan and survey methods for evaluating it], *Gaimushō Chōsa Geppō*, April 2004, 78.

20. See the 1990 comments by Upper House member Hironaka Wakako, then a member of Kōmeito, as Japan debated the extent of its participation in the Persian Gulf War. Hironaka, one of the few Kōmeito members who was not an adherent of the Sōka Gakkai religious sect, later split from the party and would become, after a number of years, a well-known member of the Democratic Party of Japan. See *Sūgi Honkaigi Gijiroku*, October 18, 1990.

21. For example, Mori Yoshirō, who would later become prime minister, drew ODA into a long but representative 1996 policy comment in the Lower House that rapidly moved toward a discussion of peacekeeping missions, revision of the UN Security Council (presumably to give Japan a seat), and the like. See *Shūgi Honkaigi Gijiroku*, December 2, 1996.

22. In a complex treatment of the subject, Oguma Eiji details the ways in which Japanese intellectuals approached "Asia" in the 1950s and 1960s, and particularly the effect of the Vietnam War on readings of Japanese war responsibility toward China. See Oguma Eiji, "Postwar Japanese Intellectuals' Changing Perspectives on 'Asia' and Modernity" (trans. Roger Brown), *Asia-Pacific Journal/Japan Focus* 5, no. 2 (2007), http://apjjf.org/-Oguma-Eiji/2350/article.pdf. Relations with Southeast Asia were rocked only infrequently, such as with the Malari riots that followed Prime Minister Tanaka Kakuei's visit to Indonesia in 1974. But even these riots were directed more at foreign investment and government corruption than at Japan's wartime legacies, however bitterly they were remembered in parts of Indonesia.

23. David Leheny, *The Rules of Play: National Identity and the Shaping of Japanese Leisure* (Ithaca, NY: Cornell University Press, 2003), 144–45.

24. Robert Wade, "Japan, the World Bank, and the Art of Paradigm Maintenance: The East Asian Miracle in Political Perspective," *New Left Review* 217 (May-June 1996): 3–36. See also David M. Seddon, "Japanese and British Overseas Aid Compared," in *Japan's Foreign Aid: Old Continuities and New Directions,* ed. David M. Arase (Oxon, UK: Routledge, 2005), 41–80.

25. For a contemporary rendering of the pro–Asian-values position, see Fareed Zakaria, "Culture Is Destiny: A Conversation with Lee Kwan Yew," *Foreign Affairs* 73, no. 2 (1994): 109–26.

26. For historical treatments of these debates, see J. Victor Koschmann, "Asianism's Ambivalent Legacy," in *Network Power: Japan in Asia,* ed. Peter J. Katzenstein and Takashi Shiraishi (Ithaca, NY: Cornell University Press, 1997), 83–110; Cemil Aydin, *The Politics of Anti-Westernism in Asia: Visions of World Order in Pan-Islamic and Pan-Asian Thought* (New York: Columbia University Press, 2007).

27. Leo Ching, "Globalizing the Regional, Regionalizing the Global: Mass Culture and Asianism in the Age of Late Capital," *Public Culture* 12, no. 1 (2000): 233–57; Koichi Iwabuchi, "Nostalgia for a (Different) Asian Modernity: Media Consumption of 'Asia' in Japan," *positions: east asia cultures critique* 10, no. 3 (2002): 547–73.

28. See, e.g., Ter Ellingson, *The Myth of the Noble Savage* (Berkeley: University of California Press, 2001).

29. Alvin L. Young, Paul F. Cecil, and John F. Guilmartin, "Assessing Possible Exposures of Ground Troops to Agent Orange during the Vietnam War: The Use of Contemporary Military Records," *Environmental Science and Pollution Research* 11, no. 6 (2004): 349–58.

30. The VA uses the Agent Orange Act of 1991 as the key guide, saying that compensation benefits are available to anyone with symptoms of exposure who "set foot in Vietnam (This includes brief visits ashore, such as when a ship docked to the shore of Vietnam or when a ship operated in Vietnam's close coastal waters for extended periods and crew members went ashore, or smaller vessels from the ship went ashore with supplies or personnel. The Veteran further must provide a statement of personally going ashore.)" or who "served on a ship

while it operated on the inland waterways of Vietnam." See http://www.publichealth.va.gov/exposures/agentorange/locations/vietnam.asp.

31. Japanese accounts at the time as well as since the war raise some questions about the ethics of representation. In *Jirai o fundara sayōnara*, Ichinose is a robust and fearless young man, charming not only because of his easy rapport with his Cambodian friends (with one he has the kind of brotherly relationship idealized in a number of Japanese films) but also because of his great courage in the face of intense personal risk. That is, a number of scenes in the film resemble those of American war films, at least low- to mid-budget ones, with chaotic physical action and a hero dodging bullets while running between trenches. Because he is armed with a camera rather than a gun, however, the audience can have its cake and eat it too; warfare becomes spectacle, but the protagonist's nonlethal tools and goals can be stand-ins for the audience's own adherence to peaceful or at least antimilitarist norms.

32. Nakamura writes that the names are traditional ways of saying "second and third sons" in Vietnamese. See Nakamura Gorō, "Viet and Duc, Their Lives Raise Some Questions," in The Group Hoping for Viet and Duc's Development (ed.), *Cheer Up, Viet and Duc*, trans. Mieko Tsuzuki (Kyoto: Kamogawa Shuppan, 1987), 3. An *Asahi Shimbun* roundup correctly notes the meaning of their ages.

33. http://www.aspeninstitute.org/policy-work/agent-orange/what-agent-orange/map-dioxin.

34. "'Nijū taiji' wa mushin ni waratta" [The conjoined twins smiled innocently], *Asahi Shimbun*, January 14, 1983, 23.

35. http://english.vietnamnet.vn/fms/society/91883/a-woman-s-fight-against-the-pain-of-agent-orange.html.

36. Tine M. Gammeltoft, *Haunting Images: A Cultural Account of Selective Reproduction in Vietnam* (Berkeley: University of California Press, 2014), 48–49.

37. "Karehazai wa jinrui no teki: shashin o motte hōbei e" [Agent Orange is the enemy of mankind: Taking the photos to America], *Asahi Shimbun*, October 27, 1982, evening edition, 18; Nakamura Gorō, *Haha wa karehazai o abita: Daiokishin no kizuato* (Tokyo: Iwanami, 1983).

38. Bunro Fujimoto, "A Wheelchair Campaign for Viet and Duc," in Group, *Cheer Up*, 8–17.

39. Fujimoto Bunrō and Takano Tetsuo, *Sensō to shōgaisha: betonamu kara no shōgen* (Tokyo: Aoki Shoten, 1981).

40. "Betonamu no shiamu futaseiji okoru kuruma-isu kansei" [Completion of the wheelchair for the Siamese twins in Vietnam], *Asahi Shimbun*, July 3, 1985, 22.

41. "Betonamu nijū taiji no ken'i Fon-sensei, itsuka ni TV de kinkyō o hōkoku" [Authority on Vietnam's conjoined twins, Dr. Phuong, to report on their circumstances on TV on the 5th], *Asahi Shimbun*, November 3, 1985, 22. For English-language discussions of the popularity of and controversies around *News Station*, see Kristin Kyoko Altman, "Television and Political Turmoil: Japan's Summer of 1993," in *Media and Politics in Japan*, ed. Susan J. Pharr and Ellis S. Krauss (Honolulu: University of Hawaii Press, 1996), 170–71; Ellis S. Krauss, *Broadcasting Politics in Japan: NHK and Television News* (Ithaca, NY: Cornell University Press, 2000), 220–40; Ellis S. Krauss, "Changing Television News in Japan," *Journal of Asian Studies* 57, no. 3 (1998): 663–92.

42. Fujimoto Bunro, Shibuya Terumi, and Sekiyama Yoshiko, "Tōkō: Betonamu no iryō, kango, kaigo wa ima—watashitachi no manabukoto wa" [Contribution—Vietnam's medical and nursing care: What we can learn], *Inochi to kurashi* 30 (March 2010): 39.

43. Kutsuwada Takafumi, "Nijū taiji no Beto-chan, nichi-aka ishidan ga kansatsu (jiji-kokkoku)" [Minute by minute: Japan Red Cross doctors observe conjoined twin, Viet], *Asahi Shimbun*, June 13, 1986, 3.

44. "Beto-chan kyūen de 4 ishi ga genchi e, shushō ga kyōryoku o hatsumei" [Four doctors sent to site to aid Viet, prime minister expresses support], *Asahi Shimbun*, June 11, 1986, 22.

45. Nakasone Yasuhiro, "Kokusai kokka nihon no dōhyō" [The signposts of international country Japan], June 29, 1986. In *Nakasone Ensetsushū* [The collected speeches of Nakasone], 343–53, and reproduced by the Sekai to Nihon Database. See http://www.ioc.u-tokyo.ac.jp/~worldjpn/documents/texts/exdpm/19860629.S1J.html.

46. See Gerald Curtis, *The Logic of Japanese Politics: Leaders, Institutions, and the Limits of Change* (New York: Columbia University Press, 1999), 34.

47. See particularly the conclusion of Miwa Kazuo, "Kamisama to Tatakikatta Isha no Zenkiroku" [The complete record of the doctors who fought against the gods], *Bungei Shunjū*, August 1989, 398–419.

48. Her answers at a press conference in mid-July were typically compelling. See "Seimei no kiki satta" [The immediate crisis has passed], *Mainichi Shimbun*, July 15, 1986, 22.

49. Miwa, "Kamisama," 407.

50. "Couple Reunited after 11 Years," *Pacific Stars and Stripes*, August 2, 1986, 11.

51. Bill Cormier, "Congresswoman Helped Cut Red Tape to Speed Reunion, Friend Says," Associated Press, August 3, 1986, http://www.apnewsarchive.com/1986/Congresswoman-Helped-Cut-Red-Tape-to-Speed-Reunion-Friend-Says.

52. "Betonamu nijiu taiji iryō, aratamete 2 joi ga rainichi e" [Two female doctors scheduled again to visit Japan for the care of the Vietnamese conjoined twins], *Asahi Shimbun*, August 12, 1986, 22.

53. "Naki-beso Doku-chan nikkori Beto-chan, nijū taiji 4-kagetsu buri kikoku" [Sobbing Duc and smiling Viet, the conjoined twins return home after four months], *Yomiuri Shimbun*, October 29, 1986, evening edition, 19; "Genki ni natta Beto-chan, Doku-chan—Shin 87," *Asahi Shimbun*, February 23, 1987, evening edition, 1.

54. Matsui Yayori, "Itō Kimiko-san 'Minamata kara betonamu e kenshinsha o okurukai' (hito)" [Itō Kimiko of the group sending mobile checkup units from Minamata to Vietnam (profile)], *Asahi Shimbun*, March 25, 1987, 3.

55. Matsutani Miyoko's picture book (with artwork by Iguchi Bunshū), *Beto-chan Doku-chan kara no tegami* [Letters from Viet and Duc] (Tokyo: Dōshinsha, 1991), is visceral and visually explicit on this issue.

56. Miwa, "Kamisama."

57. Usanami Yūsaku, "Beto-chan, Doku-chan bunri shujutsu kara 1shūkan (jijikokkoku)" [Minute-by-minute: one week since Viet and Duc's separation surgery], *Asahi Shimbun*, October 11, 1988, 3.

58. "Bunri shujutsu seikō, omowazu namida—Fon-hakushi 'shiawase desu'" ["I'm so happy"—Dr. Phuong tears up after the separation surgery's success], *Yomiuri Shimbun*, October 5, 1988, 31.

59. "Bunri shujutsu 1 yoake, Doku-chan 'ashi ga itai' to naku" [At daybreak after the separation surgery, Duc cries "My leg hurts"], *Asahi Shimbun*, October 5, 1988, 15.

60. "'Beto-chan doko?' Doku-chan, bunri kizuku" ["Where's Viet?" Duc realizes they've been separated], *Asahi Shimbun*, October 6, 1987, evening edition, 19.

61. Takamura Yōichi and Ōta Arisa, "Ketsugō taisō seiji 'Bin-chan Tan-chan' ganbare, bunri seikō no kora 'gaarufurendo ni'" [Good luck, conjoined twins "Bin-chan and Tan-chan"—previously separated twins say they'll be their girlfriends], *Mainichi Shimbun*, March 31, 1991, Osaka edition, 29. Although the word is common enough to be unsurprising, it is worth noting that *ganbare* (variously meaning "hang in there, do your best, good luck, cheer up") is the key title word in the Negau Kai's 1987 book about Viet and Duc, *Ganbare Beto-chan Doku-chan*. I have in this passage left the names of the other twins rendered in Japanese

spelling with "-chan" at the end because they are identified only in Japanese and their identities cannot be verified in English.

62. "Betonamu—ketsugō taisō joji Bin-chan, Tan-chan bunri shujutsu e, nihon ni 'sukūkai'" [Creation of the "group to save" Vietnam's conjoined girls Bin-chan and Tan-chan with separation surgery], *Mainichi Shimbun,* March 31, 1991, Osaka edition, 1. Yamamoto recalls his efforts and puts them in the context of his longer career as an peace activist in "Ibuningu Ai—View21—Tsutaetai koto—Yamamoto Naoya Shikai" [Evening eye—view 21—dentist Yamamoto Naoya, in my words], *Mainichi Shimbun,* October 12, 2000, Osaka evening edition, 1.

63. "Betonamu ketsugō taisō seiji Bin-chan, Tan-chan (Ue)—Dakenai wagako" [First part—Vietnamese conjoined twins Bin-Chan and Tan-chan—we can't hold our little girls in our arms], *Mainichi Shimbun,* April 10, 1991, Osaka edition, 22; "Betonamu ketsugō taisō seiji Bin-chan, Tan-chan—Inochi o motomete—Chū" [Middle part—Vietnamese conjoined twins Bin-Chan and Tan-chan—hanging on to life], *Mainichi Shimbun,* April 11, 1991, Osaka edition, 26; "Betonamu ketsugō taisō seiji Bin-chan, Tan-chan—Hirogaru shien no wa" [Vietnamese conjoined twins Bin-Chan and Tan-chan—the widening circle of support], *Mainichi Shimbun,* April 12, 1991, Osaka edition, 26; "Betonamu no ketsugō taisō seiji no bin-chan, Tan-chan sukūkai o setsuritsu" [Establishment of the group to save Bin-Chan and Tan-chan, Vietnamese conjoined twins], *Mainichi Shimbun,* April 23, 1991, Osaka evening edition, 10.

64. "Ketsugō taisō seiji no Bin-chan, Tan-chan kyūshi—bunri shujutsu ma ni awazu—Betonamu" [Vietnam: Conjoined twins Bin-chan and Tan-Chan die suddenly—separation surgery not in time], *Mainichi Shimbun,* May 9, 1991, 26.

65. "'Bin, Tan kikin' gienkin yaku 881-man-en o 19nichi ni zōtei" [881,000,000¥ relief fund, the Bin-Tan Fund, to be donated on the 19th], *Mainichi Shimbun,* October 15, 1991, 26.

66. Matsutani, *Beto-chan Doku-chan kara no tegami.*

67. Nomizo Takayo, "(Koe) Beto-chan no onegai tsutaeta yo" [Voice: Viet, I told them your request], *Asahi Shimbun,* October 18, 2007.

68. See Tomiko Yoda, "A Roadmap to Millennial Japan," *South Atlantic Quarterly* 99, no. 4 (2000): 629–68.

69. Esaki Misato, Tsudome Masatoshi, and Fujimoto Bunrō, eds., *Beto-chan to Doku-chan ga oshitete kureta mono* [What Viet and Duc taught us] (Kyoto: Creates Kamogawa, 2009).

70. Indeed, it was the source of the mockery in the recurring (1991–1996) *Saturday Night Live* skit "Unfrozen Caveman Lawyer," starring the program's greatest-ever cast member, Phil Hartman.

71. For an analogous analytical problem, see Jennifer Robertson, "Reflexivity Redux: A Pithy Polemic on 'Positionality,'" *Anthropological Quarterly* 75, no. 4 (2002): 785–92.

72. Nguyen Duc, "Yume wa shōgaisha o shien suru katsudō" [My dream is to help the disabled], interview by Esaki Misato in Ho Chi Minh City, 2008, in Esaki, Tsudome, and Fujimoto, *Beto-chan to Doku-chan ga oshitete kureta mono,* 3–10.

73. Tsudome Masatoshi, "Saisho no ippo o kizamu to iu koto" [What it means to mark that first step], in Esaki, Tsudome, and Fujimoto, *Beto-chan to Doku-chan ga oshitete kureta mono,* 145–46.

74. http://tuoitrenews.vn/features/13984/vietduc-separation-surgery-celebrates-25-year-anniversary.

4. Cool Optimism

1. See Karel van Wolferen's classic statement *The Enigma of Japanese Power: People and Politics in a Stateless Nation* (New York: Vintage, 1990).

2. Richard N. Rosecrance, *The Rise of the Trading State: Commerce and Conquest in the Modern World* (New York: Basic, 1986); Hanns W. Maull, "Germany and Japan: The New Civilian Powers," *Foreign Affairs* 69, no. 5 (1990/1991).

3. Bruce M. Russett, "The Mysterious Case of Vanishing Hegemony, or, Is Mark Twain Really Dead?" *International Organization* 38, no. 2 (1985): 207–31.

4. Joseph S. Nye, "Soft Power," *Foreign Policy* 80 (Autumn 1990): 155.

5. The term was popularized by French Foreign Minister Hubert Vedrine in 1999: "To Paris, U.S. Looks Like a 'Hyperpower,'" *New York Times*, February 5, 1999.

6. Ty Solomon argues that the affective component of soft power helps to make sense of the discourses surrounding it. See "The Affective Underpinnings of Soft Power," *European Journal of International Relations* 20, no. 3 (2014): 720–41.

7. David Leheny, "A Narrow Place to Cross Swords: Soft Power and the Politics of Japanese Popular Culture in East Asia," in *Beyond Japan: The Dynamics of East Asian Regionalism*, ed. Peter J. Katzenstein and Takashi Shiraishi (Ithaca, NY: Cornell University Press, 2006), 211–36.

8. See Roland Kelts, *Japanamerica: How Japanese Pop Culture Has Invaded the U.S.* (New York: Palgrave Macmillan, 2006); Sugiura Tsutomu, "Japan's Creative Industries: Culture as a Source of Soft Power in the Industrial Sector," in *Soft Power Superpowers: Cultural and National Assets of the United States and Japan,* ed. Watanabe Yasushi and David L. McConnell (Armonk, NY: Sharpe, 2008), 128–53.

9. Nissim Kadosh Otmazgin's extensive writing on the subject is the best collection of examples. See *Regionalizing Culture: The Political Economy of Japanese Popular Culture in Asia* (Honolulu: University of Hawaii Press, 2013); "Contesting Soft Power: Japanese Popular Culture in East and Southeast Asia," *International Relations of the Asia-Pacific* 8, no. 1 (2008): 73–101; "Geopolitics and Soft Power: Japan's Cultural Policy and Cultural Diplomacy in Asia," *Asia-Pacific Review* 19, no. 1 (2012): 37–61. See also Watanabe Yasushi and David L. McConnell, "Introduction," in Watanabe and McConnell, *Soft Power Superpowers,* xvii–xxxii.

10. See, e.g., Roland Kelts, "Japanamerica: Why 'Cool Japan' Is Over," *3 A.M.,* 2010, http://www.3ammagazine.com/3am/japanamerica-why-cool-japan-is-over.

11. Ian Condry, *Hip-Hop Japan: Rap and the Paths of Cultural Globalization* (Durham, NC: Duke University Press, 2006).

12. Daniel White, "The Affect-Emotion Gap: Soft Power, Nation Branding, and Cultural Administration in Japan" (PhD diss., Rice University, 2011). See also Kōichi Iwabuchi, "Pop-Culture Diplomacy in Japan: Soft Power, Nation Branding and the Question of 'International Cultural Exchange,'" *International Journal of Cultural Policy* 21, no. 4 (2015): 419–32.

13. Though not for lack of trying. For one creative and strong example, see Nissim Otzmagin's studies of the industrial structure of Japanese pop culture's spread in East Asia: Nissim Kadosh Otmazgin, *Regionalizing Culture: The Political Economy of Japanese Popular Culture in Asia* (Honolulu: University of Hawaii Press, 2013).

14. The best source on the history and transformations of J-pop in either Japanese or English is Michael Bourdaghs, *Sayonara Amerika, Sayonara Nippon: A Geopolitical Prehistory of J-Pop* (New York: Columbia University Press, 2012).

15. Geoff Burpee, "Dreams Come True Gets Asia to Perk Up Its Ears to Japanese Pop," *Billboard*, March 1, 1997, Asia-Pacific Quarterly section, 1–2, 6.

16. Steve McClure, "Japanese Pop Sweeps Across Asia," *Billboard*, January 8, 2000, 42, 86.

17. Elisa Kim, "Korea Loosens Ban on Japanese Pop Culture," *Billboard*, July 22, 2000, 68–77.

18. Yomiuri Shimbun, "Kayō CD ya Gēmu Sofuto mo, Kankoku ga Nihon Bunka Kaihō e" [Korea moves toward openness for Japanese culture—popular CDs, game software, and the like], *Yomiuri Shimbun*, September 16, 2003, http://www.yomiuri.co.jp/entertainment/news/20030916it13.htm.

19. Suh-Kyung Yoon, "Swept Up on a Wave," *Far Eastern Economic Review*, October 18, 2001, 92–94. The best study of K-pop is John Lie's superbly illuminating *K-Pop: Popular Music, Cultural Amnesia, and Economic Innovation in South Korea* (Berkeley: University of California Press, 2014).

20. Steve Mollman, "No Fly Zones," *Asiaweek*, November 30, 2001.

21. Steve Mollman, "Playing the Field," *Asiaweek*, November 30, 2001.

22. Dejitaru Kontentsu Kyōkai, *Deijitaru Kontentsu Hakusho 2003* [Digital Contents White Paper 2003] (Tokyo: METI/Digitaru Kontentsu Kyōkai, 2003).

23. See the comments by Capcom President Tsujimoto Kenzō in "Kontentsu Sangyō Kokusai Senryaku Kenkyūkai (Dai 1 Kai) Gijiroku" [Minutes of the first meeting of the Content Industry International Strategy Research Group], April 2003, 5–7, www.meti.go.jp.

24. Kōichi Iwabuchi, *Recentering Globalization: Popular Culture and Japanese Transnationalism* (Durham, NC: Duke University Press, 2002), 135–57.

25. "An Anime Culture Blossoms in Japan," *Focus Japan*, March 2003.

26. Bandai Group, *Annual Report 2002* (Tokyo: Bandai Group, 2002).

27. Kunikawa Kyōko, "Japan Meets Korian Mūbī" [Japan meets Korean film], *Pia* 1039 (February 16, 2004): 28–31.

28. "Japanese Hit Cartoon Gets US Release," April 19, 2002, *BBC Online*, http://news.bbc.co.uk/2/hi/entertainment/1939090.stm.

29. "Japanese Animated Movie 'Spirited Away' Big Hit in Korea," Kyodo News Service, July 18, 2002.

30. Comparative international and American box office data supplied by Box Office Mojo, www.boxofficemojo.com. To be fair, *Spirited Away* did edge the forgettable *Lilo & Stitch* at the global box office for the year but was behind both the competent *Ice Age* and the execrable *Scooby-Doo*.

31. Yoshiko Nakano, "Who Initiates a Global Flow? Japanese Popular Culture in Asia," *Visual Communication* 1, no. 2 (2002): 229–53.

32. For leading examples, see Jennifer Robertson, *Takarazuka: Sexual Politics and Popular Culture in Modern Japan* (Berkeley: University of California Press, 1998); D. P. Martinez, ed., *The Worlds of Japanese Popular Culture: Gender, Shifting Boundaries, and Global Culture* (Cambridge: Cambridge University Press, 1998); and Sepp Linhart and Sabine Frühstück, eds., *The Culture of Japan as Seen through Its Leisure* (Albany, NY: SUNY Press, 1998).

33. Iwabuchi, *Recentering Globalization*, 70.

34. Saya Shiraishi, "Japan's Soft Power: Doraemon Goes Overseas," in *Network Power: Japan and Asia*, ed. Peter J. Katzenstein and Takashi Shiraishi (Ithaca, NY: Cornell University Press, 1997), 234–74.

35. Tsujii Takeshi, "Nihon Bunka wa Naze Suitai no Ka?" [Why did Japanese culture decline?], *Sekai*, April 1998, 57–68; Iwabuchi Koichi, "Gurobarizēshon no Naka no Nihon Bunka no Nioi" [The odor of Japanese culture under globalization], *Sekai*, April 1998, 69–81; Chō Kyō, "Bunka ga Jōhō ni Natta Toki" [When culture becomes information], *Sekai*, April 1998, 82–91.

36. Kina Shōkichi and Shin Sugok, "Nihon Bunka tte Nan Da?" [What the Hell is Japanese culture?], *Sekai*, April 1998, 123–25.

37. Sharon Kinsella, "Japanese Subculture in the 1990s: Otaku and the Amateur Manga Movement," *Journal of Japanese Studies* 24, no. 2 (1998): 308–10.

38. Nakamori Akio and Miyadai Shinji, "Otaku-ka" [Nerd-ization], in *Poppu Karuchā* [Pop culture], ed. Miyadai Shinji and Matsuzawa Kureichi (Tokyo: Mainichi Shimbunsha, 1999), 90–95. *Otaku* was originally published in Japanese in 2001 as *Dōbutsuka suru posutomodanu: otaku kara mita nihon shakai* [Animalizing postmodernity: Japan as seen by the otaku] (Tokyo: Kōdansha gendai shinsho). Jonathan Abel and Shion Kono later translated it into English as *Otaku: Japan's Database Animals* (Minneapolis: University of Minnesota Press, 2009).

39. Michael Darling, "Plumbing the Depths of Superflatness," *Art Journal* 60, no. 3 (2001): 76–89.

40. In addition to Murakami's own book *Superflat*, see, e.g., Yamaguchi Yumi, *Tokyo Trash Web: The Book* (Tokyo: Bijutsu Shuppansha, 1999); and Nagae Akira, *Tarase no Jidai: Otaku na Nihon no Sūpāfuratto* [The age of flatness: Nerdy Japan's superflatness] (Tokyo: Hara Shobō, 2003). Yamaguchi's book (in Japanese, English title notwithstanding) is especially effective as a cacophonous visual accompaniment to her central point about the horrid beauty of modern Tokyo: everything is trash, everything is equal, everything is part of the mix. Sociologist Adrien Favell's excellent *Before and after Superflat: A Short History of Japanese Contemporary Art 1990–2011* (Hong Kong: Blue Kingfisher, 2012) provides a critical and somewhat controversial overview.

41. Douglas McGray, "Japan's Gross National Cool," *Foreign Policy* (May/June 2002): 44–54, http://www.foreignpolicy.com/issue_mayjune_2002/mcgray.html.

42. Jim Frederick, "What's Right with Japan?" *Time Asia*, August 11, 2003.

43. Takenaka Heizō, "Nihon Keizai Saisei no Kagi" [The key to Japan's economic revitalization], in *Posuto IT Kakumei "Sofuto Pawā" Nihon Fukken e no Michi* [Soft power after the information technology revolution: The road to Japan's rehabilitation], ed. Takenaka Heizō (Tokyo: Fujita Institute of Future Management, 2001), 14–30.

44. Kamiya Matake, "Sofuto Pawā to wa Nani Ka?" [What is soft power?], in *Posuto IT Kakumei "Sofuto Pawā" Nihon Fukken e no Michi* [Soft power after the information technology revolution: The road to Japan's rehabilitation], ed. Takenaka Heizō (Tokyo: Fujita Institute of Future Management, 2001), 31–64.

45. Aoki Tamotsu, "'Miwaku Suru Chikara' to Bunka Seisaku" ["The power to fascinate" and cultural policy], in *Posuto IT Kakumei "Sofuto Pawā" Nihon Fukken e no Michi* [Soft power after the information technology revolution: The road to Japan's rehabilitation], ed. Takenaka Heizō (Tokyo: Fujita Institute of Future Management, 2001), 146–76.

46. Dejitaru Kontentsu Kyōkai, *Deijitaru Kontentsu Hakusho 2003*, 24–25.

47. Uehara Nobumoto, "Kako no Seifu Hōkokusho ni Miru Kontentsu Seisaku no Ronten" [Topics in digital content policy, as seen through previous government reports], Ministry of Public Management, Home Affairs, and Posts and Telecommunications, June 11, 2003, www.ppp.am/digicon/archive/ueharjpolicy4.ppt.

48. David Leheny, *The Rules of Play: National Identity and the Shaping of Japanese Leisure* (Ithaca, NY: Cornell University Press, 2003), 133–73.

49. This is how I read Jepperson's definition of institutions, which holds that they are "socially constructed, routine-reproduced (*ceteris paribus*), program or rule systems. They operate as relative fixtures of constraining environments and are accompanied by taken-for-granted accounts." See Ronald L. Jepperson, "Institutions, Institutional Effects, and Institutionalism," in *The New Institutionalism in Organizational Analysis*, ed. Paul J. DiMaggio and Walter W. Powell (Chicago: University of Chicago Press, 1991), 149.

50. Derek Hall, "Japanese Spirit, Western Economics: The Continuing Salience of Economic Nationalism in Japan," *New Political Economy* 9, no. 1 (2004): 79–99.

51. Kankō Rikkoku Kondankai, "Kankō Rikkoku Kondankai Hōkokusho: Sundeyoshi, Otozureteyoshi no Kuni Zukuri" [Final report of the Japan Tourism Advisory Council: Building a country where one wants to travel and reside] (Tokyo: Prime Minister's Office, 2003).

See also Awata Fusaho, "'Kankōryoku' no Kōzō to Wa: Sofuto Pawā to shite no 'Nippon Bu-rando Senryaku' o Kangaeru" (What is the structure of "tourism power": Considering the "Japan brand strategy" as "soft power"), *Unsō to Keizai* [Transportation and economy] 63, no. 7 (2003): 53–62.

52. Yoriko Kawaguchi, "Common Opportunities: Japan and Canada in the 21st Century," June 14, 2002, http://www.mofa.go.jp/region/n-america/canada/p_ship21/fmspeech. html.

53. Kokusai Kōryū Kenkyūkai, "Arata na Jidai no Gaikō to Arata na Kokusai Kōryū no Yakuwari" [Diplomacy in a new era, and a new role for international exchange] (Tokyo: Japan Foundation, April 2003).

54. It has since been merged with the former Ministry of Home Affairs to become Sōmushō, which literally translates as the General Affairs Ministry but is officially known in English as the Ministry of Internal Affairs and Communications. See also Leheny, "A Narrow Place," 227.

55. Dejitaru Kontentsu Kyōkai, *Deijitaru Kontentsu Hakusho 2003,* 158–61.

56. See, once again, Tsujimoto Kenzō's comments in the "Kontentsu Sangyō Kokusai Senryaku Kenkyūkai (Dai 1 Kai) Gijiroku," 5–7.

57. These questions appear in the general working group document "Dejitaru Kontentsu WG no Kentō Jōkyō" [Investigative conditions for the Digital Content Working Group], produced by the Jōhō Tsūshin Sofuto Kondankai [Information Transmission and Software Discussion Council] (Tokyo: Sōmusho, 2003).

58. "Onna wa kawatta. Otoko wa dō da?" The writer Takeda Satetsu mocks the series in an online column about the state of the publishing industry: "Shinsho ya AERA ni umanjiru to iu koto" [What it means to reconcile yourself to booklets and *AERA*], *CINRA-Net,* September 21, 2010, https://www.cinra.net/column/norika14–2.

59. *Gaikō Foramu* 174 (January 2003), especially the international vignettes on 30–45.

60. Tadokoro Masayuki, "Sofuto Pawā to iu Gaikō Shigen o Minaoese" [Rethinking soft power as a diplomatic resource], *Chūō Kōron,* May 2003, 120–28; Susan Napier and Okada Toshio, "'Gendai Nihon no Anime' ga Amerika no Otona o Kaeru" ["Contemporary Japanese anime" are changing American adults], *Chūō Kōron,* May 2003, 142–48.

61. Nagatsuma Akira, "Sofuto Pawāto Hādo Pawā: Heiwa o Tsukuridasu Chie Nihon wa Sofuto Pawā de Sekai Toppu o Mezase" [Soft power and hard power: Japan should aim its soft power toward leading the world in the knowledge to build peace], *Huffington Post* (Japanese), August 18, 2015, https://www.huffingtonpost.jp/akira-nagatsuma/soft-hard-diplomacy_b_7996122.html.

62. See Takashina Shōji, Fukukawa Shinji, and Fujii Hiroaki, "Nihonjin wa Sofuto Pawā o motto Katsuyō Subeki" [Japanese must make more use of their soft power], *Gaikō Foramu,* January 2003, 18–27, especially comments by Fujii on 20 and Takashina on 22.

63. Paul Midford, "Japan's Response to Terror: Dispatching the SDF to the Arabian Sea," *Asian Survey* 43, no. 2 (2003): 329–51.

64. Indeed, one could easily find references to "soft power" in the Web pages of the New Komeitō (http://www.komei.or.jp/policy/detail/5-1.htm), the Democratic Party's Hatoyama Yukio (http://www.hatoyama.gr.jp/cont09/cont08.html), and the long version of the Liberal Democratic Party's 2003 "policy manifesto," available at Lower House member Kosugi Takashi's Web page (http://www.threeweb.ad.jp/~takosugi/manifesto).

65. See Joseph S. Nye, *The Paradox of American Power: Why the World's Only Superpower Can't Go It Alone* (New York: Oxford University Press, 2002); Joseph S. Nye, "The Velvet Hegemon: How Soft Power Can Help Defeat Terrorism," *Foreign Policy* 136 (May/June 2003): 74–75.

66. Although their language and goals differ from mine, Janice Bially-Mattern's and Craig Hayden's analyses of US soft power also reflect on narrative. See Janice Bially-Mattern, "Why

Soft Power Isn't So Soft: Representational Force and the Sociolinguistic Construction of Attraction in World Politics," *Millennium: Journal of International Studies* 33, no. 3 (2005): 583–612; Craig Hayden, *The Rhetoric of Soft Power: Public Diplomacy in Global Contexts* (Lanham, MD: Lexington, 2012). Solomon positions his article as a sympathetic correction of both works by focusing on affect and emotion.

67. See Donovan Schaefer's comments on addiction as a metaphor for cruel optimism in "The Promise of Affect: The Politics of the Event in Ahmed's *The Promise of Happiness* and Berlant's *Cruel Optimism*," *Theory & Event* 16, no. 2 (2013).

68. Perhaps the most widely read example is Joshua Kurlantzick's fabulously alarmist *Charm Offensive: How China's Soft Power Is Transforming the World* (New Haven, CT: Yale University Press, 2007). For a more measured and sophisticated contribution that also reflects on the competitive dynamics of soft power initiatives, see Jing Sun's *Japan and China as Charm Rivals: Soft Power in Regional Diplomacy* (Ann Arbor: University of Michigan Press, 2012). There are also many works by prominent European scholars and policy makers on the topic of soft power. Former Swedish Prime Minister Carl Bildt's 2005 op-ed in the *Financial Times* is among the most elegant such statements. See Bildt, "Europe Must Keep Its Soft Power," *Financial Times,* May 31, 2005, http://on.ft.com/1NxEwWY.

69. See David Lake's "Status, Authority, and the End of the American Century" in *Status in World Politics*, ed. T. V. Paul, Deborah Welch Larson, and William C. Wohlforth (Cambridge: Cambridge University Press, 2014), 246–69. This refers to concepts developed in Lake's widely hailed *Hierarchy in International Relations* (Ithaca, NY: Cornell University Press, 2009). Also see Deborah Welch Larson, T. V. Paul, and William C. Wohlforth, "Status and World Order," in Paul, Larson, and Wohlforth, *Status in World Politics*, 7–13.

70. Iwabuchi, *Recentering Globalization*, 33–35.

71. See the articles in the January 2003 *Gaikō Fōramu* special issue on "Nippon Burando."

72. Iwabuchi, *Recentering Globalization*, 139–57.

73. Nakano Yoshiko and Wu Yongmei, "Puchiburu no Kurashikata: Chūgoku no Daigakusei ga Mita Nihon no Dorama" [Lifestyles of the petit bourgeois: How Chinese university students watch Japanese dramas]," in *Gurōbaru Purizumu: 'Ajian Dorīmu' to Shite no Nihon no Terebi Dorama* [The global prism: Japanese television dramas as the "Asian dream"], ed. Iwabuchi Kōichi (Tokyo: Heibonsha), 183–219.

74. I thank Nakano Yoshiko for making this point in correspondence.

75. Tsūshō Sangyōsho Yoka Kaihatsutshitsu [MITI Leisure Development Office], ed., *Yoka Sōran: Shakai, Sangyō, Seisaku* [Overview of leisure: society, industry, and policy] (Tokyo: Dayamondo, 1974), 315.

76. Leheny, *The Rules of Play,* 15, 179–80.

77. Takashina, Fukukawa, and Fujii, "Nihonjin wa Sofuto Pawā o motto Katsuyō Subeki," especially Fujii on 23.

78. On the program *Cool Japan*, see Alexandra Hambleton, "Reinforcing Identities: Non-Japanese Residents, Television and Cultural Nationalism in Japan," *Contemporary Japan* 23, no. 1 (2011): 27–47.

5. Staging *The Empire of Light*

1. Akiko Takeyama, *Staged Seduction: Selling Dreams in a Tokyo Host Club* (Stanford, CA: Stanford University Press, 2016), chapter 1.

2. For an excellent study, see Jeffrey Ravel, *The Contested Parterre: Public Theater and French Political Culture 1680–1791* (Ithaca, NY: Cornell University Press, 1999), especially his arresting depiction of a 1724 performance of Voltaire's *Mariamne*, 126–31. See also Brian

James DeMare, *Mao's Cultural Army: Drama Troupes in China's Rural Revolution* (Cambridge: Cambridge University Press, 2015).

3. Barry Unsworth, *Morality Play* (London: Hamish Hamilton, 1995).

4. John K. Gillespie, "Modern Japanese Theater," in *Routledge Handbook of Asian Theatre*, ed. Siyuan Liu (Oxon, UK: Routledge, 2016), 292–95. For an extended discussion of Sadayakko's career and impact on representations of Japanese femininity, see Ayako Kano, *Acting Like a Woman in Modern Japan: Theater, Gender, and Nationalism* (New York: Palgrave, 2001).

5. Siyuan Liu, "The Impact of *Shinpa* on Early Chinese *Huaju*," *Asian Theatre Journal* 23, no. 2 (2006): 342–55. See also Siyuan Liu, "Adaptation as Appropriation: Staging Western Drama in the First Western-Style Theatres in Japan and China," *Theatre Journal* 59 (2007): 411–29.

6. Aaron Gerow weaves discussions of theatrical and cinematic *shinpa* into his analysis of early-twentieth-century Japanese film, wisely noting as well the ways in which later discussions of *shinpa* films would tend to depict them as an "aberrant curiosity," a form ready to be displaced by better, more "modern" films. See Aaron Gerow, *Visions of Japanese Modernity: Articulations of Cinema, Nation, and Spectatorship, 1895–1925* (Berkeley: University of California Press, 2010), 97. Also see Diane Wei Lewis, "Media Fantasies: Women, Mobility, and Silent-Era Japanese Ballad Films," *Cinema Journal* 52, no. 3 (2013): 99–119.

7. James R. Brandon, "'Democratic Kabuki' for a 'Democratic Japan': 1945–1946," *Asian Theatre Journal* 31, no. 1 (2014): 103–25.

8. Samuel L. Leiter, "From Bombs to Booms: When the Occupation Met *Kabuki*," in *Rising from the Flames: The Rebirth of Theater in Occupied Japan, 1945–1952*, ed. Samuel L. Leiter (Lanham, MD: Lexington, 2009), 12–31. See also Brandon, "'Democratic Kabuki,'" 108–16.

9. David Jortner, "'Imposing the Standards of Boston on Japan': *Kasutori* Performance, Censorship, and the Occupation," *Theatre History Studies* 33 (2014): 130–50. Jortner's extensive work on the place of *shingeki* in mid-century political life is instructive. See also David Jortner, "SCAP's 'Problem Child': American Aesthetics, the Shingeki Stage, and the Occupation of Japan," in Leiter, *Rising from the Flames*, 259–77.

10. Cody Poulton helpfully includes a clarifying, translated excerpt from the theater writer Hirata Oriza's book *Engeki Nyūmon* [Introduction to theater] in his essay "The 1980s and Beyond," in *The Columbia Anthology of Modern Japanese Theater*, ed. J. Thomas Rimer, Mitsuya Mori, and M. Cody Poulton (New York: Columbia University Press, 2014), 507.

11. Reiko Oya, "Kaoru Osanai and the Impact of Edward Gordon Craig's Theatrical Ideals on Japan's *Shingeki* (New Theatre) Movement," *Shakespeare* 9, no. 4 (2013): 418–27.

12. Robert Tierney, "*Othello* in Tokyo: Performing Race and Empire in 1903 Japan," *Shakespeare Quarterly* 62, no. 4 (2011), 521–22.

13. Frank S. Nugent, "'Angels with Dirty Faces,' Racy Guttersnipe Drama, with James Cagney, Comes to the Strand," *New York Times*, November 26, 1938, 18.

14. Peter Brooks, *Realist Vision* (New Haven, CT: Yale University Press, 2005), 5.

15. Masahito Takayashiki, "Language and Body: Betsuyaku Minoru and the 'Small Theater Movement' (*Shogekijō Undō*) of the 1960s," in *Legacies of the Asia-Pacific War: The Yakeato Generation*, ed. Roman Rosenbaum and Yasuko Claremont (London: Routledge, 2011), 182–97.

16. Carol Fisher Sorgenfrei, *Unspeakable Acts: The Avant-Garde Theater of Terayama Shūji and Postwar Japan* (Honolulu: University of Hawaii Press, 2005), 31.

17. For an analysis of this episode within Terayama's larger body of work, see Steven C. Ridgely, *Japanese Counterculture: The Antiestablishment Art of Terayama Shūji* (Minneapolis: University of Minnesota Press, 2011), 69–98.

18. For the best, most capacious example in English, see Tadashi Uchino's *Crucible Bodies: Postwar Japanese Performance from Brecht to the New Millennium* (London: Seagull, 2009). See also Yoshiko Fukushima, *Manga Discourse in Japanese Theater: The Location of Noda Hideki's Yume no Yuminsha* (Oxon, UK: Routledge, 2005); this analysis of one of contemporary Japan's more durable groups locates its success partly in its inclusion of provocative, manga-influenced visuals in more conventional narrative structures. However, Uchino's *Crucible Bodies* contains a brief overview of plays after the Aum Shinrikyo attack, particularly the ways in which popular plays construct a potentially conservative image of an encompassing and successful Japanese society.

19. One of Japan's leading theater critics, Nishidō Kōjin, strikes a worried tone in *Shōgekijō wa shimetsu shita ka? Gendai engeki no seiza* [Have the small theaters gone extinct? The constellation of contemporary theater] (Tokyo: Renga shobōshinsha, 1996). For an especially critical take, see Kazama Ken, *Shōgekijō, minna ga hīrō no sekai* [Small theater, where everyone's a hero] (Tokyo: Seikyusha, 1993), 207–10.

20. Fredric Jameson, "Reification and Utopia in Mass Culture," *Social Text* 1 (Winter, 1979): 130–48.

21. Lauren Berlant, *The Female Complaint: The Unfinished Business of Sentimentality in American Culture* (Durham, NC: Duke University Press, 2008), 227–29.

22. Katō Masafumi, *Kyarameru Bokkusu Hakurankai—Caramel Expo 2001* (Tokyo: Tokyo FM Shuppan, 2001), 2–15.

23. Morimoto Kazuo, *Kyarameru Mirakuru: Shōgekijō kyaramaru bokkusu no 5000 nichi* [Caramel miracle: 5,000 days of Caramel Box] (Tokyo: Tokyo FM Shuppan, 1999), 32–33. I should add a word here about sources for this chapter. Because I am trying to engage both the critical and professional atmospheres in which the play *Hikari no Teikoku* was produced, I am discussing issues that may be sensitive to members of the theater group, whose anonymity I could not reasonably guarantee given the specific focus in this chapter on one easily identifiable play. I have for that reason decided to rely on published accounts of Caramel Box and of the theater scene more broadly. I realize that this limits the certainty with which I can make some of the claims that would be helpful to my argument, particularly because the authorized and official records from Caramel Box need to be understood as such, not as histories written by disinterested outsiders. I hope that my methods have been careful enough to ensure that the limited claims I do make in this chapter seem persuasive and well-substantiated.

24. Satō Ikuya, *Gendai gekijō no fīrudowāku: geijutsu sangyō no bunka shakaigaku* [Fieldwork in contemporary theater: Artistic production and cultural sociology] (Tokyo: University of Tokyo Press, 1999).

25. Kazama, *Shōgekijō, minna ga hīrō no sekai*, 207–8.

26. Kajio's title, *Ashita no omoide*, in Japanese uses the *kanji* characters for "The Future's Memories" but transliterates the characters for *mirai* (future) as "ashita" (tomorrow). Doing so both personalizes the story and narrows it to the future of a set of characters while also suggesting a certain imminence to the narrative. The Japanese title for Narui's play is *Subete no fūkei no naka ni anata ga imasu*.

27. It also has become what seems to be the only Onda story to have been translated into English. See Onda Riku, "The Big Drawer," trans. Nora Stevens Heath, in *Speculative Japan 2: "The Man Who Watched the Sea" and Other Tales of Japanese Science Fiction and Fantasy* (Fukuoka: Kurodahan, 2011), 71–86.

28. Onda Riku, "Hikari no Teikoku" [The empire of light], in *Tokono Monogatari: Hikari no Teikoku* [Tokono tales: The empire of light] (Tokyo: Shūeisha, 2000), 134–35. This is my translation of the original "prayer" in its entirety. The gaps between stanzas represent

places where Onda breaks the poem to describe the reaction of the other children and of Professor Tsuru to the prayer the first time they hear it. The original:

Bokutachi wa, hikari no kodomo da.
Doko ni demo, hikari ga ataru.
Hikari no ataru tokoro ni wa kusa ga umae, kaze ga fuki, iki to shite ikeru mono wa kokyū suru.
Sore wa, doko de demo, dare ni demo sō da.
Demo, dare ka no tame ni demo nai shi, dare ka no okage to iu wake ja nai.
Bokutachi wa, muriyari umaresaserareta no demo nakereba, machigatte umaretekita no demo nai.
Sore wa, hikari no atatteiru to iu koto to onaji yō da, yagate kaze ga fukihajime, hana ga mi o
tsukeru no to onaji yō ni, sō iu fū ni, zuttozutto mae kara kimatteiru kimari na no da.
Bokutachi wa, kusa o hōzuri shi, kaze ni kami o makase, kudamono o moidetabe, hoshi to
yoake yumemi nagara kono sekai de kurasō. Sōshite, itsuka kono mabayui hikari no uma-
reta tokoro ni, minna de te o tsunaide kaerō.

29. Throughout the story, Onda uses the term *shimau* (to keep by putting something away, as in a desk drawer) as the family's code for their own powers of total recall.

30. Inoue Hidenori of the theater group Shinkansen, as quoted by Kazama, *Shōgekijō, minna ga hīrō no sekai*, 200–01.

31. Kazama, *Shōgekijō, minna ga hīrō no sekai*, 205.

32. Morimoto, *Kyarameru Mirakuru*, 74–76.

33. Peter Brooks, "The Text of the City," *Oppositions: A Journal for Ideas and Criticism in Architecture* 8 (1977): 9. See also Peter Brooks, *The Melodramatic Imagination* (New Haven, CT: Yale University Press, 1976).

34. David Johnson, undated conversation.

6. The Peripheral U-Turn

1. Isshiki Masaharu, *Nani ka no tame ni: Sengoku38 no kokuhaku* (Tokyo: Asahi Shimbun Shuppan, 2011).

2. For example, Kate Obenshain, *Divider-in-Chief: The Fraud of Hope and Change* (Washington: Regnery, 2012).

3. Hirokazu Miyazaki, *The Method of Hope: Anthropology, Philosophy, and Fijian Knowledge* (Stanford, CA: Stanford University Press, 2004). Miyazaki later coedited *The Economy of Hope* (Philadelphia: University of Pennsylvania Press, 2016) with Richard Swedberg, like Miyazaki a contributor to the *Kibōgaku* volumes, as are several other authors in the project.

4. Joshua Wolf Shenk, "What Makes Us Happy?" *Atlantic*, June 2009, http://www.theatlantic.com/magazine/archive/2009/06/what-makes-us-happy/307439.

5. As the center notes on its website, "While science has made great strides in treating pathologies of the human mind, far less research exists to date on positive qualities of the human mind including compassion, altruism and empathy." See http://ccare.stanford.edu.

6. Barbara L. Fredrickson, "The Role of Positive Emotions in Positive Psychology: The Broaden-and-Build Theory of Positive Emotions," *American Psychologist* 56, no. 3 (2001): 218–26.

7. See Genda Yūji, *A Nagging Sense of Job Insecurity: The New Reality Facing Japanese Youth*, trans. Jean Connell Hoff (Tokyo: International House of Japan/LTCB International Trust, 2005). See also Hirokazu Miyazaki, "The Temporality of No Hope," in *Ethnographies of Neoliberalism*, ed. Carol J. Greenhouse (Philadelphia: University of Pennsylvania Press, 2010), 239–40.

8. Genda Yūji, *Kibō no tsukurikata* [How to create hope] (Tokyo: Iwanami shinsho, 2010).

9. The *Kibōgaku* volumes were published in Japanese by the University of Tokyo Press in 2009. See http://www.utp.or.jp/series/kibougaku.html.

10. Genda Yūji, "Joshō: Kibōgaku ga mezasumono" [What Kibōgaku aims for], in *Kibōgaku*, ed. Genda Yūji (Tokyo: Chūō Shinsho Laclef, 2006).

11. Uno Shigeki, "Shakai kagaku ni oite kibō o kataru to wa: shakai to kojin no arata na kessetsuten" [What it means for social science to discuss hope: New nodes for individual and society], in *Kibōgaku 1: Kibō o kataru—shakai kagatu no arata na chihei ni* [Kibōgaku 1: Talking about hope—toward new horizons for the social sciences], ed. Genda Yūji and Uno Shigeki (Tokyo: University of Tokyo Press, 2009), 280–81.

12. Uno Shigeki, *"Watashi" jidai no demokurashii* [Democracy in the age of "me"] (Tokyo: Iwanami Shinsho, 2010); Uno, "Shakai kagaku ni oite kibō o kataru."

13. The Japanese-language scholarship on the population change and rural governance is extensive, thoughtful, and informative. See, for example, Furuta Takahiko, *Jinkō hadō de mirai o yomu* [Reading the future through population change] (Tokyo: Nihon Keizai Shinbunsha, 1996); Ōmori Wataru, ed., *Jinkō dōtai to gyōsei sābisu* [Population dynamics and government services] (Tokyo: Gyōsei, 1993). More specifically on rural subgovernance, see Endō Hiroichi and Kamo Toshio, *Chihō bunken no kenshō* [Investigating regional decentralization] (Tokyo: Jichitai Kenkyūsha, 1995); Kanai Toshiyuki, *Jichi taisei* [Local governance] (Tokyo: University of Tokyo Press, 2007); Morita Akira, Taguchi Kazuhiro, and Kanai Toshiyuki, eds., *Seiji Kūkan no hen'yō to seisaku kakushin 3: Bunken kaikaku no dōtai* [Policy renovation and the transformation of political space 3: Dynamics of decentralization reform] (Tokyo: University of Tokyo Press, 2008). For a superb English-language overview that focuses analytically on many of the causes of rural depopulation, see Peter Matanle and Anthony S. Rauch with the Shrinking Regions Research Group, *Japan's Shrinking Regions in the 21st Century* (Amherst, NY: Cambria, 2011).

14. Michael W. Donnelly, "Conflict over Government Authority and Markets: Japan's Rice Economy," in *Conflict in Japan*, ed. Ellis S. Krauss, Thomas P. Rohlen, and Patricia G. Steinhoff (Honolulu: University of Hawaii Press, 1984), 336.

15. See Marilyn Ivy's *Discourses of the Vanishing: Modernity, Phantasm, Japan* (Chicago: University of Chicago Press, 1995); and Jennifer Robertson, "Furusato Japan: The Culture and Politics of Nostalgia," *International Journal of Politics, Culture, and Society* 1, no. 4 (1988): 494–518.

16. Christopher S. Thompson summarizes much of this in English in his substantial and positive review of volumes 2–3 of *Kibōgaku* in *Social Science Japan Journal* 13, no. 2 (2010): 241–47.

17. Nakamura Naofumi, "Kioku no genryū: Kamaishi chiiki no kindaishi" [The origins of memories: The modern history of the Kamaishi region], in *Kibōgaku 2: Kibō no saisei—Kaimaishi no rekishi to sangyō ga kataru mono* [Kibōgaku 2: The rebirth of hope: What Kamaishi's history and industry teach us], ed. Genda Yūji and Nakamura Naofumi (Tokyo: University of Tokyo Press, 2009), 32–35.

18. Henry Oinas-Kukkonen, *Tolerance, Suspicion, and Hostility: Changing U.S. Attitudes toward the Japanese Communist Movement, 1944–1947* (Westport, CT: Greenwood, 2003), 78–79. On Shōriki's legacy, see "Matsutarō Shōriki: Japan's Citizen Kane," *Economist*, December 22, 2012, http://www.economist.com/news/christmas/21568589-media-mogul-whose-extraordinary-life-still-shapes-his-country-good-and-ill-japans.

19. Uno Shigeki, "Kamaishi shichō to shite no Suzuki Tōmin: Chiiki no Fukushi Seiji to Rōkaru Aidentiti" [Suzuki Tōmin as Kamaishi's mayor: Regional welfare governance and local identity], in *Kibōgaku 2: Kibō no saisei—Kamaishi no rekishi to sangyō ga kataru mono* [Kibōgaku 2: The rebirth of hope: What Kamaishi's history and industry teach us], ed. Genda Yūji and Nakamura Naofumi (Tokyo: University of Tokyo Press, 2009), 109–43.

20. See Masatoshi Yorimitsu, "The Decline and Renaissance of the Steel Town: The Case of Kamaishi," in *Japanese Cities in the World Economy,* ed. Kuniko Fujita and Richard Child Hill (Philadelphia: Temple University Press, 1993), 203–23.

21. Aoki Hiroyuki, Umezaki Osamu, and Nitta Michio, "Soshiki no kibō: Kamaishi seitetsujo no kako to genzai" [The hope of organizations: Kamaishi's steelworks in the past and present], in *Kibōgaku 2: Kibō no saisei—Kaimaishi no rekishi to sangyō ga kataru mono* [Kibōgaku 2: The rebirth of hope: What Kamaishi's history and industry teach us], ed. Genda Yūji and Nakamura Naofumi (Tokyo: University of Tokyo Press, 2009), 61–107.

22. John Sargent and Richard Wiltshire, "Kamaishi: A Japanese Steel Town in Crisis," *Geography* 73, no. 4 (1988): 354–57.

23. Aoki, Umezaki, and Nitta, "Soshiki no kibō." See also Nakamura Keisuke, "Kigyō yūchi to jiba kigyō no jiritsu" [Attracting enterprises and the independence of local industry], in *Kibōgaku 2: Kibō no saisei—Kaimaishi no rekishi to sangyō ga kataru mono* [Kibōgaku 2: The rebirth of hope: What Kamaishi's history and industry teach us], ed. Genda Yūji and Nakamura Naofumi (Tokyo: University of Tokyo Press, 2009), 145–96. Nakamura's chapter is in many ways the most detailed and informative of the entire *Kibōgaku* project.

24. Matanle and Rauch, *Japan's Shrinking Regions,* 321–22.

25. The most important English-language work on the topic is Robert Pekkanen, *Japan's Dual Civil Society* (Stanford, CA: Stanford University Press, 2004), which emphasizes the crucial role the state has played in the development of Japan's civil society. The essays in Frank J. Schwartz and Susan J. Pharr, eds., *The State of Civil Society in Japan* (London: Cambridge University Press, 2003), also give a superb overview.

26. See Kim D. Reimann, *The Rise of Japanese NGOs: Activism from Above* (Oxon, UK: Routledge, 2010); Petrice Flowers, *Refugees, Women, and Weapons: International Norm Adoption and Compliance in Japan* (Stanford, CA: Stanford University Press, 2009); David Leheny, "Conclusion—Remaking Transnationalisms: Japan and the Solutions to Crises," in *Japanese Aid and the Construction of Global Development,* ed. David Leheny and Kay B. Warren (Oxon, UK: Routledge, 2010), 270–86.

27. See the six volumes of the *20 Seiki Shisutemu* project, all published in 1998 by the University of Tokyo Press.

28. Hirowatari Seigō, "Kibō to henkaku: ima, kibō o kataru to sureba" [Hope and change: If we're to discuss hope now], in *Kibōgaku 1: Kibō o kataru—shakai kagatu no arata na chihei ni* [Kibōgaku 1: Talking about hope—toward new horizons for the social sciences], ed. Genda Yūji and Uno Shigeki (Tokyo: University of Tokyo Press, 2009), 3–29.

29. Mark Granovetter, "The Strength of Weak Ties," *American Journal of Sociology* 78, no. 6 (1973): 1360–80.

30. For a good early English-language discussion of the literature, see Richard Wiltshire, "Research on Reverse Migration in Japan: (I) Reverse Migration and the Concept of 'U-Turn,'" *Science Reports of Tōhoku University,* seventh series (geography) 29 (1979a): 63–68.

31. Ishikura Yoshihiro, "Chiiki kara tenshutsu to 'U-Taan' no haikei: dare ga itsu modoru no ka?" [Background on the move from the periphery and the "U-turn": Who returns, and when?], in *Kibōgaku 3: Kibō o tsunagu—kamaishi kara mita chiiki shakai no mirai* [Kibōgaku 3: Connecting hope—the future of regions, viewed from Kamaishi], ed. Genda Yūji and Nakamura Naofumi (Tokyo: University of Tokyo Press, 2009), 205–36.

32. Nishino Yoshimi, "Kamaishi-shi shusshinsha no chiiki idō to raifukōsu—Kamaishi o hanareru, kamaishi ni modoru" [The regional migration and life course of Kamaishi natives—leaving Kamashi, returning to Kamaishi], in *Kibōgaku 3: Kibō o tsunagu—kamaishi kara mita chiiki shakai no mirai* [Kibōgaku 3: Connecting hope—the future of regions, viewed from Kamaishi], ed. Genda Yūji and Nakamura Naofumi (Tokyo: University of Tokyo Press, 2009), 163–204.

33. I thank Satsuki Takahashi for picking up on this aspect of *Ama-chan*, which I otherwise would have missed.

34. The Kamaishi miracle has been covered extensively. For the most comprehensive account, see *Kamaishi no Kiseki: Donna bōsai kyōiku ga kodomo no "inochi" o sukueru no ka* [The Kamaishi miracle: What kind of disaster planning education will save children's lives?] (Tokyo: NHK Special Unit, 2015).

35. Satoshi Kodama, "*Tsunami-Tendenko* and Morality in Disasters," *Journal of Medical Ethics* 41, no. 5 (2013): 361–63.

36. See Atsushi Arai's response to Kodama in "*Tsunami-Tendenko* and Morality in Disasters," *Journal of Medical Ethics* 41, no. 5 (2013): 365–66.

37. Richard Lloyd Parry's *Ghosts of the Tsunami: Death and Life in Japan's Disaster Zone* (London: Jonathan Cape, 2017) is a profoundly moving and beautifully reported portrait of the tragedy and its aftermath.

38. Russell Banks, *The Sweet Hereafter* (Toronto: Vintage Canada, 1997), 237.

39. Ikegami Masaki and Katō Junko, *Ano toki, Ōgawa Shogakkō de nani ga okita no ka* [What occurred at Ōgawa Elementary School?] (Tokyo: Seishisha, 2012). See also Ikegami Masaki and Katō Junko, *Ishinomaki shiritsu Ōgawa Shogakko "Jiko Kentō Iinkai" o kentō suru* [Investigating the Ishinomaki Public Ōgawa Elementary School "Accident Investigation Committee"] (Tokyo: Poplar, 2014).

40. I do not disagree with Genda, although my own discomfort about the Kamaishi miracle emanates primarily from my imagination of what it must have been like for Ōgawa parents to see any of the myriad Kamaishi miracle stories in the newspapers or on television.

41. Genda Yūji, "Kamaishi no kibōgaku: shinsaizen, soshite shinsaigo" [The social sciences of hope in Kamaishi: Before and after the disaster], in "*Mochiba*" *no Kibōgaku* [Social sciences of hope: People in charge], ed. University of Tokyo Institute of Social Science, Nakamura Naofumi, and Genda Yūji (Tokyo: University of Tokyo Press, 2015), 26–29.

42. The word *mochiba* in the book's title is perhaps best translated as "one's post," implying stoicism and responsibility among the victims working to rebuild Kamaishi. The official English version of the title is *Social Sciences of Hope: People in Charge*.

43. Nakamura Naofumi, "Kamaishi ni okeru shinsai no kioku" [Memories of the disaster in Kamaishi], in *'Mochiba' no Kibōgaku* [Social sciences of hope: People in charge], ed. University of Tokyo Institute of Social Science, Nakamura Naofumi, and Genda Yūji (Tokyo: University of Tokyo Press, 2015), 45–111.

44. Richard J. Samuels covers Kan's work extensively in his *3.11: Disaster and Change in Japan* (Ithaca, NY: Cornell University Press, 2013). Jeff Kingston offered a shrewd and nuanced appraisal as early as late 2011: Jeff Kingston, "Ousting Kan Naoto: The Politics of Nuclear Crisis and Renewable Energy in Japan," *Asia-Pacific Journal*, September 26, 2011, http://apjjf.org/2011/9/39/Jeff-Kingston/3610/article.html. Kenji Kushida places Kan's struggles in the broader context of leadership change. See Kenji E. Kushida, "The Fukushima Nuclear Disaster and the Democratic Party of Japan: Leadership, Structures, and Information Challenges during the Crisis," *Japanese Political Economy* 40, no. 1 (2014): 29–68.

45. This is a central element in Kan's own account of the disaster. See Kan Naoto, *My Nuclear Nightmare: Leading Japan through the Fukushima Disaster to a Nuclear-Free Future*, trans. Jeffrey S. Irish (Ithaca, NY: Cornell University Press, 2017).

46. Frank J. Schwartz, *Advice and Consent: The Politics of Consultation in Japan* (Cambridge, Cambridge University Press, 2001).

47. "Higashi Nihon Daishinsai Fukkō Kōsō Kaigi (Dai 1-Kai) Giji Yōshi" [Summary record of the first meeting of the Great East Japan Earthquake Reconstruction Design Council] (Tokyo: Prime Minister's Office, 2011).

48. Richard J. Samuels, "Japan's Rhetoric of Crisis: Prospects for Change after 3.11," *Journal of Japanese Studies* 39, no. 1 (2013): 97–120.

49. The record of the meeting is not in the form of *gijiroku* (minutes) but rather of *yōshi* (summary/main points), which divide speakers' comments but without identifying the speakers themselves except in certain circumstances. The speaker's focus and tone strongly suggest that it was Satō Yūhei, Fukushima's governor at the time. See "Higashi Nihon Daishinsai Fukkō Kōsō Kaigi (Dai 1-Kai) Giji Yōshi," 10.

50. "Higashi Nihon Daishinsai Fukkō Kōsō Kaigi (Dai 1-Kai) Giji Yōshi," 14–15.

51. Shōbayashi Mikitarō, "Nōson, shoshite nōgyō no shiten kara shinsai chiiki no fukkō ni kan suru kentō kadai" [Working issues for the reconstruction of disaster zones from the perspective of farming villages and agriculture], Meeting 3, April 29, 2011; Saigō Mariko, "Machizukuri kaisha ni yoru jizoku kanō na machizukuri" [Sustainable community planning from community planning firms], prepared for Meeting 8 of the Great East Japan Earthquake Disaster Reconstruction Council Working Group, June 14, 2011.

52. In the first paragraph of the extract I use the official English translation from the council's announcement. See "Seven Principles for the Reconstruction Framework," Reconstruction Design Council, May 10, 2011, http://www.cas.go.jp/jp/fukkou/english/pdf/7principles.pdf. The extract is from "Higashi Nihon Daishinsai Fukkō Kōsō Kaigi Kentō Bukai (Dai 8-Kai) Giji Yōshi" [Summary record of the eighth meeting of the Great Eastern Japan Earthquake Reconstruction Design Council Working Group] (Tokyo: Cabinet Office, 2011), 8–9. Again, speakers are not identified by name, but the specific and personal reflections on the *Kibōgaku* project make it clear that this is Genda's statement. Genda elaborates on these thoughts in English in Genda Yūji, "Future Employment Policy Suggested by the Post-earthquake Response," *Japan Labor Review* 4 (Autumn 2012): 86–104.

53. "Hope Beyond the Disaster," in *Final Report of the Reconstruction Design Council* (provisional translation), 8–9.

54. I am deeply indebted to Kerim Yasar for his having suggested this formulation.

55. http://www.hurex.jp/column/i-turn.

56. Indeed, this is one of the lessons from "In the Mud," chapter 7 of Anne Allison's *Precarious Japan* (Durham, NC: Duke University Press, 2013).

57. See http://ishinomaki2.com.

58. Ishii Kōta, *Itai: Shinsai, tsunami no hate ni* [The bodies after the tsunami] (Tokyo: Shinchōsha, 2011), 260. Original text: *Minasan, Kamaishi ni umarete yokatta desu ne.*

59. Samuels, *3.11: Disaster and Change in Japan*, 151–79. On different perspectives on *machi-zukuri*, see Gagugei Shuppansha Henshūbu, ed., *Higashi nihon daishinsai, genpatsu jiko: fukkō machizukuri ni mukete* [The great Eastern Japan earthquake and nuclear disaster: Toward recovery and community development] (Tokyo: Gakugei, 2011).

7. Everything Sinks

1. Originally titled *Baburu e GO! Taimu-Mashiin wa doramu shiki*, or more precisely translated as *Go to the Bubble! The Washer's a Time Machine.*

2. See, for example, Kosuge Nobuhiko, "Fukushima genpatsu jiko: ekonomisuto no shiten kara" [The Fukushima nuclear disaster: An economist's view], *Gurobaru komyunikeshon kenkyū* 1 (March 2014): 87–112; Yoshimi Shun'ya, "Radioactive Rain and the American Umbrella," trans. Shi-Lin Loh, *Journal of Asian Studies* 71, no. 2 (2012): 319–31. Yoshimi emphasizes especially the work of the young sociologist Kainuma Hiroshi in this regard. See *"Fukushima" ron: genshiryokumura wa naze umareta no ka?* [On Fukushima: Why nuclear power was developed] (Tokyo: Seidosha, 2011).

3. Hiroki Azuma, "For a Change, Proud to Be Japanese," trans. Shion Kono and Jonathan Abel, *New York Times,* March 16, 2011.

4. "Ganbare Nippon—Gaikokujin ga mita higashi nihon dai shinsai," NHK BS-1, June 18, 2011, http://www6.nhk.or.jp/cooljapan/past/detail.html?pid=110618.

5. Caramel Box, "Tōhoku ōen muryō tsuō" [The Tōhoku support free tour], http://www.caramelbox.com/stage/tohoku/tour.

6. For a brilliant analysis, see Hoyt Long, *On Uneven Ground: Miyazawa Kenji and the Making of Place in Modern Japan* (Stanford, CA: Stanford University Press, 2011).

7. Uwajima Suisan kōkō, "'Ehime maru' ni yoru higashi nihon daishinsai hisaichi shien katsudō," http://uwajimasuisan-h.esnet.ed.jp/sien/sien_kannsou.html.

8. "Watashi wa nihon kara ikiru kibō o moratta. Kondō wa watashi kara hisai shita hitotachi e êru o okuru ban desu." See "Kokkyō o koete—Guen-Doku hisaichi no kizuna" [Overcoming national borders: Nguyen Duc's bonds with the disaster zone], *NHK Heartnet,* October 2, 2012, http://www.nhk.or.jp/heart-net/tv/calendar/2012-10/03.html.

9. "'Toward an Alliance of Hope'—Address to a Joint Meeting of the US Congress by Prime Minister Shinzo Abe," April 29, 2015, https://japan.kantei.go.jp/97_abe/statement/201504/uscongress.html.

10. For example, Susan J. Napier, "Panic Sites: The Japanese Imagination of Disaster from *Godzilla* to *Akira*," *Journal of Japanese Studies* 19, no. 2 (1993): 327–51; Jessica Langer, "Three Versions of Komatsu Sakyō's *Nihon chinbotsu* (Japan Sinks)," *Science Fiction Film and Television* 2, no. 1 (2009): 45–57.

11. Tsutsui Yasutaka, "Nihon Igai Zenbu Chinbotsu," 1973, reprinted in *Nihon Igai Zenbu Chinbotsu: Tanpenshū* (Tokyo: Kadokawa, 2006).

12. Yamada Yoshiko and Daniel Clausen, "Risk Management, Disaster Diplomacy, and the Struggle for National Identity in Japan," in *Risk State: Japan's Foreign Policy in an Age of Uncertainty,* ed. Sebastian Maslow and Ra Mason (London: Ashgate, 2015). See also David Leheny, "Conclusion: Remaking Transnationalisms—Japan and the Solutions to Crises," in *Japanese Aid and the Construction of Global Development: Inescapable Solutions,* ed. David Leheny and Kay B. Warren (Oxon, UK: Routledge, 2010), 270–86.

13. Kawashima Shin, "Japanese Studies Overseas: A Target for More Strategic Support," Nippon.com, October 23, 2014, http://www.nippon.com/en/editor/f00030.

INDEX

Page numbers in italics refer to illustrations.

CPSIA information can be obtained
at www.ICGtesting.com
Printed in the USA
BVHW03*0525091018
528826BV00001B/2/P

9 781501 729072